The British Tanks 1915–19

THE
BRITISH TANKS
1915–19

David Fletcher

The Crowood Press

First published in 2001 by
The Crowood Press Ltd
Ramsbury, Marlborough
Wiltshire SN8 2HR

British Library Cataloguing-in-Publication Data
A catalogue record for this book is available from the British Library.

ISBN 1 86126 400 3

Photograph previous page: an official photograph of Mother, or His Majesty's
Landship (HMLS) *Centipede*, from the front, showing the 57mm guns in their
sponsons and the face of the driver's cab with the two armoured flaps,
separated by a machine-gun mounting.

Typeset by Florence Production Ltd,
Stoodleigh, Devon EX16 9PN
Printed and bound in Great Britain by
Antony Rowe, Chippenham

Contents

Introduction

You will not find books about First World War tanks on the bookshelves every day, which is odd because titles on that wretched war seem to be extremely popular at the present time. Yet this upsurge of interest is very narrowly focused, upon the infantry in their wet and crumbling trenches and in particular upon that dreadful summer on the Somme. Many people will have fathers, grandfathers and even great-grandfathers who served in the trenches and they seem to be fascinated by their grim misery. They are almost all gone now and we are left to contemplate the horrors they suffered.

In a sense the existence of the tank spoils that image. Where the collective folk memory conjures up images of trenches, mud and barbed wire, swept by a merciless torrent of machine-gun fire we imagine stolid British infantrymen advancing to victory and death. In such a timeless scene of Gothic horror the tank appears to intrude. It reminds us that this was not some ancient, heroic conflict like King Harold's defence at Hastings but a war of modern times in which machines played a significant part. Mud, misery and fear we can all understand and so many survivors have recorded their impressions that we can identify with them. Indeed, as John Terraine has pointed out, the Great War was the first war that involved the British middle class on a massive scale and they were an articulate generation; no wonder that we perceive their war in such a personal way. We somehow resent the idea, that, behind the scenes, politicians, engineers, scientists and even enlightened soldiers were striving to develop new ways of overcoming the impasse of trench warfare.

What we forget, of course, when it comes to tanks is that there were men inside those machines who were suffering just as much, who were just as fearful as their comrades in the trenches and just as likely to come to an unpleasant end. Indeed as the entire story of the Great War teaches us something about human courage so that of the tank tells us more about human adaptability. For the average Briton in pre-war years the closest they came to mechanization was when they crammed into a train or rattled around London on a solid tyred bus; they had no more idea of how the tank worked than most of us do about the inside of a computer. Yet, by 1918, thousands of these men had learned to drive a 28t (28,448kg) armoured vehicle, delve into the intricacies of its mechanism and repair it, sometimes under enemy fire.

In a book such as this it is impossible to avoid technical matters but it would also be foolish to ignore the human element. Thus we endeavour to show how the tank was invented and by whom. Personalities, both strong and forthright, played their part in overcoming others whose attitudes were every bit as entrenched as the enemy they sought to defeat. And when the tanks go off to war the men who go with them have to do more than just learn new skills, they must set aside their fears and learn to nurse these vulnerable machines across appalling ground while every German gun within range attempts to destroy them. It is not easy to comprehend their dedication, much less the strange affection they began to feel for these heartless lumps of steel. Sometimes it is difficult to decide who was protecting whom. If a tank broke down in action, and the engine stopped, the crew would suddenly hear the deadly rattle of machine-gun fire, playing like hail upon the armour and they felt vulnerable. Yet they would work like demons to get the thing going again, not just to drown out the noise but with every intention of continuing the fight or, at best, shepherding their faithful 'old bus' back to the British lines rather than abandoning it to the foe.

The author can only hope that something of this comes across in the text, but even if it does he cannot claim very much credit for it. After all, anyone who attempts to write history is only really rearranging other men's words, and most of these writers can no longer pass judgement. As if that were not enough he owes more to friends of his own time but at least he can acknowledge them. So to George Forty, John Glanfield, Philippe Gorczynski, Dick Harley, Max Hundleby, John Reynolds and Mike Verrall and others, many thanks.

1 Firepower, Protection and Mobility – Early Developments

In 1854, by his own account, a certain James Cowen submitted his design for a steam-powered armoured fighting vehicle to Lord Palmerston, the British Prime Minister. It was intended for service in the Crimean War. Cowen believed that the Premier approved the scheme; others claim that 'Pam' thought the weapon barbarous while a military committee, sitting at Woolwich Arsenal, rejected it out of hand. Since the Crimean War did not really get underway until September 1854 and Palmerston did not become Prime Minister until February 1855, it seems that Cowen got some of his facts mixed. In any case by the time he published his complaint against the 'washed out old women and senile old tabbies' at Woolwich, Cowen, who was described as a 'social, medical and political reformer', was apoplectic and clearly in no mood to be fussy about trivial details like dates.

If we can assume that Cowen meant 1855 then his scheme makes more sense, even if the design appears to be totally impractical. In the three great battles of 1854, those of Alma, Balaclava and Inkerman, the British Army had been highly successful, in a haphazard sort of way. Since then they had suffered the rigours of an appalling winter – watching as the Russians fortified themselves inside Sebastopol – and settled down for a good, old-fashioned siege. Trench lines were dug, artillery massed in fixed batteries and all the traditional characteristics of positional warfare practised. If Cowen ever meant to sell his idea to the Army then it could only be at a time when they had need of it. A period of stalemate with high casualty rates and no progress on the ground is the very time when soldiers are casting about for new methods of attack.

That Cowen's design was turned down is hardly surprising. Such details as survive suggest that the machine could not have worked, and it is probable that the committee at Woolwich realized this. Mechanical land transport was in its infancy and the idea of turning a primitive traction engine into an armoured vehicle, carrying cannon and sporting scythes around the rim of its hull, was probably too ambitious. Of course, one is tempted to echo Cowen's complaint and blame the fuddy-duddies; somehow it seems typical of the British way of war. The British Commander-in-Chief, Lord Raglan (known as 'the Old Woman' to his men) is a classic example. A veteran of Waterloo, where he lost an arm, he had not seen active service for forty years. Yet one would be wrong to assume that everything about his army was old-fashioned.

Even before the Duke of Wellington died, in 1852, Britain had embarked upon the age of steam, and the industrial revolution was getting into its stride. In 1854 steam-powered warships and transports took the army to the Crimea. By April 1855 a steam railway was delivering ammunition from the dockside to the battlefield and in 1856, when it was too late to matter, a steam traction engine was being built to tow a huge mortar into action. On balance, it seems reasonable to suppose that it was not simply a reactionary committee that doomed James Cowen's 'Land and Sea Locomotive Steam Ram and Battery'.

If Cowen suffered the fate of so many pioneers it should not detract from the fact that he was right in principle. Subsequent events would prove that, as firepower became more intense, a self-propelled, armoured vehicle, capable of returning fire, was an effective solution to positional warfare. Yet everything has its time, both in terms of technology and social acceptability and a machine that combines various forms of technology has to wait a good deal longer before all the various factors mature. Armoured fighting vehicles, as defined by their title, combine the characteristics of protection, firepower and mobility and in fact all three had been developed, up to a point, by the end of the nineteenth century. Then, however, they had to wait upon the ultimate factor, social acceptability or, more specifically in this case, an imperative military requirement. Cowen's concept may have appeared barbarous to Lord Palmerston in 1855, but nobody, at least nobody in Britain, is quoted as saying the same thing about tanks in 1916. The Germans made such claims, but they had different, and predictable, views on the subject.

ARMOUR PROTECTION

Armour, in the sense of protective plate, goes back a long way. The medieval armoured knight is a good example but in his case the metal was formed to deflect a lance or sword blade. The clothyard shaft from a Welsh longbow could go straight through it and even pin the knight to his saddle. By the time of the English Civil War body armour, thin enough to be worn by a human, was virtually redundant in the face of firearms. As armour gets thicker it becomes heavier and there is a limit to what man and horse can bear, so its subsequent application was at sea. But armour is not just iron plating, as the Royal Navy discovered when it ordered five iron warships in the 1850s. Iron plate of that time, brittle and full of impurities, shattered like glass under shellfire. Improvements in metallurgy wrought such rapid change that by 1861 the world's first truly armoured ship, HMS *Warrior* was commissioned.

It was said of her, at the time, that she was more powerful than all the other warships in the world put together. She never got the chance to test her might one way or the other but in March 1862 the USS *Monitor* did. Its famous battle with the Confederate armoured ship CSS *Virginia* in Hampton Roads proved that, for the time being, the power of defence ruled over that of attack.

Developments in armour protection advanced rapidly in the 1890s. Starting with Hayward Harvey in the United States, improved by John Brown & Co., Cammells and Vickers in Britain and then refined by Krupp in Germany, it changed the nature of naval warfare out of all recognition in just forty years. Hayward's process involved pressing a heated metal plate against a carburized surface and then cooling it with water, which created face-hardened plate; Krupps created a homogeneous alloy with high nickel chrome content. Yet quality was not a substitute for thickness; warship armour, at this time, was often around 10in (25cm) thick.

Armour such as that had no value on land, except as an adjunct to fixed fortifications. It was far too thick and heavy to move about. Thinner armour plate could be produced, assuming there was a use for it, but it would still be too heavy for a horse to manage. Armoured trains had been constructed in the American Civil War and employed by the British in the Sudan some twenty years later but they either used boiler plate or locally acquired materials of dubious protective value. By the outbreak of the Boer War designs had become quite sophisticated and, when John Fowler & Co. of Leeds constructed a steam-powered, armoured road train for the British Army in 1899, so had the armour. The locomotives and wagons were covered in ¼in (6mm) nickel steel plate, supplied by Cammells but to Krupp patents, which was described as being able to resist Mauser rifle bullets at close range. A petrol-driven armoured car, built as a private venture by Vickers, Sons & Maxim in 1901, to the design of F.R. Simms, used ¼in (6mm) Vickers armour plate which was said to be capable of stopping a .303in

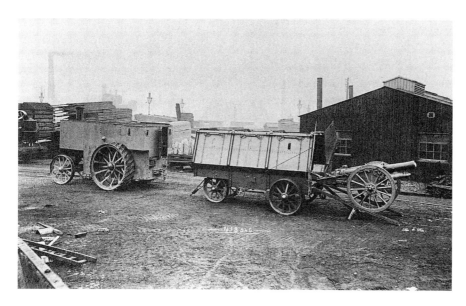

Built by Fowlers of Leeds to War Office specifications the big compound road locomotive is seen here winching a gun into one of the special armoured wagons, three of which would make a typical road train.

bullet at any range. This armour was also curved at both ends, which not only enhanced the appearance of the vehicle, but must have had some potential to deflect shot as well.

FIREPOWER AND MOBILITY

When it comes to firepower one has to be a bit more selective. This is no place to tackle the entire history of ordnance. Rather one needs to examine two aspects – automatic weapons which fire a continuous spray of bullets and armour-piercing ammunition. The former only concern us inasmuch as they came to revolutionize warfare and initiated the design of the tank, but their history is well recorded. Classic examples from the past include Puckle's gun of 1718 which operated on the Gatling principle, the Gatling itself of course and the Maxim brothers' machine-gun being designed in 1881.

Armour-piercing ammunition is every bit as complex as armour and has a surprisingly long history. A strange, bottle-shaped round developed during the American Civil War, employed a central, hardened metal rod which acted as the penetrator. Approximately a decade later a British cavalry officer developed a technique for hardening the nose cap of a shell to improve penetration, which proved very successful against thick naval armour. There being no obvious requirement for small-calibre armour-piercing rounds, none were developed until 1903. Even then an armour-piercing bullet developed by Roth of Vienna found no ready market since there was no apparent demand.

Mobility, like firepower, demands examination of two factors that directly affect the subject – one is the power source, the other the means of traction. James Cowen advocated steam for his 1855 patent because it was the only source then available. Fowlers employed steam for their armoured road train of 1899 because it delivered adequate power, although the internal combustion engine existed at that time. However there are many objections to using steam as a power source for armoured vehicles. Fuel and water are bulky loads, rapidly consumed. The firebox has to be served directly by a human being, which is demanding in space and rather risky if munitions are being handled near an open firebox door. There is a further risk to the crew from escaping steam if the boiler is damaged and, of course, there is little to recommend the experience of being shut up inside an armoured box that also contains a furnace and boiler.

THE COMING OF TRACKED VEHICLES

The internal combustion engine was rejected at first because it lacked power. The early products of Benz and Daimler could be used to propel small vehicles but few in authority took them seriously. Even when it was appreciated that they could be made capable of doing heavier work, and were more practical than steam engines, the military looked at them askance and dismissed automobiles as a rich man's toy, a fad that would soon pass. Petrol was volatile stuff, not to be used anywhere near munitions, and indeed it was banned for such work in the British Army until 1911. Unfortunately the alternative had other defects. Engines could be made to operate on paraffin (kerosene) although they did not deliver the same power as petrol and gave off a truly

awful smell. However there was no denying the commercial imperative. By 1908 the streets of London were thronged with motor buses and the horse bus was becoming redundant. Motor taxicabs rendered the elegant Hansom obsolete; more and more tradesmen were replacing their horse-drawn carts with lorries and vans while those wealthier citizens who could afford a motor car were also disposing of their horses. The War Office was becoming alarmed by the massive reduction in the number of horses in Britain, which might be available for military use in time of war. So where commerce led, the army was obliged to follow and, as the demand grew, so did the power and reliability of petrol engines.

In 1713 an enterprising Frenchman, one Monsieur D'Hermand, designed a small cart, to be pulled by goats, upon which children were given rides around a Paris park. Instead of wheels the little cart ran on a system of linked rollers which worked, in effect, like a crawler, or caterpillar track. Similar concepts were patented by the British engineer Richard Edgeworth in 1770 and by Thomas German in 1801. A rival idea, that of fitting feet to existing wheels, was pioneered by

A steam tractor by Robey & Co. of Lincoln fitted with Diplock's Pedrail wheels on the hind axle. Contemporary reports claim that the noise, as each foot hit the ground, was incredible and the haulier who purchased this machine soon replaced the Pedrails with conventional wheels.

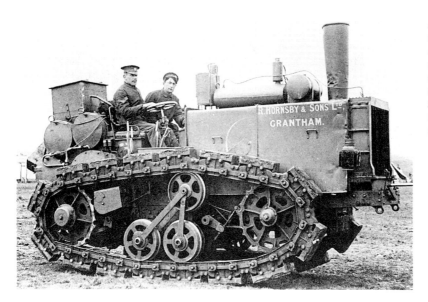

Hornsby's 1909 War Office tractor fitted with David Roberts' patent tracks. The engine starts on petrol, drawn from the little tank above the engine and then switches to paraffin carried in the three large drums at the back.

James Boydell in 1846; followed by Andrew Dunlop in 1861 and Bramah J. Diplock in 1899. The original impetus for this modest flurry of invention was to provide a means of moving heavy vehicles smoothly over rough or soft ground. Public roads, even in the industrialized world, were generally in an atrocious condition and with the advent of the railway they became even worse.

In effect these inventors were attempting to improve traction on roads by adopting railway principles. They were trying to interpose a firm, smooth surface between the wheels of a vehicle and the ground; indeed the term 'portable railway' was used in more than one patent application for what we know as crawler tracks. At this time, when the power source was animal, they did not have to concern themselves with the problem of steering a tracked vehicle by its tracks since it followed whereever the animal towed it. Once mechanical power was applied to these machines the technical difficulties multiplied. John Heathcote's ploughing engine of 1836 was one of the first examples of a self-propelled, tracked vehicle and various patents were taken out in Britain and the United States in the latter half of the nineteenth century. All would have been steam powered but few were actually built. In addition

to the steering problem one had to devise an effective way of transmitting drive to the wheels and engaging them with the tracks. These are theoretical matters but such prototypes as were built also suffered from weakness in the structure of their tracks. Tracks are subjected to a tremendous amount of stress, especially during steering movements or on rocky surfaces and the metals available at the time were simply not up to it.

It is worth noting that with perhaps one exception, none of the tracklaying machines devised or built in the nineteenth century were intended for military use. Improvements in agriculture and heavy haulage on roads were the prime motivating factors. It is a commentary on their modest success, and on the lack of interest shown by the War Office, that such machines were not taken seriously by the military until the First World War.

Progress was made during the first decade of the twentieth century, but only slowly. The British Army tested some tracklaying vehicles by Hornsbys of Grantham over this period, and even purchased two, which was not sufficient to encourage the manufacturer to expand production. Hornsbys constructed a total of six tracklaying machines between 1904 and 1912, four of which they managed to sell. The trouble was that they

A 75hp Holt tractor, the four-cylinder model widely used by the Army Service Corps as an artillery tractor on many fronts. The small wheel at the front acts as a pilot when the machine is turning.

were aiming primarily at the farming community, which was the wrong target.

By any contemporary standards agriculture in Britain was highly developed by the middle of the nineteenth century. Farms may have been quite large but fields were small so the demand for machinery was limited. In any case a system of ploughing, using steam engines and cable-hauled ploughs, was already well established. Things were different in the United States. There farms were huge with much new land waiting to be broken, and the demand for tracklayers increased rapidly. Among the most prolific manufacturers was the Holt Company of Stockton, California, which registered the trade name *Caterpillar* in 1910. They survived the San Francisco earthquake of 1906 and financial crises of 1910 and 1912, and in the latter year acquired the tracklaying patents of Hornsbys in Britain. Their success encouraged others, particularly in the Mid-west, to the extent that there were at least six builders of commercial tracklaying vehicles in the United States by 1914.

Those that survived in Britain did so on a shoestring. Bramah Diplock continued to develop his *Pedrail* footed wheel system up to 1908, then switched to a crawler track scheme, albeit of a highly individual type. A small agricultural concern in Lincoln, William Foster & Co. Ltd., marketed a half-track type, similar to the Holt and known as the Centipede, in 1913. Records indicate that they only sold one, and that for export. Fosters had also co-operated with Hornsbys on the last of their tracklayers, a steam-powered machine built for a customer in the Yukon. Contemporary reports suggest that William Tritton, managing director of Fosters, had a poor opinion of tracks. In his experience they tended to pick up stones which then got trapped between the links and could cause them to break. Since it has a bearing on our subject it should also be noted that, from 1911, Fosters produced a range of petrol-engined tractors – in effect traction engines with petrol motors – which enjoyed some success on the export market. The original heavy-duty model had a two-cylinder Hornsby engine while the smaller type employed a 40hp Daimler sleeve valve unit.

Technically, then, all the ingredients needed to create a tracked, armoured fighting vehicle existed by 1914 and could be said to be in a relatively advanced stage of development. All that was

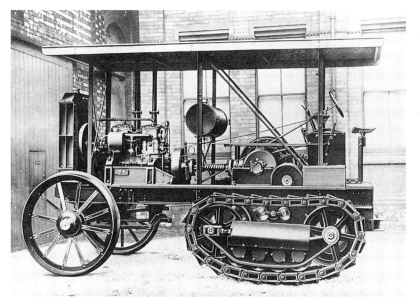

A retouched publicity photograph of the Fosters Centipede tractor in the yard of the Wellington Foundry at Lincoln. Notice how the tracks were curved, where they touch the ground, a feature Tritton would later apply to the Bullock tracks imported from Chicago.

lacking was the incentive, at least where it mattered. Writing in 1898 a Polish author, I.S. Bloch, had forecast that any future war between European nations would result in stalemate. Everything, from the use of temporary earthworks to the intensity of small-arms fire favoured the defence. In 1903, one of Britain's most popular and imaginative authors, H.G. Wells, had published a short story in the *Strand Magazine* that featured Land Ironclads. He described them as 'something between a big blockhouse and a giant's dish-cover ... from 80 to 100ft long, moving up gentle slopes at six miles an hour and crossing 30ft trenches by means of Diplock pedrails'. Wells, however, was not attempting to prove a military point. He wished to show how a modern, industrialized society might fare against one that relied upon traditional martial virtues.

A retired British Army officer, Capt T.G. Tulloch, put forward the idea of armouring the Hornsby type tracklayer as a means of overcoming the defensive power of the machine-gun. Tulloch was described as an expert in explosives and ballistics. He was employed by the Chilworth Powder Company and his work involved a lot of foreign travel, particularly to Germany. Tulloch returned from a visit to Germany late in 1911, concerned that they were manufacturing vast numbers of machine-guns. He therefore resurrected his original idea and improved upon it. His new design, which he sketched out, was a double-ended arrangement, based upon two Hornsby tractors, which mounted six quick-firing guns (12-pounder, 3in), twelve machine-guns and up to 100 men, all covered by armour. It was an ambitious scheme by any standards, seemingly typical of the type of inventor who wishes to run even before he can walk.

A year later an Australian engineer, Lancelot de Mole, submitted his own idea for an armoured tracklayer to the War Office in London. The interesting thing about de Mole is that he had no known military background and no obvious reason for suggesting such a thing at the time. While Tulloch's scheme was no more than the adaptation of an existing vehicle de Mole advocated something entirely original. He produced detailed drawings and even a large-scale model which shows a fully tracked machine, entirely clad in armour plate and he even went so far as to propose a novel steering system that involved bending the tracks.

Fig.1.

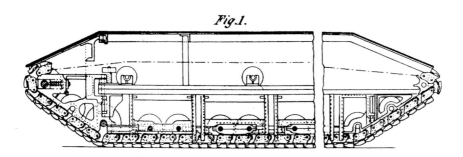

Fig.2.

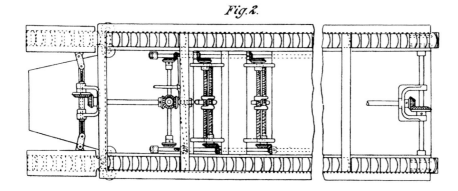

Part of Lancelot de Mole's patent drawing for his 1912 landship design. Notice how the complicated drive train enables the tracks to pivot at the front to enhance steering.

Walter Gordon Wilson (1874–1957), a versatile engineering genius who ultimately made a name for himself as a designer of sophisticated vehicle transmission systems.

While Tulloch's design included weapons it seems clear that de Mole was primarily interested in solving the mechanical problems associated with mobility. Some years later, when comparing his design with the British tanks as built, de Mole remarked that his machine could extricate itself from a shell hole in either direction more readily than the existing model. This hardly suggests deep tactical thinking and may well be no more than hindsight yet there is no doubt at all that, in terms of design, de Mole's machine was very advanced and ahead of its time in 1912. It should be no surprise at all to learn that the military authorities in London could see no particular value in it, and appear to have relegated the drawings to one of those pigeon-holes, in the basement of the War Office, reserved for the brainstorms of mad inventors. It is only fair to add that similar ideas, developed in Austria and Russia at this time, met with a similar fate.

Finally, before looking at events during the war, three significant individuals should be introduced. Walter G. Wilson was an inventor in the Victorian tradition, in that he experimented in many fields. He devised a revolutionary sail for small boats, co-operated in the design of an early aircraft, which sadly crashed and killed his partner and worked on the design of an automobile which featured an advanced transmission system. From 1904 his cars, known as Wilson-Pilchers, were manufactured by Armstrong-Whitworth in Newcastle-upon-Tyne, a company better known for manufacturing armaments. In 1906 Wilson designed an armoured car, which could also serve as an artillery tractor, for the company but they could not persuade anyone to purchase it. In 1913 Armstrong-Whitworths obtained an order, reputedly for thirty-six turreted armoured cars, from the Imperial Russian government. Very little is known about them but they were clearly a rather crude design, with wood spoked wheels and solid tyres. It would be particularly interesting to know something about the armour plate used in their construction but no details appear to have survived.

In 1910, when Robert Falcon Scott was planning his second, disastrous Antarctic Expedition he was advised to take some caterpillar-type tractors to haul sleds across the snow. The advice came from a fellow naval officer, Captain Murray Sueter, and the tractors were built by the Wolseley Motor Company. Wolseleys was then a Vickers subsidiary, with no apparent experience of making tracklayers, and the result seems to confirm this. They did not even bother to devise any form of steering gear. Each tractor was equipped with a sort of bowsprit and a change of direction was achieved simply by men swinging the machine around upon the snow using the bowsprit as a lever. Sueter, who played a pioneering part in the development of the submarine and in aviation for the Royal Navy, was Director of the Admiralty's Air Department in 1914.

R.E.B. Crompton was born in 1845. At the age of ten he contrived to visit the Crimea as a temporary naval cadet aboard his cousin's ship, HMS *Dragon*. Crompton had a brother in the Army out there and was able to examine the trench lines before Sebastopol. He later served with the Rifle Brigade in India where he was placed in charge of some steam road trains, acquired by the government for use on the Grand Trunk Road and for military manoeuvres. Returning to Britain he became involved with the newly developed electrical industry while maintaining an interest in transport matters. Following service in the Boer War he was retained by the War Office as a consultant on transport and road construction. His interest in military mechanization and his vast experience made him something of a legend. He, along with others already mentioned, will appear again in our story. When he does, do bear in mind that 1914 was his sixty-ninth year.

2 Armoured Cars – the Navy Shows the Way

When the War Office Mechanical Transport Committee compiled their annual report in April 1914 they had no idea that war was just a matter of months away. In fact the document was never issued, it got no further than the proof stage, and in the glare of hindsight it makes interesting reading. They devote no more than a brief paragraph to Armoured Motor Cars, noting that several different models had been constructed on the Continent. The General Staff told them that there were many more important things that they should concentrate upon and the matter could stand over for the present.

They also commented on Chain Tractors, the term they used to describe the Hornsby and other caterpillar machines. They explained that the surviving military Hornsby had seen service at Okehampton and on Salisbury Plain but they failed to point out that the company had stopped building such machines two years previously. In earlier reports they had commented upon the American Holt tractors. Little had been heard of the type since 1913 but they believed that it was still being manufactured in the United States. Thus we learn that, notwithstanding subsequent claims, the British War Office was at least aware of caterpillar tractors, even before the war began.

Small as it was, the British Army that went across the Channel in 1914 was very professional and highly mechanized. However this mechanization did not extend beyond the supply services. The fighting arms, infantry, cavalry and artillery, used modern weapons but employed horses or their feet to get about. The Royal Flying Corps (RFC) and its naval counterpart, the Royal Naval Air Service (RNAS) were the exceptions. Aviation was, by definition, mechanized and it attracted the modern young man who also had a passion for powerful motor cars and the resources to indulge it. In 1914 only the RFC went overseas with the British Expeditionary Force (BEF); the RNAS was charged with the defence of Britain, from the predicted attack by German airships. How they chose to interpret this role is another matter.

THE USE OF AIRPOWER

The only complete RNAS unit in Britain when war broke out was the Eastchurch Squadron, based at the airfield of that name on the Isle of Sheppey in the Thames Estuary. Commanded by the diminutive but intrepid Charles Rumney Samson it was more like an exclusive flying club than an arm of the prestigious Royal Navy but its pilots were itching for action. Samson's immediate superior was Murray Sueter, now a Commodore and Director of the Air Department at the Admiralty in London.

With the backing of his chief, First Lord of the Admiralty Winston Churchill, Sueter agreed to Samson's proposal that his squadron could achieve much more if it was based on the Continent. Operating from Antwerp the flying sailors would be within bombing range of German airship sheds at Cologne or Düsseldorf. Leading the way in a BE biplane Samson took his squadron across the English Channel on 27 August 1914. They landed at Ostend and set up a base.

The seven aircraft were a mixed lot and the same could be said of the squadron's transport that consisted of various impressed lorries and a selection of powerful private cars, belonging to the officer pilots.

ARMOURED CARS AND THE DEVELOPMENT OF ARMOUR PLATE

While plans were made to mount bombing raids against the Zeppelin bases, Samson's squadron became involved in reconnaissance flights for British and French troops around Ostend and Dunkirk. But these early aircraft were only fair-weather flyers and there were many days when it was too dangerous to get airborne. As an extra outlet for his squadron's enthusiasm, Samson started to organize reconnaissance trips by road, probing the flanks of the German advance on Paris and getting into occasional scraps with their cavalry. Thus began a process that tank designers later knew as the gun/armour race. On their first raids the sailors carried rifles and a machine-gun. The Germans responded in kind. Samson then fitted panels of steel plate to his cars and, within months, the Admiralty was supplying armoured cars to a standard pattern and expanding the size of the force. By December 1914 an entirely new design of armoured car was entering production, complete with a revolving turret containing a machine-gun. Demands for greater firepower were met by fitting small naval guns to armoured lorries and by the time Samson left France, in February 1915, the RNAS was operating a considerable force of armoured fighting vehicles in support of the British Army. Yet opportunities to use them were diminishing.

Conditions in France started deteriorating by the winter of 1914 as far as the armoured cars were concerned. Roads were breaking up under shell-fire and both sides were starting to entrench. The cars were virtually helpless when confronted with

A Wolseley armoured car of Samson's force leading a convoy into Antwerp. The protection afforded by its armour was minimal but Samson was never short of volunteers and here Royal Marines appear to have joined the Naval crew.

a trench and the extensive use of barbed wire spoiled things even more. Many of the more adventurous spirits who worked with Samson had already gone, looking for opportunities and excitement elsewhere, but others had been impressed by this new style of fighting. They had acquired a taste for mechanized, armoured warfare and a belief in its potential, and they had ideas if only someone could be persuaded to listen. The Admiralty, meanwhile, handed its armoured cars over to a reluctant War Office and they were still operating in France in April 1917.

From Samson's rather informal arrangements an entire Armoured Car Division of the RNAS had been created by the end of 1914. That it was still little more than a nominal force hardly mattered at the time since it was commanded by a group of men determined to make it succeed. Into this company, in December 1914, came Lt Albert Stern RNVR. The division was then based in the *Daily Mail* airship shed at Wormwood Scrubs in west London. The shed had been built with funds raised by the newspaper in 1910 as part of an attempt to awaken interest in aviation in Britain. Presented to the Admiralty by Lord

Albert Stern, seen here in the uniform of a Colonel of the Machine Gun Corps. A remarkably forceful, many would say ruthless, character he had little time for the finer points of military etiquette, political machinations or the deliberations of elderly inventors. Without him the advent of the tank might have been delayed for years.

Northcliffe it was now being used by lighter-than-air machines of the RNAS which, presumably, shared it with the armoured cars.

When Stern arrived at Wormwood Scrubs he described the Airship Shed as the only building available, the rest of the area being a sea of mud. That they needed more space was obvious and they found it, virtually just around the corner, at the Clement-Talbot motor works in Barlby Road, Notting Hill. The Talbot Company supplied chassis to the Royal Navy and also built aero engines and it seems that the RNAS men occupied lean-to buildings along the side of the main factory and used the adjacent land for experimental work and trials. Contemporary accounts tend to speak of both sites as Wormwood Scrubs but other evidence suggests that the centre of gravity shifted to Barlby Road as the armoured car force expanded. The initial work carried out

there had to do with the development of armour plate.

When Samson had his armoured cars constructed in France they used boilerplate, which was hardly bullet proof at all. The first armoured cars supplied by the Admiralty were little better. They were fitted out at the Sheerness naval dock-yard with 4mm armour plate backed by a 3mm layer of wood. This was just about adequate to resist rifle fire at 300yd (270m) but no closer. Having discovered that the War Office was no better informed on the qualities of light armour plate, the RNAS contacted William Beardmore & Co. Ltd., of Glasgow. Working in conjunction with Sqn Cdr Hetherington and Lt Symes RNVR they evolved 8.5mm nickel chrome alloy plate that would stop a German rifle bullet, or the British Mark VII service bullet, at 10yd (9m) and this was adopted for the next batch of armoured cars, the turreted type.

Early in 1915 reports reached London that the Germans had developed a new technique. They had somehow discovered that if you removed a bullet from its cartridge case and replaced it with the point reversed: that is, with the flat base forwards, this would go through the 8mm plate at 75yd (68m). Of course, in doing this the Germans ruined the aerodynamic effect of the bullet and adversely affected its accuracy but 12mm plate,

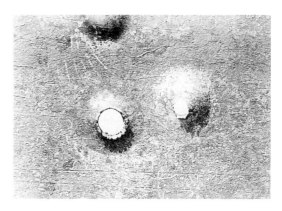

A sample piece of armour plate, tested by the Royal Naval Air Service, showing penetration effected by a reversed German rifle bullet.

supplied by the Firth Company, which could resist the reversed bullet at 10yd (9m), was too heavy for the armoured cars.

Incidentally, in April 1915 a certain M. Dercole, in France, was offering a concept that consisted of two layers of 4mm plate separated by a patent jelly of his creation. Some of this material was acquired by the RNAS and found to be ineffective against the reversed bullet and, according to Hetherington, they tried replacing the jelly by an ordinary domestic doormat which, by all accounts, did not work either.

Since no means had then been found of welding armour plate, the armoured cars were built by riveting the armour to a framework of angle iron bolted around the chassis. A further complication arose when curved armour plate was required for the turrets of these new cars and this was another matter that Beardmores solved in a very short time. Production of the turreted cars began in December 1914 but experimental work on armour went on well into the New Year. Indeed it became standard practice to test one piece of armour from every batch with a reversed bullet to ensure that the quality did not diminish.

In a sense the whole essence of military success is movement so, in an industrial age, when mechanization was available, the problems facing all arms are more or less the same. Artillery is a case in point. Technology and the strength of materials enabled bigger guns to be produced which, in turn, made them heavier and more difficult to move. It was a matter that the Austro-Hungarian Army had investigated. Their huge Skoda 30.5cm howitzers were designed to be broken down and hauled along the roads by equally large Austro-Daimler tractors. The Germans had made similar arrangements to move their even larger Krupp 42cm weapons. A battery of two of the latter appeared before the impregnable Belgian fortress of Liège and systematically battered its strongpoints to rubble in a matter of four days, commencing on 12 August 1914. By 21 August they had moved to Namur, where they were joined by a battery of two Skoda heavies.

Four days later the circle of forts that protected that city were in ruins.

It made a lasting impression on the Allies. Thus it was that when, in September, Admiral Sir Reginald Bacon of the Coventry Ordnance Works offered a similar weapon to Winston Churchill the deal was swiftly approved. The weapon in question was a 15in (38cm) calibre monster, of clumsy appearance compared with its Teutonic cousins. Churchill agreed to purchase some for the Royal Marine Artillery rather than take the obvious course of passing details on to the Royal Artillery but it was a condition of the deal that they could be transported, like the big German weapons. In order to comply Admiral Bacon approached the British Daimler Company who passed him on to William Tritton of William Foster & Co. Ltd. In Lincoln, Fosters had already built a huge, internal combustion-engined tractor, powered by a Daimler 'Silent Knight' 105hp engine which was rapidly adapted for the task. Known as the Foster-Daimler tractor it was, in effect, a typical traction engine of the period with the steam boiler replaced by a petrol engine. The nickname 'Silent Knight' applied to this engine incorporated the name of Charles Yale Knight, an American engineer whose sleeve-valve system for petrol engines made them a lot quieter than their conventional counterparts. Knight's principle could be applied to any size of engine although it was most popular with firms like Daimler who were building cars for the luxury market (and in particular for the Royal Family) where silence was a virtue. Whether it was ideal for heavy tractors is another matter for many commentators suggest that, in terms of power output, the sleeve valve system was not as effective as the more typical poppet valves employed by most designers.

The German advance on Paris was first halted on the River Marne and then, in a series of actions of shifting fortunes, pushed back to the River Aisne. Here, for the first time, the German Army entrenched itself in an effort to hold off further Allied attacks and, when these petered out, the British C-in-C Sir John French ordered his troops

A 105hp Foster-Daimler Tractor nicknamed Sloazhell in Army service. The Daimler engine and gearbox are effectively hidden by the rear wheels, one man sits astride the petrol tank ahead of which is the huge, box-shaped radiator.

to dig in. His order, confirming this, is dated 15 September 1914 – a significant date, as we shall show. Gen Joffre, the French commander, had arrived at the same conclusion. Despite lessons from recent history, notably the American Civil War and the Russo-Japanese War, it is clear that none of the armies in France had been prepared for such an eventuality. The Germans had permitted themselves forty days to subdue France while the French, at all levels, had a strong aversion to the very idea of going to ground. Both sides regarded these circumstances as temporary but there were those, mainly behind the lines, who perceived things differently.

Notable among them was Col Ernest Swinton of the Royal Engineers. Whatever his professional skills may have been Swinton had made a name for himself as a writer, in particular for a series of futuristic short stories with a military theme which he had produced during the Boer War. He had also written genuine military history and it was this reputation, as an imaginative writer, that got him the job of official war correspondent, or 'Eyewitness', at General Headquarters in France. From the reports that passed through his hands, what he saw with his own eyes and heard from friends, he had an excellent overview of the situa-

ation. His historical experience warned him of the risk of stalemate and he spent a lot of time considering the matter.

Portable bridges

Writing in 1923 (*The World Crisis*, Vol. 1), Winston Churchill quotes from a letter of his

Major-General Sir Ernest Swinton

Ernest Swinton, a sketch made between the wars when he was Colonel-Commandant of the Royal Tank Corps.

dated 23 September 1914. It is addressed to a Col Ollivant of the Royal Naval Division Administration and in it he proposes that armoured cars and other transport should be equipped with planks which could serve as portable bridges for vehicles to use when they encountered trenches dug across the road. This was certainly done, for bridging planks were a standard feature of the turreted type of armoured car which first appeared in that December. Yet in a footnote, referring to this letter, Churchill goes on to say that it was September 1914 when he suggested to Admiral Bacon that his Foster Daimler artillery tractor might be fitted with a portable bridge that it could lay over a gap, pass across and pick up automatically when it was over. This, he claims, was the first stage in the process that led to the invention of the tank. Other evidence suggests that he may have telescoped events and confused two separate issues.

The Caterpillar Tractor

To make matters worse, in his second volume Churchill treats the subject in more detail and refers to 'eight enormous caterpillar tractors' supplied by Admiral Bacon. He then writes that it was one of these that he directed the Admiral to fit with a portable, trench-crossing bridge, in November 1914. Here he is definitely in error. The caterpillar tractor came from an entirely different source; two sources in fact.

On 7 November 1914 Wg Cdr F.L.M. Boothby RN, who was described as the Officer Commanding Armoured Cars, Aeroplane Support, wrote to Murray Sueter submitting a report by Sub-Lt R.F. Macfie, on the subject of Caterpillar Tractors. Macfie, whose family had overseas interests in agriculture, was then serving with the armoured cars at Wormwood Scrubs. His report covered a photograph, which had appeared in the *Daily Mail* of 2 November 1914, showing a tractor hauling guns for the German Army. Macfie recognized the machine as a Holt Caterpillar Tractor and he went on to explain that they were built in California.

Unaware of the steps already taken by Churchill, Macfie pointed out that there could come a time when the British might need to get heavy artillery to deal with German fortifications over ground which was unsuitable for wheeled vehicles. Using a series of simple diagrams he went on to show how the caterpillar track, with its long bearing surface in contact with the ground, would be much more effective in such conditions than a conventional wheel. He went to some lengths to describe techniques for crossing rivers but it is quite clear that he was only talking about hauling artillery. Nothing in his paper suggests anything, which could in any way be mistaken for a tank. Macfie clearly realized that his readers, select as they were, would know little or nothing about the properties of caterpillar tracks but what he did not know was that the War Office did. As we have seen Holt tractors had been mentioned in a pre-war report and, in October 1914 a Holt had been demonstrated by company representatives, to military experts in Britain and some were soon ordered, for delivery in March 1915.

There are two footnotes to Macfie's report on the Holt. One, from Flt Cdr Hetherington, the Chief Transport Officer at Wormwood Scrubs, suggested to Boothby that one of these machines should be acquired for experimental purposes and that it could be useful for recovering broken-down armoured cars. The other is from Murray Sueter but strangely, dated 14 October 1916, it reads 'this tractor work is well known to the Army. They are hauling about guns daily.' One is surprised that he didn't add 'so there!' If the date of this note is correct then it is a bit late. The tank had been invented and, indeed, used in action by then; Boothby had moved on to other things and Macfie had become embroiled in a farce, as we shall see. If, for 1916, we should read 1914, then it pre-cedes Boothby's original letter by three weeks, which is clearly ridiculous. Even in October 1915 the whole matter would have been of no more than academic interest.

Ernest Swinton has already been mentioned. In July 1914 he was an assistant secretary to the Committee of Imperial Defence (CID) when he received a letter from a friend from his Boer War days. Hugh Marriott was a mining engineer and, having seen a Holt tractor in Antwerp, thought that Swinton should know about it. Marriott was a student of military matters and saw the tractor as being suitable for cross-country transport. Swinton passed this information on to his superior at the CID, Col Maurice Hankey, and to other War Office departments. The official response was not encouraging but the war had not begun at that time and Swinton left it at that. By September he was in France, with a pad of foolscap paper and some pencils.

By October 1914 Hankey was Secretary to the War Council. Sometimes referred to as 'the man of a million secrets' he was supremely well placed to exert influence at the highest level and was widely respected for his intelligence and discretion. By his own account Swinton called upon Hankey in London late in October 1914 to discuss the situation. In doing so he reminded his erstwhile boss of the earlier discussions about Holt tractors. Early the following month Swinton wrote to Hankey from France and again raised the subject. Indeed on more than one occasion he referred to it as Hankey's idea but it is instructive to note that, in later years, Hankey made no such claims for himself. The two men then agreed to press the idea of using caterpillars to break the deadlock in their respective spheres; Swinton at GHQ and Hankey with the War Office. Before leaving London, Swinton also made appointments to see Asquith and Lord Kitchener. The first took place at 10 Downing Street and the Prime Minister questioned Swinton about conditions in France. Oddly, since he did not feel that he had the authority, Swinton failed to raise the subject of fighting machines and when his appointment with Kitchener had to be cancelled at the last minute he seems to have abandoned the idea of pressing it further. In his book *Eyewitness*, Swinton cites the aborted meeting with Kitchener

as a missed opportunity but he does not appear to have made any attempt to arrange another.

Over Christmas 1914 Hankey put together a well-argued paper which reviewed the entire war situation but placed particular emphasis on conditions developing across the Channel. Drawing examples from history he explained how, when such problems had arisen before, new means had been devised to overcome them. His personal suggestion, to deal with the present situation, visualized an enormous, bullet-proof roller, pushed from behind by a motorized caterpillar device, the driver of which was encased in an armoured cab and provided with a Maxim machine-gun. Numbers of these things would be launched at the enemy lines, the roller crushing down barbed wire and the Maxim providing fire support to infantrymen who would advance into action behind the roller and then spring out, once they were safely through the wire, to assault the enemy's trenches. This paper of Hankey's was widely distributed where it mattered. On the civilian side it was read by the Prime Minister, the Chancellor of the Exchequer and A. J. Balfour, while its military readers included Lord Kitchener and, of course, Winston Churchill at the Admiralty.

Hankey's paper was generally well received but not particularly productive. No one in the Cabinet was galvanized into immediate action; the politicians were either too busy or ineffective. At War Office level things simply moved too slowly and the only immediate response, as might be expected, came from Churchill. His letter of 5 January 1915, although addressed to the Prime Minister, was clearly inspired by Hankey. He foresaw no great difficulty in building forty or fifty armoured, steam tractors containing soldiers and machine-guns, which would be used at night to storm the German trenches. Their weight would be sufficient to crush down barbed wire, and caterpillar tracks would enable them to cross trenches. Machine-guns on each vehicle would sweep the enemy trenches, accompanied by hand grenades lobbed over the top. Once across the first

The big 120hp version of the Holt, powered by a six-cylinder engine. The long gap between the leading wheel and the driving tracks made it entirely unsuitable for trench-crossing tests devised by the War Office experts.

line trench they would halt, forming strongpoints upon which following infantry could rally. This accomplished they would advance again to deal with the German second line. In his characteristic way Churchill made light of any difficulties but rounded off his proposal by claiming that these things would be cheap enough to make and if they proved to be useless, what harm was there?

Churchill had two other ideas up his sleeve. One was artificial smoke and, by implication, poison gas; the other was a man-propelled shield for infantry. Something similar had been proposed during the 1911 Siege of Sidney Street, a terrorist incident in London which Churchill, as Home Secretary, had attended. He now told the Prime Minister that he already had twenty such shields on order.

For a while things seemed to move swiftly. Swinton, back in London on a few days' leave, saw Gen Scott-Moncrieff, the Director of Fortifications and Works, at the War Office and put forward his ideas for armoured cars equipped with caterpillar tracks. Capt Tulloch maintained the pressure when Swinton returned to France and within a few days a small, but influential committee had been formed to take the matter further. On 13 January members of this committee went down to Aldershot to inspect a couple of Holt tractors, one of which was subsequently sent to

Shoeburyness, on the opposite side of the Thames Estuary from the Isle of Sheppey.

A month later, on 17 February, a trial was arranged at Shoeburyness. The Holt, one of the big, six-cylinder 120hp models, was unarmoured but, in order to simulate the weight of weapons and armour, it was coupled to a trailer loaded with sandbags to a total weight of 5,000lb (2,268kg). The trailer may well have been one of those marketed by the Holt Company, which also ran on caterpillar tracks, but it was hardly a fair way of testing the machine. Even so the Holt dealt reasonably well with some of the prepared trenches and wire entanglements, despite the fact that the ground, which is soft there at the best of times, had become waterlogged from heavy rain. Yet the committee, no doubt suffering themselves from the climate, could only see the negative aspects. They elected not to try the tractor against obstacles that they were sure would defeat it and made much of the obvious problems. They worried about the weight factor and the vehicle's vulnerability to enemy fire. They believed that it would take too long to develop a suitable machine, presumably on the grounds that the war would be over before it was ready. This might have been the only optimistic result of the trial, depending upon who they supposed was going to win, but ultimately pessimism won the day. Try as they may they could think of no one in the engineering profession who might be able to design such a thing and with that, for the time being, appear to have thrown up their hands in dismay and gone back to London.

Meanwhile, at the Admiralty, optimism was the order of the day, tempered by frustration. Summoned to the First Lord's room, Murray Sueter remembered how Churchill paced up and down declaiming 'We must crush the trenches in . . . We must crush them in. It is the only way. We must do it. We will crush them. I am certain it can be done.' Thinking, no doubt, of Hankey's roller idea Churchill ordered Sueter to get hold of a couple of steamrollers and begin trials at once. Sueter was not so sure. Two days later, on 20 January he also went down to Aldershot to inspect a Holt. For his benefit it was coupled up to a 16-ton (16,256kg) traction engine which it proceeded to drag around over muddy ground without the least difficulty. An order, however, is an order so Sueter arranged to borrow two steamrollers and then had a trench dug at Wormwood Scrubs that they were supposed to crush in. Churchill's idea was to join the two machines side by side, with one extra wide roller at the front and the inner rear rolls connected at the back. Thus prepared they would move along the trench, rather than across it, pushing down the parapets and by dint of their combined weight, suitably augmented with ballast, collapse the trench.

Sueter had neither the time nor the resources to rebuild the two machines. The best he could do was to try to couple them side by side and see what happened. The result was total failure. As soon as they started to move the two machines broke apart and, whenever they encountered resistance, the wheels simply spun around on the damp ground. Steamrollers are fitted with smooth wheels, ideal for levelling roads but incapable of obtaining any sort of grip in adverse conditions. Hemp rope was tied around the driven wheels to obtain grip but it made no difference. In desperation Sueter ordered a single roller to get up steam and charge at the trench from the side but, as soon

as it met the slightest slope it stopped, the rollers spun and excavated a hole which totally trapped the machine. Murray Sueter prepared a report for the First Lord and sent the rollers back to their municipal duties.

In Lincoln, meanwhile, Fosters had completed the first of their 105hp tractors to the Admiralty order and a trial was arranged in a nearby park at the beginning of December 1914. Admiral Bacon was among the observers and he watched as a party of sailors erected a wooden bridge over a ditch and the tractor made its way across. Recalling Churchill's earlier requirement, Bacon asked William Tritton if it might not be possible to fit one of the tractors with a bridge that it could carry, lay and recover as a means of crossing trenches. By January Tritton had a small model finished which was shown to Churchill who approved of the idea so Fosters started work on converting a tractor. By February the project had been overtaken by events and Fosters were told to stop the work but by then it was quite advanced so it was completed and its ultimate fate will be recorded later.

The various schemes recorded here all played their part in achieving the ultimate goal but there are some which, for one reason or another, stand out as milestones. They are not all necessarily logical milestones in fact, one or two appear, with hindsight, to be quite ridiculous. Sometime around the middle of January Maj Hetherington was toying with the idea of an enormous wheeled machine, capable of crushing wire, squashing trenches and even wading through small rivers and he discussed this with Murray Sueter. Sueter told Hetherington to come up with a more detailed design and arranged for him to meet Churchill and the Duke of Westminster to explain it. The meeting took place in Grosvenor House on or around 17 February 1915 and the only thing that everyone seems to remember about it was Hetherington's fantastic image of a war machine running upon gigantic wheels. Writing in 1919 Hetherington insisted that he also discussed Pedrail and caterpillar tracks, and there is evidence to bear this out.

A Pedrail tracked truck, loaded with half-a-ton of bricks, of the type examined and tested by Winston Churchill on Horse Guards Parade.

Pedrail Tracks

Two days later Churchill came down to Horse Guards Parade, from his rooms at the Admiralty. Waiting for him was a small truck mounted on a Pedrail track, which was loaded with 30cwt (1,524kg) of stone. This truck was of a type marketed by Diplock's company, mostly for overseas sales, that was designed to be hauled by a draught animal. Hetherington, Boothby and Sueter all claimed to have been responsible for this trial but its purpose was to explain the caterpillar principle to Churchill. The First Lord was invited to push the little vehicle, which must have weighed around 2t (2,032kg) all told, and he did it with ease. Churchill was shown how an endless track, or portable railway, offered less rolling resistance than wheels bearing the same weight which meant, of course, that a heavy tracked vehicle, powered by a moderately powerful engine could move around more easily than a comparable wheeled machine, especially over rough ground. The point appears to have been made. Churchill told Hetherington to call on Lord Fisher, the First Sea Lord. Fisher, in turn, called in the Director of Naval Construction, Eustace Tennyson D'Eyncourt, who evidently could not see what it had to do with him. Hetherington remained on tenterhooks for two days.

The Big-Wheel Machine

Experts at the Admiralty Air Department had, meanwhile, been evaluating Hetherington's other proposal, the big-wheel machine. They improved upon the original idea to the extent that it mounted three naval turrets equipped with 4in guns, the kind of thing normally carried by a destroyer. The platform upon which these turrets were mounted was supported by three wheels, each 40ft (12m) in diameter; two at the front and one in rear for steering. Much of the structure appears to have been a lattice work of girders that not only reduced weight but presented enemy gunners with a less solid target. Where armour was applied it would be up to 4in (10cm) thick and power was supplied by two Sunbeam marine diesel engines, as used in submarines, driving dynamos and electric motors that powered the wheels. Overall dimensions were given as 46ft (14m) high and 100ft (30m) long with an estimated weight of some 300t (304,800kg). Impressive and appealing it might be but it was clearly out of court in so many respects that it was abandoned without further consideration.

Yet there can be little doubt that for those leaving Grosvenor House after dining with the Duke of Westminster that evening it was the potent image of Hetherington's Big Wheel that stuck in their minds. It was like something from H.G. Wells's *War of the Worlds*. Churchill was clearly inspired. Two days later, on the morning of Saturday, 20 August, a select group met in Churchill's room at the Admiralty. The First Lord had a cold and conducted the meeting from his bed. Among those present were Hetherington, Tritton, Col Dumble and Tennyson D'Eyncourt, the last named being still rather reluctant to get involved. It was now that Tritton was told to stop work on his Trench Crossing Tractor. Churchill was at his most persuasive and when the meeting ended D'Eyncourt had agreed to chair a small committee, which would take the matter forward.

The Admiralty Landships Committee met for the first time on Monday, 22 February. It comprised the same party that had met in the First Lord's room on Saturday. They agreed that their first duty was to decide between the merits of large wheels and caterpillar tracks as the means of traction and agreed that a weight of about 25t (25,400kg) was the most they should consider. They further resolved that the best way of arriving at a decision was to construct an example of each. Despite the fact that D'Eyncourt had ruled out Hetherington's Big Wheel, the Committee was not prepared to say at this stage whether 25t (25,400kg) should be the ceiling weight or whether the two prototypes, when built, should be regarded as models for larger machines. In fact they were not very wide of the mark for the first production tanks tipped the scales at around 28t (28,448kg).

After further consideration they decided that the wheeled machine should be based around one of Fosters' big tractors but they were less sure about the caterpillar type. They believed the first stage should be to evaluate the different types of track then available. Lt Macfie, who had attended the first meeting in an advisory capacity, had stressed the advantages of tracks but, in order to obtain more mature experience, the Committee applied to the Road Board for the temporary loan of Col Crompton who attended their next meeting on 25 February. The veteran engineer accepted the challenge with alacrity although there is no evidence that he had any previous experience of caterpillar tracks. Indeed he already had a design of his own on the drawing board, and it was a wheeled machine.

Crompton had been anxious to involve himself in war work from the very beginning but without much luck. An early suggestion to replace all existing army lorries with a more suitable design of his own was rebuffed for practical reasons but early in 1915 Col Dumble had asked him to come up with a design for what would be known as a trench straddling machine. Crompton envisaged this as being based upon a Foster-Daimler Tractor. His idea was to surround the tractor with a platform, about 18in (46cm) from the ground, which

could carry a trench-storming party of fifty men. This platform would be 36ft (11m) long by 11ft (3.5m) wide and encased with armour sufficient to protect the men from rifle, machine-gun and shrapnel fire. Crompton even describes it as a travelling fort. The method of operation was hardly the stuff of a surprise attack since the tractor's mobility, over uneven ground, was strictly limited.

Crompton's plan was to have the tractor cross specially prepared sections of the British trench line and move slowly into no-man's land. A team of men would move ahead of the vehicle, levelling rough ground and filling in shell holes as close to the enemy line as they could. This, according to Crompton, was probably best done by night although he did not regard this as essential. Of course, at this time, Crompton had not seen the front and he could have had little idea of the concentration of firepower that might be brought against the working party. He says nothing of the tractor carrying any armament of its own, merely that the storming party would have two machine-guns. Once the ground had been prepared the storming party would make its way out to the tractor and climb aboard. With everything ready the tractor advanced cautiously into the German lines until the overhanging front end of the platform was above the enemy trench. Hatches would open in the floor and the storming party jump down to clear the trench. This done they would return to the tractor, construct a small bridge across the trench and the machine would then winch itself over, ready to move on. It was hardly a practical idea but probably no worse than many others floated at the time.

In the meantime the Committee had discussed their ideas with the First Lord and Churchill told them to get on as quickly as possible. They were, at this time, also considering something along the lines of a trench straddling machine, capable of transporting fifty fighting troops across no-man's land to be dropped off in the German trenches.

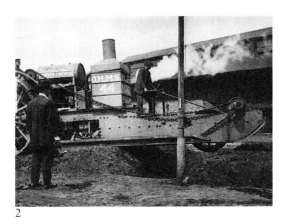

1

2

3

4

5

A sequence of five views showing the modified Foster-Daimler Tractor, known as the Tritton Trench Crosser, tackling a narrow trench in the factory yard.

1. *Shows the machine being prepared for the trial.*
2. *The tractor's nose is across the trench and the leading wheel is on the far side.*
3. *Now the driver has released the ramps that form a simple bridge over the trench.*
4. *The tractor's rear wheels now cross the trench, by means of their own bridge.*
5. *The ramps are now dragged clear so that the machine can reverse over them, hoist them back into place and continue upon its way.*

3 The Landships Committee

With the formation of the Admiralty Landships Committee we reach another significant stage in the development of the tank. From this date, late February 1915, a course was set which would lead directly to the creation of a true landship under the guiding hand of D'Eyncourt and the driving force of young Albert Stern. There would be other schemes, to be sure, but they would prove to be dead ends. Some of the present actors would be sidelined in due course, and others would appear, but even a committee takes on a life of its own and survives change; possibly even thrives on it.

Yet at the start it was the amazing energy of the septuagenarian Crompton that got things moving. On 26 February Crompton went up to Lincoln to meet William Tritton and initiate work on the wheeled landship model. Tritton had ideas of his own but for the present he was no more than a contractor, building to the Committee's wishes and Crompton's design. Even so Tritton was undoubtedly happier to be working on a wheeled design. His limited experience of track-laying vehicles, when his firm built the Centipede Tractor, convinced him that tracks would get tangled up in barbed wire and probably break. Crompton obtained the services of an old friend, L.A. Legros, then President of the Institution of Automobile Engineers, who was deputed to supervise Tritton's work.

Early in March, Crompton made contact with J.B. Diplock, whom he had advised on an earlier project. He then began negotiations with the traction engine and lorry manufacturer Fodens, of Sandbach in Cheshire, who would be the main contractor for the tracked landship model. Churchill was shown scale models of both designs and authorized contracts for six-wheeled and twelve-tracked machines at an estimated cost of £70,000.

From the first trenches established on the Aisne in September 1914 the lines had by now spread in both directions, towards the Channel coast and the Swiss frontier. The Germans made a powerful attack around Ypres later in the year and then came to the conclusion that they could not break the deadlock. Their reaction was to improve the existing defences and then transfer large numbers of men to their Eastern Front. This was not such a blessing to the Allies as one might suppose. If German reinforcements in the east could force a decision there it would only be a matter of time before the entire German Army, with its Austro-Hungarian allies, would be back with a vengeance. It was therefore incumbent upon the British, French and Belgians to maintain the pressure from their side and keep as many Germans as possible in France. At Neuve Chapelle, on 10 March 1915, the British opened the season with a well-organized assault on the German-held village. Described as the first planned offensive to be undertaken by the British in this war it showed, in its early stages, a remarkable grasp of the problems of trench warfare with a surprise attack in the wake of a well-directed artillery barrage. It lasted for five days and failed, in the end, for reasons that would become familiar. Poor information filtering back from the fighting line, lack of adequate reserves to exploit success and, in this case, a shortage of guns and ammunition.

Cdre Murray Sueter, it will be noted, was not among those selected to sit on the Landships Committee. Whether he was not asked, or declined an invitation is not known, but the former is suggested by his subsequent actions. That he had not lost interest in the project is indicated by the fact that, on 4 March 1915, he submitted a design of his own before

D'Eyncourt's committee, which had been prepared in conjunction with Diplock's Pedrail Transport Company of Fulham. The general design was similar to the tracked landship that Crompton was preparing, also with Pedrail track units in mind. The similarities are strong in other respects. It would have employed a pair of Rolls-Royce engines and weighed, in theory, 25t (25,400kg). Sueter claims that he used experience, gained from earlier work on submarine design, which resulted in upturned ends to the hull, to clear uneven ground, and a central conning tower containing a giant ship's wheel. The machine would have been 38ft (11.5m) long, 10ft 6in (3m) tall, and capable of travelling in either direction. There is no mention of a crew, nor obvious evidence of room for fifty infantrymen. When he first publicized the design, in 1937, Sueter mentioned a 12-pounder gun but claimed that no weapons were shown on the original drawing for reasons of secrecy. One is inclined to suspect that he was being disingenuous, with the advantage of hindsight, because by that time tanks were expected to have guns. What the Landships Committee made of it is not clear and there is no evidence at all that it was developed any further.

Late in April 1915 Sueter claims that he had some surplus funds in his budget and offered Lt MacFie £700 to work out a design of his own. Following some investigation MacFie found a Mr Nesfield, with a garage in Ealing, who was prepared to work with him. They acquired the chassis of a 5t (5,080kg) Alldays & Onions lorry at the Talbot works which was towed over to Ealing where the two men began to draw up their design. By the end of June they had produced a small working model that they planned to show to the Landships Committee.

In the meantime Sueter heard that MacFie and Nesfield had fallen out and, as he writes, 'a regular dog-fight ensued over this model'. Sueter decided to keep out of it and requested that Cdr Boothby should intervene as peacemaker but this failed. Both designers laid claim to the model and MacFie resorted to placing armed sailors, as

sentries, in Nesfield's workshop to guard the unfinished prototype. Sueter then ordered MacFie to have the chassis returned to Wormwood Scrubs but although MacFie refers to a 'semi-completed caterpillar mechanism' there is no evidence to show that he had actually got very far. The truth appears to be that, while their model showed many ingenious features, notably the outline of its tracks which were raised at the front, they had not descended to such practical matters as the type of track to be used, the nature of the suspension (if any) or the arrangements for driving and steering the machine. With these fundamental aspects unresolved one can hardly make any quantifiable claims for their work and it is instructive to note that, when the project was offered to the Ministry of Munitions for further development it was declined. Sueter may well have wasted his £700.

Meanwhile poor old Col Crompton was meeting with endless frustration. At Fodens they were experiencing industrial trouble and Crompton took himself up to Cheshire in an effort to sort it out. He failed. On 20 April it was announced that Fodens had lost the contract and that the tracked landship would now be built in Birmingham, by the Metropolitan Carriage, Wagon and Finance Company Ltd. The very next day Crompton was off to France. He crossed the Channel with Thomas Hetherington and Albert Stern. Crompton's diary gives the date as 21 March and claims that his plan was to examine the lines around Neuve Chapelle and, no doubt, get a first-hand feel for the conditions and problems of trench warfare. Stern, in his *Logbook of a Pioneer*, gives the date as 20 April and this is confirmed by official sources. Crompton says that the mission failed because much of Neuve Chapelle was still in German hands while Stern claims that they were turned back on orders from British GHQ at St Omer because they had no official sanction for the visit. Not an uncommon fate for prophets.

In fact they were acting on orders from Churchill, who was interfering in his usual way. Crompton had been trying to get such information from the War Office, without much luck, but Churchill's writ did not run in France and the best that his party could achieve was to examine the roads between Dunkirk and St Omer. Crompton later claimed that it was from this expedition that he appreciated the need to articulate his landship design, in order that the machines could pass through French villages. There was, however, another factor involved. It seems that the method of attack had been changed, even before the first machine was completed. Now, instead of a direct assault upon the enemy's trenches, the machines would, as it were, sidle up to the enemy lines and deposit the troops on the edge of the trench. The approach would be a zig-zag route across no-man's land, with the landships finally drawing up alongside the trench. This could be another good reason for creating an articulated design.

Such a fundamental change, of course, altered the entire picture as far as the Landships Committee was concerned. It was back to the start in terms of design so production of all but one of the Pedrail machines was abandoned with one other, designed to run on imported American tracks, authorized for construction. Crompton's first three designs are fairly easily described. The original, rigid type, dating from March 1915 looked, on paper, like a small industrial building on tracks, complete with its gabled roof. Corridors were provided along both sides to accommodate the fighting troops. The original articulated version, drawn in April, was similar, except that it was in two halves, and further modified so that the sides could be raised to enable the infantry to debus directly into a trench when the machine was stopped alongside. The third was identical except that parallel pairs of American Bullock tracks replaced the full-width Pedrail units. This version was drawn in May 1915.

The American connection came about thus. Crompton, although he was prepared to create a design around the Pedrail system, had some reservations about it. He regarded it as too complex and believed that a large vehicle based upon Diplock's system was likely to be unstable. But

With human ballast in place the little Killen-Strait tractor leaps over a grassy mound in the grounds of the Talbot Motor Works at Barlby Road.

he also knew that it was the only such system available in Britain since Fosters had abandoned their *Centipede* design. In the United States, on the other hand, a number of firms were manufacturing caterpillar tractors for agricultural and industrial use and Crompton was anxious to examine them. He knew that the Holt type was out of the question, since their production was all required for artillery work, but he could see no harm in looking at the others.

Some years before the war Crompton had designed an ingenious, if impractical, military steam tractor and during the design stage he had hired a young assistant named George Field. Crompton now enlisted Field to go to the USA on his behalf. Field was granted a commission as a Lieutenant in the Royal Naval Volunteer Reserve (RNVR) and duly set off. The first result of his research was a small machine known as the Killen-Strait tractor which Crompton first saw at Barlby Road towards the end of March. Built in Appleton, Wisconsin, the Killen-Strait ran on three sets of tracks like a tricycle; two at the back for driving, one in the front for steering. It was powered by a four-cylinder petrol engine and appears to have had a very lively performance.

A Bullock Creeping Grip Tractor inspected by members of the Landships Committee on the Greenhithe Marshes, close to the River Thames in Kent.

When it first arrived it was even fitted with a fancy canvas canopy with scalloped edges which made it look like something belonging on a fairground. Mr William Strait, proprietor of the American company, was in Britain at this time, either with the tractor or on business of his own, and he was able to make some helpful suggestions.

George Field also went to Chicago where he saw a larger type of machine, generally similar to the Holt, built by the Bullock Creeping Grip Tractor Company. He learned that one of their models had recently been exported to Britain and that it was working on the Greenhithe Marshes, near Dartford in Kent, presumably on some sort of land reclamation project. On 28 April, in company with other members of the Landships Committee, Crompton went down to Kent on what appears to have been a cold and windy day. Evidently the tractor impressed Crompton sufficiently for him to instruct Field to place an order for two of the Bullock Company's largest machines on behalf of the Admiralty. He then went back to his drawing office and redrew his articulated landship design around the new track system. The order was confirmed on 10 May and, in fact, was increased to include two pairs of extra long Bullock tracks which would be used on the prototype design. Crompton does not appear to have been put off by Field's report that the staff at the Bullock Tractor plant did not work to the

highest standards of accuracy. Field claimed that if, in the final assembly, the tracks failed to mesh correctly with the teeth of the drive sprocket the workmen simply beat them with sledgehammers until they did!

Otherwise, from the landships point of view, May 1915 seems to have been a fairly quiet month. On the 16th Maj Hetherington went up to Lincoln to inspect the mock-up of the Big Wheel machine at Fosters. This was as close as anyone in Britain ever came to creating anything like Hetherington's original Big Wheel concept and it would be interesting to know if Hetherington ever found out that the Imperial Russian Army did, in fact, build such a thing. Meanwhile, back at Wormwood Scrubs, there was a brief revival of interest in Pedrails. Apparently in response to reports from Gallipoli, a party of twelve ratings and a Chief Petty Officer from the Repair Depot, Royal Naval Armoured Car Division, fitted a wooden pattern for an armoured shield to one of the Pedrail one-ton tracked trucks. The thing had been designed by draughtsmen from Vickers, at the request of Cdre Sueter, and improved upon by Lt Symes. Ballasted with ingots of pig iron to represent the weight of the real thing in steel it was found quite possible for two men to move it across rough ground. Cdr Boothby suggested that it could be powered by a motorcycle engine but, after some two

The type of Bullock tractor seen at Greenhithe was the 50bhp Creeping Grip Senior model which had the four-cylinder engine located at the front, behind a conventional radiator.

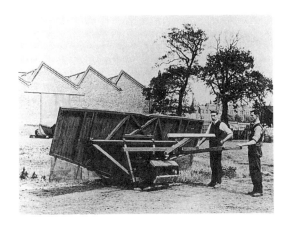

The wooden mock-up of the man-propelled infantry shield on a set of Pedrail tracks, seen on land adjacent to the Talbot works on Barlby Road.

Here the Killen-Strait is seen, fitted with the body from a Delaunay-Bellevile armoured car from which the turret has been removed. Wider track shoes appear to have been fitted at the rear, presumably to spread the extra weight.

months' work, the entire scheme was abandoned. Whether there is any link between this device and the shields which Churchill claims that he ordered is not clear but given the dates it seems unlikely.

Events on Gallipoli seem to have inspired another project based upon the Killen-Strait tractor. In March 1915 two sections of Rolls-Royce armoured cars from Numbers 3 and 4 Squadrons had been landed on the peninsula. The effort proved almost pointless since ground conditions, and the tiny area occupied by British troops, seriously restricted their use. Boothby seems to have come up with the idea of fitting an armoured car body to the Killen-Strait which he hoped would prove more effective and this was duly done at Wormwood Scrubs. The body of one of Samson's old armoured cars, with the turret removed, was fitted to the tractor and driven around the site. It seems to have worked perfectly well but was never developed although, in theory, it was the first example of a tracked, armoured fighting vehicle ever built.

Early in June the Landships Committee, possibly on Hetherington's advice, decided to abandon the wheeled landship project. Crompton

Tritton and Wilson, with another officer, examine the wooden mock-up of the Big Wheel machine at the Wellington Foundry. The chalk circle, drawn on the planks, shows the size and location of one of the 15ft wheels.

The chassis of the Pedrail Landship rolls out from the Stothert and Pitt works near Bath. The Aster engines are located transversely across the track units but the tracks themselves are virtually hidden by the frames. Note the rollers at each end to assist it over obstacles.

seems to have taken some delight in writing to Tritton on the 9th that 'it appears unlikely that the Admiralty will proceed with a high vehicle'. Crompton was clearly not impressed with his rival. At about the same time the Admiralty decided to create another new Royal Naval Air Service Squadron dedicated to undertake development work and the testing of landships. Lt-Cdr McGrath took over 20 Squadron which was, of course, based at Wormwood Scrubs.

If things had been quiet on the Admiralty front in May there had been even less activity from the War Office. On 7 June Tom Tulloch wrote to Col Louis Jackson, the officer responsible for trench warfare matters in the Directorate of Fortifications and Works. Tulloch was bemoaning the lack of progress and the dearth of imagination in Britain which, he claimed, invariably left the initiative to the Germans. Jackson was in a receptive mood. He had got wind of a suggestion that the Germans were building an armoured flame-thrower and when Tulloch came up with a similar idea it inspired him to follow it up. Designs were prepared for a 35t (35,560kg) machine, running on Pedrail or similar tracks, mounting a flame-thrower and three machine-guns in a body described as 'egg-shaped' which overhung the tracks at each end.

According to the history of the Ministry of Munitions, negotiations had already begun with the Aster Company for a pair of six-cylinder engines and with Diplock's Pedrail Company for the tracks, but there may be some confusion here. The machine they ended up with was almost certainly the Pedrail landship initiated by Col Crompton. Since the industrial trouble at Fodens this machine, whatever may have been built of it, became an abandoned orphan. Crompton himself was already working on alternate designs, and work on the original machine had been passed on to the Metropolitan Company in Birmingham and from there, briefly, to Fosters of Lincoln. It is doubtful, however, if much was done because the Admiralty, by this time, had clearly lost interest. It was officially taken over by the War Office in July 1915 and transferred to another engineering company, Messrs Stothert & Pitt of Bath. It seems to have been completed, at least as a running chassis, by August 1915 and then taken to the Trench Warfare Department's experimental ground at Porton Down on Salisbury Plain. It was never fitted with armour, nor with the flame-thrower, but it underwent some cross-country trials before being abandoned.

This period was also a frustrating one for Ernest Swinton. In April he travelled to Boulogne

The completed Pedrail Landship photographed at Porton Down. It has been posed in such a way that it appears to be attacking the sandbagged parapet of a trench; in fact it could not have coped with such an obstacle and has been parked in a prepared gap.

Hetherington steers the Killen-Strait through a barbed-wire entanglement at Barlby Road during a demonstration for Churchill and Lloyd-George. The weather vane at the front shows the driver which way the track is pointing. Below it is the 'secret' net-cutting attachment that upset the Admiralty.

to witness the first arrival, in France, of British Territorial Army regiments. He was immediately struck by their excellent appearance and behaviour so it was with additional misgivings that he pondered upon their fate. In his occasional contacts with Maurice Hankey he could learn nothing new; there seemed to be no progress whatever on their joint scheme. His work as a war correspondent was also being undermined as more reporters from British newspapers were gaining a foothold in France. In May he prepared a lengthy paper setting out a case for Armoured Machine-Gun Destroyers. It is a remarkably prophetic document both in the tactical and mechanical sense but, as may be anticipated, it met with little enthusiasm at General Headquarters. A few days later Swinton bumped into an old acquaintance, a fellow officer just out from England, who told him roughly what the Admiralty had been up to. What he did not know was that, back at home, the War Office and the Admiralty were finally preparing to share the problem.

On 30 June a demonstration was arranged at Barlby Road to show the Minister of Munitions

the kind of work 20 Squadron was doing. The Army would soon be taking over. Just a week before, it had been announced that Col Jackson's department, hitherto part of the Directorate of Fortifications and Works, should become an independent Trench Warfare Department in its own right, under the direct control of the Ministry of Munitions. David Lloyd-George, the Minister, arrived at Wormwood Scrubs accompanied by Winston Churchill and a bevy of officers. They were treated to displays of the Pedrail Infantry Shield and Killen-Strait tractor. The latter, driven by Maj Hetherington, tackled a variety of obstacles and it was said that Hetherington's skill as a steeplechase jockey made it an exciting display. The tractor had been fitted with a lethal-looking attachment, something after the style of a giant can-opener, which sliced its way through complex barbed wire entanglements. The device had been created for use on submarines, to help them cut a way through anti-torpedo nets hung out by enemy warships and it was still very much on the Secret List. The staff at Wormwood Scrubs got a severe dressing down for using it in this way. Later the Killen-Strait was shown again, fitted

The Bullock tractors ordered from Chicago were the 75bhp Texas–California Giant version. This had the engine at the back, adding weight where it mattered, and a curious drum-shaped radiator at the front.

with the body of the Delaunay-Belleville armoured car, which illustrates just how quickly the change could be effected.

Churchill used this event to help persuade Lloyd-George that his Ministry should take over the project and this was confirmed by the Prime Minister about two weeks later. Even so the Ministry of Munitions could not create an experimental team out of thin air so it was agreed that, for the time being, the Admiralty experts and 20 Squadron should continue with the experimental work and only hand over to the Army on the eve

of production. Thus, by early August 1915, 20 Squadron had moved to the new Trench Warfare Department's testing ground at Wembley Park, to the north-west of its previous site.

Among the engineering firms involved in work on behalf of the Landships Committee were Messrs McEwan & Pratt from the famous beer brewing town of Burton-on-Trent. The firm had produced gears for the Pedrail Landship and they were now contracted to do work on two Bullock Creeping Grip Tractors imported from the United States. The two machines were delivered from Liverpool on 16 June when tests began. They were of the manufacturer's largest model, the 75hp California Giant, and W.G. Wilson, who was based at Burton at the time, was scathing about their condition. They had been shipped across the Atlantic as deck cargo and each showed signs of surface rust. To make matters worse they had not been at Burton for very long before someone left one of the tractors in gear with the engine running. It ran into its twin and both canopies were damaged to the point that they had to be removed.

In fact these canopies would probably have been taken off before long anyway because the purpose of the trials at Burton-on-Trent was to test out Col Crompton's theories about articulated landships. McEwan & Pratt fitted a

The articulated Bullock tractors, apparently stuck in a trench during trials at Burton-on-Trent. This whole, bizarre concept was doomed from the start.

complicated coupling system to Crompton's design. The two tractors were arranged back to back and connected by a complex system of pulleys and wire ropes in tension. The idea was to keep the two machines firmly but flexibly locked together and the cables were extended forward in an effort to keep the steering wheels at each end clear of the ground. Thus the result, at least in theory, was to create a four-tracked machine with a flexible coupling in the centre, but the trials were disappointing. The contraption was run over a series of trenches and earthworks and it invariably got stuck. Crompton's theory that, in such an event, one tractor would haul the other out of trouble proved to be untenable. For one thing it was discovered that reverse gear did not match any of the ratios of the three forward gears so that, with one tractor driving forwards and the other in reverse, extra strain was placed upon the coupling.

These trials were soon abandoned and orders arrived that the two Bullocks should be sent down to Wembley Park. However before they went, they gave an impressive demonstration of wire crushing and one of them was involved in a more bizarre experiment. Known as Elephant's Feet it is attributed to Maj Ernest Baguley, who had purchased the failing McEwan & Pratt Company in 1912. The Elephant's Feet idea was as basic as it was peculiar. One of the tractors was fitted with an external frame from which swung six long wooden poles, each with a large disc (or elephant's foot) on the end.

If the tractor got stuck, while crossing a trench, the wooden legs would take the weight before it fell too far and, in effect, pole-vault the vehicle over the gap. It looked incredibly ramshackle, not at all the work of a skilled engineer such as Baguley was said to be, and it seems to have been abandoned very quickly.

By the end of July the two Bullocks were despatched to London. Oddly they did not go by rail, as one might expect, but apparently travelled all the way, 120 miles, by road. It is said to have taken three weeks and would have been as much

The crude Elephant's Feet system on trial at Burton. The track unit has slipped into a trench, one foot supports the machine while the other hangs over the trench, although the engine is running it seems safe to assume that the tractor is stuck fast.

a trial of the crew as it was of the tractors. On 3 August two pairs of extended Bullock tracks arrived in Liverpool aboard the SS *Orduna*. They had been ordered by Crompton, through George Field, and were to be the basis of his first full-size prototype. Now, however, matters would speed up dramatically and bring with them a good deal of change.

Early in July it was agreed that in future landship designs the emphasis would be on combat, as distinct from troop carrying. Whether this was a result of the War Office take-over is not clear but it could equally well have been a case of natural evolution. Crompton's first design along these lines featured two drum-shaped turrets on each unit. Each turret was apparently going to carry a 75mm gun. At the end of the month Crompton drew a lower profile model which lacked the upper turret. The first turreted design was 9ft 6in (2.9m) high and may have been considered top-heavy; the second model was 7ft 6in (2.3m) high while a third, which appeared on his drawing board about a month later, was just 6ft (1.8m) high overall. It retained the basic shape of the second model but with a lower profile body for each unit. Unfortunately, by the time this third design was ready Crompton was no longer working for the Landships Committee.

William Ashbee Tritton, managing director of Fosters of Lincoln. His rapid elevation to knighthood and national fame made no impression on this solid, practical businessman.

In his *Reminiscences,* written in 1928, Col Crompton devotes a chapter to his work for the Landships Committee but it ends, enigmatically, in August 1915. When his colleague, L.A. Legros wrote an account of the invention of the tank for *The Automobile Engineer* in 1922 he virtually ignored developments from August 1915 until 1918 as if they had no bearing on the matter. A modern psychologist might describe the condition as one of being in denial.

On 19 July William Tritton sent his chief draughtsman, William Rigby, down to London to assist Crompton and Legros in the preparation of drawings. Rigby set up his drawing board in Crompton's house, Thriplands in Kensington Court. It therefore follows that Rigby would have been involved in drawing work on Crompton's two final designs. Yet it is altogether possible that, even before Rigby came down to London, Crompton's fate had been sealed. Stern, who clearly interpreted his role as secretary to the Landships Committee as one of some substance, was finding Crompton's approach altogether too

slow. Looked at with hindsight, and keeping Crompton's age and the novelty of his task in mind, it all seems remarkably rapid but that might be misleading. The fact is that Crompton was, at heart, a Victorian engineer dedicated to quality and perfection. Stern was a businessman in the modern sense and he needed to see results.

One suspects that the bluff approach which Tritton would have brought to the proceedings appealed to Stern far more than Crompton's gracious style, and in any case the time was rapidly approaching when a manufacturer must become involved. Thus, on 22 July, a contract was issued to William Foster & Company of Lincoln for the construction of a prototype landship. It would not be an articulated machine, such as Crompton was working upon, but a single unit running on a pair of tracks.

These tracks would be the lengthened set manufactured by the Bullock company in Chicago which arrived at Liverpool early in August and were sent at once to Lincoln. On 5 August Crompton's appointment was officially terminated. He must have known that it was coming but that did not lessen the disappointment. Indeed he was later to complain that the first design to come out of Lincoln was based on drawings that Rigby had done for him and when he saw the second prototype he referred to it rather unkindly as 'The Slug'.

There is some substance to Crompton's complaint. When Tritton was interviewed by Stern in London at the end of July, and learned that he was to take over the project, he sent an urgent telegram to his office in Lincoln instructing them to begin work on a landship 'such as Rigby drew', they were to install a 'Daimler Set' and fit the tracks that would be arriving from Liverpool. The Daimler Set refers to the 105hp Daimler/Knight engine, two-speed gearbox and worm differential from the Foster-Daimler tractor. Although Tritton denied it later, under oath, the only designs that Rigby may have drawn up to this time should have been those he did under Col Crompton's guidance.

4 Testing the Ideas

Work began in Lincoln even before Tritton left London. When he did arrive back at Fosters he was joined by Walter Wilson, from Burton, who was appointed overseer on behalf of the Admiralty. Wilson had worked with Tritton before, when they were building a mock-up of Crompton's wheeled landship design where the two men, quite different in background, temperament and engineering outlook, had learned to respect one another. There seems to be little doubt that from the very start Tritton regarded Wilson more as a colleague than an inspector, and one whose inventive genius fitted in well with his own practical, commercial approach to engineering matters.

When the two men inspected the long Bullock track units they were dismayed. Wilson already had some experience of them during the trials at Burton and among other things he had noted the crude workmanship and the fact that, when they were driven over trenches the tracks tended to sag away from the rollers. Construction work on the new landship began on 11 August and six days later Tritton came up with the idea of a wheeled tail, attached to the rear of the vehicle. This was designed partly as a steering aid but also as means of supporting the rear end of the vehicle when it tackled an obstacle. To that extent it was something like the rump of Crompton's scheme to build articulated machines.

Yet if Tritton, at this time, was thinking up ways of perfecting the existing design, Wilson appears to have been way ahead of him. On 17 August Wilson explained to Tritton his vision of a landship design in which the tracks passed all the way around the body of the vehicle. Given the present state of development this was an amazingly perceptive step. The following week

A photograph of the Number 1 Lincoln Machine under construction at Fosters factory. The workmen are completing the turret but notice the shaft at the bottom onto which the Bullock track units would be mounted.

Tritton went down to London for an interview with Tennyson D'Eyncourt. Having outlined the problems of the original concept he soon persuaded the Director of Naval Construction to authorize work to begin on Wilson's improved design. D'Eyncourt noted in his diary 'Proposal for next (Landship) with equivalent of 50ft wheel. All parts can be made in England. I think well of this. Wilson's idea.' The reference to a 50ft (15m) wheel concerns the lower radius of the tracks where they met the ground. In profile Wilson's design was an irregular rhomboid with rounded corners.

This was all very well but if it could all be made in England (or Britain as D'Eyncourt should more properly have said) it would need British tracks, and there was the rub. Meanwhile work still went ahead on the original design

The Number 1 Lincoln Machine on trial with wagon covers thrown over the turret to disguise its purpose. The curvature of the track, on its lower run, shows up well.

which, if nothing else, might serve as a test bed. The first machine, fitted with the lengthened Bullock tracks was run, briefly, in Foster's yard on 9 September 1915. The design, of course, was dictated by the tracks although, to avoid confusion it should be explained that what the Chicago company supplied was not just a set of tracks; it was an entire suspension system of frames, springs and rollers which included an adjustable idler wheel at the front and a toothed drive sprocket at the rear. This was mounted on a shaft, extending from each side of the vehicle. The body, which was little more than a riveted box, was raised above the tracks and this, in turn, was surmounted by a simple, drum-shaped turret.

Inside the body was the Daimler engine, gearbox and differential along with a radiator and, of course, the driving controls. The turret itself was a dummy, it was not even made to rotate; however situated where it was, almost directly above the engine, it would probably have been impossible for gunners to occupy it anyway. Stern had been concerned about the turret but for different reasons. Writing to Tritton on 3 September he suggested that the turret be mounted on rails so that it could slide forwards in order to give the gun a better field of fire when the machine was operating on rough ground. This, in turn, meant that the top of the vehicle would not

be fully covered but Stern claimed that he had been told there was no need to protect the crew from shrapnel so a fully enclosed body would not be necessary.

As soon as the tracks were fitted Tritton and Wilson noted another problem. Where they touched the ground they were flat, from front to back, making it almost impossible to steer the vehicle. Tritton quickly worked out a modification which he described as giving the tracks a fish-belly shape at the bottom to reduce ground contact. In this form the prototype, now variously known as the Tritton, or Number I Lincoln Machine, was tested on Cross O'Cliff Hill, an area of rough ground close to the city. To disguise its purpose the turret was shrouded in a large sheet of tarpaulin bearing the company's name but the trials were not a success. As Wilson had forecast the tracks sagged away from the rollers every time it went over a trench and they kept coming off. The sag did not really matter on the shorter tracks fitted to production Bullock tractors, although they were not designed for trench crossing either, but the new set, being 9ft (2.7m) long, came off with monotonous regularity. More than that they showed signs of breaking up since they had never been intended to support the weight of a such a machine which was calculated at around 16.5t (16,764kg).

In July Ernest Swinton heard that he was being recalled to London. His role as 'eyewitness' was redundant and his old boss, Maurice Hankey, had a new job for him. Hankey's title, at this time, was Secretary of the Cabinet Dardanelles Committee. He was planning to visit Gallipoli and decided that Swinton would make an excellent deputy. Despite its rather specialized title the Dardanelles Committee was, in fact, the old Committee of Imperial Defence under a new guise. It answered directly to the Cabinet and, in practice, was called upon to consider any matter concerning the progress of the war that ministers deemed relevant. It gave Swinton unparalleled access to virtually everyone who mattered in London and enabled him to deal with both services. He determined that this should serve as a key to the promotion of his Machine Gun Destroyer idea but he was still cautious in his approach.

For example, late in July he had occasion to visit Lord Kitchener on Committee business and, despite a friendly reception, decided not to take the opportunity to broach his pet scheme. We have seen that Swinton was already aware of what the Navy was doing and his instincts seem to have told him that by informing Kitchener he might jeopardize the entire project. As things turned out this may well have been a wise decision. Even so his reservations did not stop him from visiting Tennyson D'Eyncourt at the Admiralty a few days later and through him getting in touch with Stern. On the strength of this, Swinton was invited to attend the initial trial of the Number I Lincoln Machine at Cross O'Cliff Hill in Lincoln, after which he was ushered into a securely locked building to view the full-size wooden mock-up of Wilson's new design.

THE DESIGN OF THE TRACKS

The story of the design of the tracks for Wilson's improved model landship hardly sounds like the stuff of high drama. In fact it was probably the one most significant factor in the entire story of the British tank, apart from the original idea itself. It has already been shown that no tracks made in Britain up to that time would answer and it was now clear that the American types would not do either. Tritton and Wilson ensconced themselves in a room at the White Hart Hotel in Lincoln, determined to thrash the problem out. Some ideas got no further than the fireplace; each day's work was burned. Better ideas were sent down to the factory and tested; each one failed. One of the last materials tried was Balata belting, a thick, reinforced rubber used in heavy-duty conveyor belts. It also went up in flames. The problem was solved by Tritton and announced to Stern in a famous telegram dated 22 September 1915:

Balata died on test bench yesterday morning STOP *New arrival by Tritton out of Pressed Plate* STOP *Light in weight but very strong* STOP *All doing well, thank you* STOP (signed) PROUD PARENTS.

Tritton had gone back to basics. His engineering instincts told him that the problem could only be solved by rugged construction so he created a track which looked crude and heavy by contemporary American standards but was as simple and tough as it needed to be. Each link consisted of a panel of pressed steel with a raised lip at one end that was riveted to heavy-duty castings on the inner face. It was these castings which connected the links of track together by means of steel pins, but they were also fitted with flanges that engaged in rails along the inner faces of the track frames in such a way that they could not drop away when the machine was driven over a trench.

Of course the tracks could not move upwards either and this meant that the vehicle would not have a sprung suspension of any kind. It might mean a very rough ride for the crew but there was no alternative without a considerable period of further development and there was no time for that. This track design is the key. No other tank designers, either in Britain or abroad, made this step at the time so they were all condemned to create designs around existing commercial track systems and they all ended up with machines which, to a greater or lesser extent, were like Tritton's original concept; an armoured box riding above a set of tracks. It was not just that these new tracks were stronger, they gave the two designers a free hand when it came to perfecting the outline of the final design. There was now no reason at all why the tracks could not be stretched right around the frame just as Wilson had intended. This, in practical terms and simple as it sounds, was the masterstroke and it is this that Swinton saw, in mock-up form, in the locked hut in Lincoln.

The wooden model of Wilson's design, which had been created by carpenters at Fosters, arrived at Wembley Park on the back of a lorry late in September. On the 29th of that month Tennyson D'Eyncourt hosted a meeting in his office at the Admiralty. It brought together, probably for the first time, members of the original Landships Committee and their team along with people from the War Office, the Ordnance Board, Ministry of Munitions and GHQ in France. Ernest Swinton was also present and accompanied the party to Wembley Park. He describes how the model was viewed inside a screened-off enclosure such as one might see on a fairground. It was, he said, just as if one were visiting a sideshow to throw balls for coconuts or see the fat lady.

It was immediately clear that when it was finished this new design would exceed the original parameters in many respects so an effort was made to redraft some features. For a start it was agreed that the frontal armour should be thick enough, at 10mm, to resist the German reversed bullet. Wilson had specified a speed of 2mph but the meeting required that this should be doubled and they calculated that the crew should number eight men.

THE *CENTIPEDE* AND *LITTLE WILLIE*

Once approval had been gained to continue with the new design the staff at Fosters got to work. For a short time the two prototypes were sitting side by side at the Wellington Foundry. Wilson's design, known at this time as the *Centipede*, was rapidly coming together while the Number I Machine, soon to be rechristened *Little Willie*, was being fitted with Tritton's tracks. In its new form *Little Willie* was tested at Burton Park, Lincoln. The turret had been removed, since it made the vehicle top heavy, but ballast weights were added to the frames to maintain the weight. The new tracks, which were 3ft (0.9m) longer than the Bullock pattern, were wrapped around external frames so that none of the rollers, nor the driving sprockets or idlers, were easily visible. In this form *Little Willie* performed very well but it was already redundant.

Before *Little Willie*'s turret was removed the plan had been to fit it with a 40mm, 2-pounder Maxim gun, supplemented by up to six Danish Madsen machine-guns. This was a considerable reduction on Crompton's original plan to use

Little Willie, *viewed from the front, with the maker's plate and a lucky horseshoe prominent. The solid construction of Tritton's tracks is immediately obvious.*

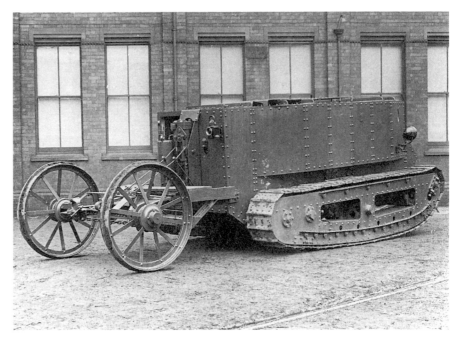

A rear three-quarter view of Little Willie *running on the new tracks, photographed in Foster's yard. The track frames hide the idler, drive sprocket and track rollers. A circular plate has been placed over the turret aperture on the roof.*

75mm weapons but an improvement on the Admiralty's first notion to equip the vehicle with machine-guns only. A turret being out of the question on the new design for various reasons, the wooden model was shown with gun sponson extending from each side which reminded one observer of bow windows. These sponsons were shown with a 2-pounder gun in one side and a 2.95in howitzer (the celebrated 'Mountain Gun') in the other.

Neither weapon satisfied the authorities. The 2-pounder was too puny for such a big machine and the Mountain Guns were in short supply so, by December 1915, the Admiralty had agreed to supply fifty pairs of 6-pounder quick-firing guns of 57mm calibre which would be mounted, one each side, in the completed Landships. Swinton, Stern, D'Eyncourt and others went up to Lincoln to observe progress on 6 December and found the *Centipede* nearly complete. It was clearly such an improvement on *Little Willie* that all further work on the latter ceased. On 12 January 1916 *Centipede* ran for the first time in Foster's Yard and the next day it was driven, under conditions of some secrecy, to Burton Park where it was tested over a trench and against other obstacles.

Stern claims that the *Centipede*, which he knew more familiarly as *Mother*, first ran as early as 3 December 1915 in Lincoln and that, soon afterwards it was taken to a field outside the city where Tennyson D'Eyncourt wished to see the 6-pounder gun fired. Evidence suggests that only one weapon was mounted at this time and that D'Eyncourt, as designer of the sponsons, wanted to see how they stood up to the shock. Stern tells a good story; of how the gun failed to fire at the first attempt but went off of its own accord a few seconds later while they were examining the breech. However he goes on to say that the machine was not completed until 26 January 1916 when it was taken by rail to Hatfield in Hertfordshire, which more or less agrees with the Ministry of Munitions account.

Despite the fact that personnel from 20 Squadron RNAS had prepared a series of obstacles at Wembley Park this site was now deemed unsuitable for demonstrations. It was too public and probably too restricted for practical manoeuvring. Stern and D'Eyncourt finally settled on Lord Salisbury's estate at Hatfield Park and, having obtained His Lordship's permission set about digging up land adjacent to his private golf course. Once again the Naval party created a range of obstacles including British and German style trenches, a shell hole and wire obstacles for *Mother* to defeat. The machine made an initial run at Hatfield on 29 January and, four days later on 2 February, took part in a full-scale demonstration before such dignitaries as Lord Kitchener, the First Lord of the Admiralty and the Minister of Munitions accompanied by a large party of lesser beings. The trial was a complete success, despite the fact that Lord Kitchener left early, having been overheard to say that the war would never be won by such 'pretty mechanical toys'. On 8 February the King came up to Hatfield and watched a repeat demonstration, as a result of which Tennyson D'Eyncourt wrote an enthusiastic account for Winston Churchill in which he referred to the new machine as a 'Tank'.

Quite when the word was first coined, and by whom, is a matter of some argument. Swinton and Stern both make the claim, explaining that they believed the term landship to be too descriptive, but once again Stern tells the better story. By his account they cast around for a term which was descriptive of what the thing looked like but far removed from its true purpose and finally hit upon the term Water Carrier. This, indeed was a reasonable description of a large, riveted steel structure but it still would not do for Bertie Stern. Bearing in mind the military practice of reducing everything to sets of initials he felt that there was little merit to be gained in being known as secretary to the WC Committee and selected the shorter, and even more ambiguous word Tank instead.

Since it formed the basic pattern for the majority of tanks that served the British Army over the next three years *Mother* deserves a fairly thorough description. The tank was just over 31ft (9.5m) long by 8ft (2.5m) high and some 13ft 8in

(4m) wide when the six-pounder sponsons were mounted. The elevated driving cab was built from 10mm nickel steel plate except at the front where it was 12mm thick. The sides and rear plate were also nickel steel and 8mm thick while the roof and underside were in high tensile steel and 6mm thick. The tank was of riveted construction, the armour plates being attached to a skeletal girder frame. And it is interesting to observe that on this model the rivets were set close together, at boilermaker's pitch. *Little Willie*, and all the production tanks, had more widely spaced rivets in what is known as girder-maker's pitch. Indeed the very structure of the tank was built upon girder principles to ensure the maximum possible strength. This was particularly important in areas around major openings such as the gaps in each side where the sponsons were fitted. It was vital that the hull remained structurally sound at all times. It could be subjected to substantial stresses on rough ground.

The body of the tank was not unlike *Little Willie* but it was more or less invisible since the track frames, upon which *Little Willie* rode, had now been enlarged and extended until they were larger than the tank's own hull. Indeed it was these frames that gave the tank its shape and the hull was sandwiched between them. These frames, in their turn, contained a series of twenty-six rollers, alternately flanged and smooth, .that followed the lower profile of the frames. Another roller carried the tracks over an angle near the back but elsewhere the track was carried upon skid rails. A larger roller at the very front was a toothed idler wheel and this could be adjusted to make the track tighter as it stretched. At the very back was a toothed drive sprocket which meshed with the tracks in order to move the tank along.

The tracks, that have already been described, were 20.5in (52cm) wide; there were ninety plates on each side. As they passed around the idler at the front and ran down towards the ground successive links were picked up by fixtures known as switch plates that engaged the flanges on the track links with rails on the inner faces of the frames to prevent them from dropping away. Further switch plates at the rear released the tracks before they reached the drive sprocket.

Inside the tank, roughly at the centre, was the engine, a six-cylinder Daimler-Knight, sleeve-valve unit of 13.5ltr rated at 105hp when running at 1,000rpm. It was started by a crank handle inside the tank and exhausted directly through the roof. There was no silencer but baffles were placed over the exhaust apertures which cut down the noise and, to some extent, dispersed the fumes. The engine flywheel contained a cone clutch and from this drive passed into a two-speed and reverse gearbox of the type used in Foster-Daimler tractors. These machines also supplied the enormous worm drive differential located at the back. Half-shafts from here transmitted the drive to exposed, secondary, two-speed gearboxes in the track frames and from here, via long loops of heavy-duty roller chains to gears that meshed with the sprockets and thence to the tracks.

The engine was water-cooled and a large, box-shaped radiator was installed at the very back of the tank. This was cooled by a big fan which drew its air from inside the tank, while heat was dissipated through a grid of small holes in the roof plate directly above the radiator. Petrol was carried in two tanks located within the frames, either side of the driver's cab. There was a round manhole cover in the roof of the tank and large, hinged flaps in front of the driver and commander. When these were closed the crew observed through a variety of slits and loopholes or thick glass blocks.

The gun sponsons were bolted on each side, around apertures cut for them in the frames. Each sponson had a hinged door at the back, the normal means of access, and a large opening at the front through which the gun projected. Each gun was mounted on a pedestal and could rotate approximately 90 degrees from straight ahead to the flank. Each gun was protected by a curved shield which filled the aperture and through which a slot was cut to accommodate the telescopic sight. The

gun itself was a Hotchkiss design, dating from 1885 although the particular version supplied for *Mother* and the first production tanks was a mass-produced model built for the Royal Navy in 1915. It consisted of a single-piece, rifled barrel, 40 calibres long (89.76in (228cm)) with a vertical sliding breech block. It had a hydro-spring recoil system and the recoil distance was just 4in (10cm). It had a maximum range of 7,500yd (6,858m) and a muzzle velocity of 1,818ft (554m) per second. The calibre was 2.244in (57mm) and it fired a single piece round in a brass cartridge case.

The matter of secondary armament does not appear to have been settled by this stage. The Danish Madsen machine-gun has already been mentioned but the Lewis and Hotchkiss were also considered. There was only one proper machine-gun mounting built into the hull, in the front plate between the driver's and commander's visors; but there were hinged flaps in the sides of the sponsons through which a gun might be fired in an emergency.

Where the tracks and track frames extended ahead and behind the hull these sections were

Mother from the rear showing the tail wheel assembly, the hydraulic lifting apparatus and the small door at the back of the hull. Notice also the ventilating holes on the roof, above the radiator.

Here Mother *attacks an obstacle comprising poles and sandbags during trials at Burton Park, Lincoln. Quite what this obstacle represented is not clear but it certainly did not hinder the tank's progress.*

known as the horns. The steering tail was fitted between the rear horns and was a more sophisticated version of the one Tritton had first designed for the No. I Lincoln Machine. The wheels themselves were not unlike the front wheels of a traction engine. They were carried on stub axles which pivoted against a frame and steered on the Ackerman principle, being worked from a wheel in the driver's cab via long lengths of cable. They must have been very hard work to operate. The entire frame was pivoted against the inner faces of the horns and could be raised or lowered by a pump attached to the back of the hull. This allowed the tail to be raised clear of the ground if the tank was to steer on its tracks alone or lowered as necessary. When the tail wheels were pressed against the ground, contact was maintained by sets of coil springs which enabled the wheels to operate even while the tank was moving over uneven ground. The tail could also be used to support the rear end of the tank when it crossed a wide trench or even alter the centre of gravity as it went over a knife edge or similar obstacle.

Four of the crew served the guns; a gunner and loader on each side. The others were all required to operate the controls. The driver, sitting to the right of the commander, was effectively there to make the tank go. Apart from the steering wheel, that was almost useless, he had no control whatever over turning, or swinging the tank to use the contemporary term. He controlled the primary gearbox, clutch and footbrake which acted on the transmission shaft along with the ignition and throttle controls. The commander operated the steering brakes and either man could work the differential lock which was above, between and behind them. The two extra men worked the secondary gearboxes at the back, on instruction from the driver who had to work the clutch at the same time.

It was, according to the instruction book, possible to steer the tank by selecting a different ratio in each of the secondary gearboxes although experience soon proved that this would result in twisted gear shafts. Thus, except for slight deviations when the steering brakes were used, the standard procedure for steering was to halt the tank, lock the differential and take one track out of gear. First was then selected in the primary box and the other secondary box, the brake was then applied to the free track and the tank would swing in that direction. Conditions inside are almost impossible to imagine. The noise and heat from the engine dominated and it was quite impossible

Leaving the sandbag obstacle in pieces, Mother *then tackles the trench that, once again, fails to stop the machine.*

to hear anything else when it was running. The big engine also tended to leak exhaust fumes from joints in the manifold and exhaust stacks and, despite the fact that air inside the tank was always on the move, the amount of carbon dioxide swirling about inside the hull was enough to choke on.

Bearing in mind that parts of the engine and adjacent plumbing were too hot to touch, plus the fact that, without springs every bump in the ground was transmitted through the tracks and rollers to the hull and thence the crew, you have a recipe for severe discomfort. To make matters worse the petrol supply placed the crew in

extreme danger. On *Mother* and the first 250 production tanks, fuel was carried in two 23gal (105l) tanks located in the frames on either side of the cab. Supply to the carburettor was by gravity and it could fail if the tank stalled nose down in a trench. The risk of fire was ever present and if the fuel was ignited, either by accident or an incoming shell, the chances of all eight men getting out unscathed were slim.

The King came up to Hatfield on 8 February and watched while *Mother* was put through her paces. He appeared to be impressed and this put the final seal of approval on the new invention. The question now was, would anyone take it?

An enlargement from an original snapshot of Mother, *the only one which identifies the location as Hatfield Park. The two men in naval uniform would be members of 20 Squadron.*

5 The First Tanks – Training and Fighting

Stern says that at the end of the Hatfield demonstration on 2 February 1916 Reginald McKenna, Chancellor of the Exchequer, told him that the money was available if the War Office decided to order tanks. Yet, in a sense, the decision had already been taken for on Christmas Eve 1915 the Committee of Imperial Defence had ordained that, in the event of War Office approval, a Tank Supply Committee should be formed to oversee production.

This came into being on 12 February 1916, on the same day that the Army Council placed an order for 100 tanks. Such work was beyond the capacity of Fosters who could only handle an order for twenty-three, the remainder to be built by the Metropolitan Carriage, Wagon and Finance Company of Birmingham, a much larger firm more particularly concerned with the manufacture of railway rolling stock and tramcars. Armour plate would come from Beardmores, Vickers and Cammell Laird, engines, gearboxes and differentials from the Daimler Company and 6-pounder guns from the Admiralty. Hotchkiss machine-guns were now selected as the secondary weapons, specifically the model 09/13 Light Hotchkiss of .303in calibre.

It is worth remarking that with British industry geared up to war production on an undreamed-of scale it was not going to be easy to find firms with spare capacity. Fosters had certainly been seeking war work but they were small fry – typical of the smaller rural engineering companies that abounded in Britain at this time. There must have been hundreds of firms like them but it was clearly unreasonable to entrust the manufacture of a brand new weapon to dozens of small companies scattered all over the land. Metropolitan Carriage, on the other hand, was a huge company formed by a series of amalgamations in 1902. It had a number of factories in the Birmingham area and others scattered throughout Britain. The tanks would be built at the works of one of its constituent companies, the Oldbury Railway Carriage and Wagon Company Ltd.

As tank production got underway it now became necessary to enlist men to operate them and, if anything, this was an even more scarce resource than factory space. Starting at the top Ernest Swinton learned, in February 1916, that he had been selected to command the new arm, which at that time was known as the Tank Detachment. Despite the fact that the term 'tank', at this time, did not equate to armoured fighting vehicle in the average man's vocabulary, there appears to have been some concern about its use. Thus the title was changed, very rapidly, to the Armoured Car Section of the Motor Machine-Gun Service which, if anything, was even more descriptive.

The Machine Gun Corps (MGC) had been formed in 1915 in belated recognition of the importance of this weapon and it had sprouted the Motor Machine Gun Section (MMGS) to operate its own motorcycle machine-gun units and the fleet of armoured cars taken over from the Royal Navy. There was, however, little use for motorcycle machine-guns or armoured cars on the Western Front by this time so many of the officers and men from this branch were available for transfer to the tanks, including the commanding

A fine study of the Machine Gun Corps in action, a Vickers team under cover in an abandoned farm building.

Vickers-Clyno machine-gun combinations of the Motor Machine Gun Service, photographed during a training session. It looks like stirring stuff but in reality, conditions on the Western Front inhibited mobility and may of these men were transferred to the tanks.

officer of the MMGS, Lt-Col John Brough, who was selected to command the new force in the field. Among those who came to the tanks in this way was Pte A. E. Lee who joined the MMGS in 1915. He was posted to Bisley in Surrey where the MGC had taken over the National Rifle Association's shooting range and camp. Lee noted that most of his fellow soldiers, who had not been issued with the motor-cycle machine-gun combination, were ultimately posted to infantry divisions while he, with some others, ended up in the Armoured Car Section.

It also made sense to transfer the men from 20 Squadron RNAS to the Army, on the grounds that they had more experience of tanks than anybody. Indeed in 1915 the Admiralty had decided to raise three more squadrons; Nos. 21, 22 and 23 to operate its landships but these were never completed. In the event none of the personnel from 20 Squadron wished to change service, since they were of higher rank and on a much better pay scale as sailors than they would be under the War Office. Thus the only Naval personnel to transfer to the Army were specialists such as Stern and Wilson while 20 Squadron was retained as a Naval unit – despite an attempt by the Admiralty to reclaim it in May 1916 – and remained responsible for testing tanks and delivering them to the docks in Britain until the end of the war.

The War Office also hoped to entice officers from other regiments who had mechanical expertise into the new force. Stern implies that only officers with the right qualifications were accepted but there is evidence to show that this was not always the case. More than one officer, with no mechanical aptitude whatever, found himself seconded to the new unit probably because he did not get on terribly well with his current commanding officer. Basil Henriques, a subaltern in the Buffs in 1916, recalled being told by his commanding officer that he had been specially selected for a new posting. He and a fellow officer were interviewed by Swinton in London, both confessed to having few, if any, mechanical skills yet they were accepted immediately; it seems to have made no difference at all that Henriques himself was over 6ft (1.8m) tall! Skilled mechanics were also recruited from civilian life, largely through the agency of Mr Geoffrey Smith, editor of *The Motor Cycle* magazine who was given the task of examining would-be volunteers in various centres around the country.

In May 1916 the unit title changed again. Now it would be known as the Heavy Section, Machine

Gun Corps. Swinton, meanwhile, was addressing the business of organization. His original idea was rejected and the War Office finally agreed upon an establishment of six companies, lettered A to F, each comprising four sections of six tanks and one spare. By this time the number of tanks on order had been raised by fifty, all of which would be built by Metropolitan. It will not have escaped notice that 150 tanks, shared twenty-five apiece between six companies, did not leave any reserves nor, indeed, any for training which must be seen as a short-sighted view. At the time when this increase in numbers was authorized, in April 1916, another change was introduced. It was now agreed that only seventy-five tanks would be completed, like *Mother*, with a pair of 6-pounder guns. The remainder would be fitted with redesigned sponsons that would only carry machine-guns.

Male and female tanks

One reason for this was a shortage of 6-pounder guns although more had been ordered from Armstrong-Whitworth. A more pressing one was a belief that tanks might be overwhelmed by mass attack from German soldiers and, since case shot was not available at this time, a heavy machine-gun was seen as a good alternative. The new sponsons were probably more like the so-called bay window design seen on the wooden mock-up of *Mother*. They were designed to hold a pair of water-cooled Vickers machine-guns, a specially adapted version with raised foresights, which would be fitted in armoured jackets. The two guns in each sponson had a combined arc of fire which could sweep virtually 180 degrees along each side of the tank. This, of course, ruled out the large rear door of the 6-pounder sponsons, and the tiny door that was adopted instead made the machine-gun tanks virtual death traps for the crew if they caught fire. To distinguish between the two types, those with 6-pounder guns were referred to as Male tanks, those with machine-guns only were, therefore, Females.

Stern, as chairman of the Tank Supply Committee, was now starting to wonder about his future. There was no immediate prospect of further orders for tanks so he began to cast around for other work. Two new designs had been mooted in April; one was for a tracked carrying vehicle capable of transporting heavy artillery up to the 5in field gun (otherwise known as the 60-pounder) or the 6in howitzer. This was authorized on 5 June and two weeks later an order was placed for something even more spectacular. This was to be a tank carrying armour thick enough to resist enemy field-gun fire. In April Lieutenant Symes had carried out preliminary trials using a captured German weapon against armour plate 2in (5cm) thick and by June the proving ground at Shoeburyness was conducting trials on various types of plate supplied by Beardmores. Tritton was responsible for the design and in order to produce adequate power the Daimler Company was instructed to develop a double version of its 105hp engine. This is not to say a V12 but two complete engines sharing a common crankcase. Each engine would drive its own four-speed gearbox.

In fact three or four designs were presented and the version chosen for production was estimated to weigh 100t (101,600kg). In addition to the main tracks at each side a subsidiary set was carried beneath the hull which would support the tank on soft ground. A single 6-pounder gun, with an arc of fire of about 80 degrees, was located at the front with three machine-guns along each side. In the event it was never completed. According to Stern, the War Office believed that mobility provided better protection than thick armour but one is also inclined to suspect mechanical problems. The massive tank design was known as the 'Flying Elephant'.

Machine-gun training was the main feature of the time at Bisley. Six-pounder guns were in such short supply to begin with that the two fitted to *Mother* herself had to be dismounted and sent to Bisley. Attempts to fire them there were soon quashed when it became clear that their range was too great for safety. Gunnery training then moved

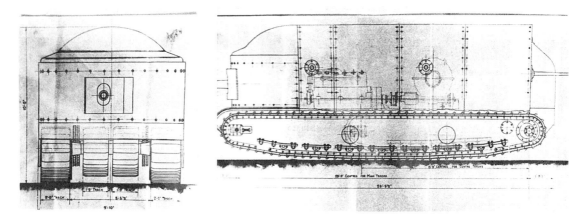

Front and side elevation drawings of one version of Foster's Flying Elephant *design. It would not, in fact, have been much larger than a Mark I tank but considerably heavier, due to the thick armour. Notice the auxiliary tracks, beneath the frames, the location of the double engine and differential, and the unspecified secondary armament at the rear.*

to the Royal Artillery camp at Larkhill on Salisbury Plain while the Royal Navy also came to the rescue. Since they were instructing on the 6-pounder anyway the Navy began taking tank gunners and training them at their gunnery school, commissioned as HMS *Excellent*, located on a reclaimed mud bank known as Whale Island in Portsmouth Harbour. Live firing was practised from the deck of a Monitor in the English Channel and some claimed that the motion of the ship would not be dissimilar to a moving tank. Others believed this to be entirely unrealistic and devised, instead, a form of rocking sponson to simulate the motion on dry land.

Both Stern and Swinton were convinced that the ideal projectile would be case shot, which is, essentially, an anti-personnel round. However the authorities rejected this in favour of a high explosive round, containing black powder and a carbon steel cap, which had a modest armour-piercing capability. Even these were in short supply until it was discovered that a large shipment had been supplied to the Imperial Japanese Navy, which had no use for them so they were shipped back. It was also discovered that the original batch of 6-pounders, those of single-tube construction,

were not strong enough to contain the full charge of the regular 6-pounder round so those issued to the tanks had a reduced charge which resulted in a lower muzzle velocity and shorter range.

At the same time more thought was given to protection. Although the tanks were theoretically capable of resisting machine-gun fire it was now agreed that improved protection might be afforded against enemy shellfire. Thicker armour was the obvious answer but that meant an unacceptable increase in weight. One alternative would be to add a burster plate; in effect a panel of armour spaced away from the main body of the tank which would set a shell off before it struck home. Tests showed that 4mm plate, spaced about 30cm (11.8in) from the hull, would have this effect and it was agreed that this plate should be perforated in order to reduce weight. Even so this proved impractical and was never adopted although a shield was provided at the rear to cover the hydraulic apparatus for the tail.

Back in October 1915 Swinton had also applied himself to the problems of devising tactical procedures for the use of tanks. By March 1916 these had been polished to the point where they were ready to be issued and copies were circulated to the War Office. The paper, entitled 'Notes on the Employment of "Tanks"' is far too long to reproduce here but it is fair to say that it was a remarkably perceptive document which dealt with every aspect of the subject in forty-five well-considered paragraphs. As far as the incumbents at the War Office were concerned it might just as well have been a work of fiction for all the attention it received; it was not placed before the people that mattered, those who actually operated the machines in action, until they had managed to work out most of its precepts for themselves by trial and error.

Tank production was, inevitably, slow in getting underway but the demand for them became increasingly urgent. Towards the end of April, Swinton had received a communication from Sir Douglas Haig in France, requesting as many tanks as possible to be ready by 1 June. And by ready Haig meant in France, with trained crews, fully prepared for action. This, of course, was in connection with the forthcoming offensive on the Somme which was due to commence on 1 July. Swinton knew that this was quite impossible and said that the best he could offer was a few tanks by that date, and only then if machine-guns could be found for them from stocks in France. He would undertake to supply more, complete with weapons and trained crews by 1 August. In the event even this proved to be an optimistic promise.

TRAINING TANK CREWS

In any case, before any crews could be trained somewhere had to be found for them to train with the tanks. Continued secrecy was vital so an officer, working on Swinton's behalf, began to scour the country for a suitable site. It had to be a thinly populated area from which the existing population could be removed. Somewhere close to a railway line and preferably not too far from the main factories or the Channel Ports. They settled, in the end, for Lord Iveagh's private estate at Elveden, on the Norfolk–Suffolk border near Thetford. A siding was laid from Barham station on the Thetford to Bury St Edmunds line of the Great Eastern Railway which was provided with a ramp at the end, down which tanks could be unloaded. Work began at once in converting a part of the estate into an extensive replica of a section of the British and German lines in France, complete with detailed trenches revetted with sand-

---

The Mark I Tank
Data for a male machine with tail

Crew:	8
Weight:	28 tons
Length:	32ft 6in (9.91m)
Width:	13ft 9in (4.19m)
Height:	8ft 2in (2.49m)
Armour:	12mm (½in) max.
Speed:	3.7mph (6km/h) max.

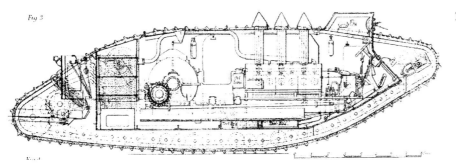

Fig 3

The Mark I tank.

*Mark I male tank No. 742, running without sponsons, probably at Thetford. Two of the inverted **V** exhaust baffles can be seen on top of the hull along with the apparently misspelt Russian inscription 'With Care to Petrograd'.*

bags and protected by barbed wire. Explosives were used to create replica shell holes, and to extend the fiction about what was going on the site was referred to, on admission passes, as the Elveden explosives area.

Despite all this effort Basil Henriques described the area as parkland, intimating that it was not ideal preparation for the realities of the Western Front, whereas Capt H.P.G. Steedman, of 711 Company ASC, stated that before very long the site had become a quagmire. The officer in charge of the digging was, like Swinton, a Royal Engineer, Maj Giffard le Q. Martel who served with the tanks for the rest of the war. Meanwhile yet another RE officer, Maj Hugh Elles, was sent over to Elveden as Sir Douglas Haig's representative.

The first production tanks, later to be designated Mark I, differed from the prototype *Mother* in a number of details. To begin with they were built with the rivets at girder-makers pitch, like *Little Willie*; that is with fewer rivets and more widely spaced than on *Mother*. On top of the hull the exhaust outlets were now covered by inverted V-shaped baffles and the circular manhole hatch in the roof had been moved further back. The roof plates above the radiator were not perforated, as they were on *Mother* but a louvered panel had been inserted at the back instead while the number of springs attached to the tail assembly had been doubled. On male tanks the sponson doors had

been enlarged and rehung to open away from the hull sides.

From early June the tanks began to arrive and crew training began. At this time the tanks were all painted grey but some thought now had to be given to camouflage. To this end yet another Royal Engineer arrived, the artist Solomon J. Solomon, a member of the Royal Academy then serving as a Lt Col of Sappers. According to Basil Henriques, Solomon began on the hull of *Mother* that, in a short space of time, was sporting a complex pattern of colours that looked like some sort of impressionist landscape. Each tank crew was then ordered to make their own copy from the master on their own machines although the quality of the work seems to have varied. Henriques goes on to say that, soon after the tanks arrived in France they were made to repaint them in a less gaudy scheme with each patch of colour outlined in black to create a sort of crazy paving effect.

Towards the end of June a body of Army Service Corps drivers arrived at Elveden, to be known as 711 (Motor Transport) Company ASC under the command of Maj Knothe. These men had previously been employed at Avonmouth Docks, near Bristol, where they were responsible for handling Holt Caterpillar Tractors *en route* from the United States to the Western Front. Thus they had some experience of tracked vehicles yet, when confronted with the tanks, they are said to

What is believed to be another picture from Thetford, a female Mark I in the Solomon camouflage showing a structure on the roof that may well be an early wireless aerial.

have been so nervous of them that they denied all knowledge of internal combustion engines and were sent back to Avonmouth. Even when this was sorted out conditions were said to be far from satisfactory. The men disliked the isolation and secrecy and are said to have been on the point of mutiny until Knothe was posted to France and Capt Steedman took over. Steedman was very critical of the fact that tanks invariably had to be unloaded from the trains at night, presumably to maintain security, which proved to be very dangerous.

Another new arrival was Philip Johnson, a highly qualified engineer who had originally enlisted under Swinton as a tank driver. He recollects that Elveden, when he arrived, was in a state of chaos. Crews were being trained on tanks which did not have their sponsons fitted so they were some eight tons lighter than they would be in fighting trim and, no doubt, not too uncomfortable to drive since there would be plenty of fresh air passing through. Nor was his the only critical voice. W.G. Wilson, who was now based at Birmingham, supervising the construction of tanks, complained bitterly about the standard of workmanship, only to be told brusquely by Stern that it was his job to ensure that it was done correctly.

There is some evidence to suggest that, even at this early date, experiments had been carried out using portable wireless sets in tanks; although the term portable should not be taken too literally. The problems must have been daunting. It was not a question of size, sets were already being carried in aircraft, nor necessarily the proximity of a petrol engine for the same reason. What is hard to understand is how anyone might have expected a set to operate in such an environment. Noise levels alone would have made it impossible to hear anything, even Morse code, while the vibration coursing through an unsprung tank on rough ground must have shaken a 1916 valve set to pieces.

On 21 July a large-scale demonstration was organized at Elveden to be attended by Lloyd-George. As Minister of Munitions he was largely responsible for tank production but, since the death of Lord Kitchener, when the cruiser HMS *Hampshire* was lost on 5 June, he was also Secretary of State for War. Gen Sir William Robertson, Chief of the Imperial General Staff, was also present along with representatives from GHQ in France. The demonstration consisted of a mock attack by twenty-five tanks, all complete with weapons, over a succession of trenches and included a counter-attack by 'German' infantry.

2nd Lt Allan's Mark I female C6 Cordon Rouge, photographed on the Albert Road on 22 September 1916. It still appears to be sporting the Solomon camouflage and notice, also, the two objects protruding from the cab roof that are small periscopes.

The action was photographed by aircraft from the Royal Flying Corps airfield at Thetford and was generally judged to have been a great success, the only drawback being that some of these early tanks, as a result of continual use, were showing distinct signs of wear and tear. In particular the steering tails were subject to fractures and the whole lot had to be removed from the tanks and shipped back to Fosters in Lincoln for strengthening.

In mid-August 1916 the first tanks were sent out to France, starting with Maj A. Holford-Walker's C Company. This means that these men could have had no more than eight weeks of training, a remarkably short time for such a new weapon. The tanks went by rail to Avonmouth where they were loaded aboard ship for the crossing to Le Havre; the crews went via Southampton. If the men were inexperienced, the tanks were in poor condition due to the extensive training, and staff from the builders in Birmingham were sent to Thetford to help to restore them. There were many who regarded the move to France as premature. Stern, for one, used all the influence at his disposal to impose delay and he had a lot of support which was not confined to Britain. Col Baptiste Estienne, who was endeavouring to design tanks for the French Army and had already been to Elveden in order to observe British progress, also pleaded for delay and Stern

enlisted the aid of Monsieur Breton, the French Minister of Munitions. It was all to no avail. Lloyd-George and the British Prime Minister also believed that Stern was right but they were not prepared to overrule Haig, and Haig was adamant; he needed tanks, even a few tanks, as soon as possible. Col Brough fell foul of Haig at this point and was replaced by Lt Col R.W. Bradley from England.

GHQ in France had selected a site at the village of Yvrench, near Abbeville on the Somme as the centre for the tanks. Abbeville is south of St Valéry, well away from the front but centrally placed; it was also a major railway junction with

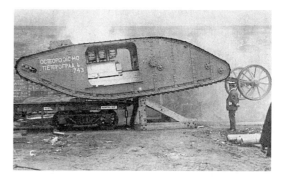

Mark I tank number 743 climbs onto a railway wagon at Foster's Wellington Foundry. Details to notice are the machine-gun ammunition racks between the exhaust stacks and the light steel cover over the engine.

A Mark I crew in Palestine demonstrates the use of lifting girders and chain hoist. In this case they appear to be fitting a gun rather than actually attaching the sponson but the principle remains the same.

lines radiating to different parts of the front. This was vital since all tank movement was by rail. Not that it was easy; before a tank could travel by rail the sponsons had to be dismounted and loaded onto special trailers. Tanks then climbed onto a train, one at a time from the end and made their way precariously over the wagons, towing their sponson trailers, until they were all loaded, chained down and covered in tarpaulins. When it arrived at its destination the train was shunted up

against another ramp and the tanks trundled off, to be reunited with their sponsons.

Two girder frames were placed onto the roof of each tank, from which the sponsons were slung while the securing bolts were put in place. It was a long and tiresome business, made worse by the fact that the bolt holes would not always line up. Without the sponsons, and despite their inherent strength, the tank hulls would twist out of shape in transit and it was often necessary to ream out new holes to take the bolts when the sponsons were offered up.

D Company, commanded by Maj F. Summers, arrived at Yvrench at the end of August. A Company (Maj C.M. Tippetts) followed two weeks later but by then C and D Companies had moved again. Trains had transported them to a vast railhead known as the Loop, near Bray-sur-Somme where they were being prepared for action. Haig had decided that he would use whatever tanks he could get to bolster a planned attack on German defences south-west of Bapaume. Gen Rawlinson described it as a gamble. The infantry were exhausted after two months hard fighting on the Somme and there were no reserves. Haig hoped that the tanks could force the issue by smashing through the German

Male Mark I C15 crosses a British trench. It carries the grenade-deflecting roof and notice that the tail wheels are being carried off the ground so the tank would be steering on its tracks only.

57

lines and permitting the infantry to take Bapaume itself. If this succeeded it would be a major blow to the Germans and, to some extent, redeem the horrendous casualty lists of the original offensive.

Visiting France at this time Swinton was horrified to see how the tanks, training with the infantry, had become a major attraction in the area. Carloads of British and French officers were turning up every day to watch the show and expected the tanks to perform all kinds of silly stunts which were bound to cause damage. Even so the men of C Company had managed to improve their tanks by fitting a grenade-proof roof. This was a gabled affair of timber with a screen of wire netting stretched across it. The idea was to prevent grenades from being thrown on top and damaging the roof plates. Oddly it does not seem to have been adopted by D Company and this may be due to the extra time C Company had in France to prepare for the battle.

The battle which began on 15 September 1916 is often known as Flers–Courcelette after two villages which were captured during the attack. For three days before the attack was launched a concentrated barrage of some 1,600 guns

pounded a five-mile (8km) stretch of the German front line while nine infantry divisions prepared to follow the tanks into action. On the night before the battle two companies of tanks moved forward. C Company made for a brickworks near Trones Wood while D Company aimed for a site known on the military maps as Green Dump.

Of the forty-nine tanks which set off from the Loop, seventeen either broke down or became ditched leaving thirty-two to spread out to their various starting points just behind the British lines. It was not that Swinton's instructions had been ignored but that nobody had yet had a chance to read them. Even so the logic of launching the tanks as a concentrated striking force was lost on the planners who saw them rather as a means of dealing with various German strong points which had been identified before the battle; sites such as the Quadrilateral in front of the village of Morval which was effectively a machine-gun fort at ground level.

Inevitably everyone was working in the dark as far as the new weapon was concerned and it proved impossible to calculate how the tanks would keep pace, in the advance, with the infantry. In the end it was agreed that, if the tanks

German soldiers pose with the wreck of 2nd Lt Sampson's tank D13, Delilah, where it ended its combat career in High Wood. This tank appears to have the extra roof studs, that would have held the burster plates or spaced armour, to use a more modern term.

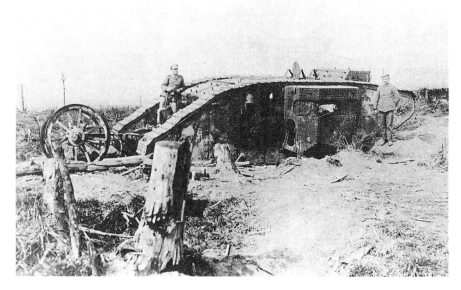

could be onto their objectives five minutes before the infantry came up this should be ideal. To this end the artillery plan included a requirement that from about 0600 hours, twenty minutes before the infantry were due to move off, they would leave a series of lanes, each about 100yd (91m) wide, through the barrage. The tanks would move along these aisles towards their first objectives and subdue them as the infantry followed in their wake.

No arrangements had been made for tank commanders to do any reconnaissance before the battle and they probably would not have gained much from the opportunity anyway. Many of them, and their drivers in particular, were newcomers, not just to the Western Front but to the fury of battle in general and they had no means of estimating the state of the ground. Furthermore it seems reasonable to suppose that many of those involved in planning the battle had a false idea of what the tanks were capable of, partly from optimistic speculation and, no doubt, from their own impressions gained while the tanks were training. To make matters worse some of the plans that had been made over the preceding days were changed at the last minute and there were only enough maps to supply one to every three tanks.

At 0600, while it was still virtually dark and with a light mist hanging over the ground, the tanks started to move. Nine of them did quite well, keeping ahead of the infantry and dealing with whatever obstacles they encountered. Nine more made such slow progress that they were overtaken by the infantry and another nine all broke down for one reason or another. The final five ended up stranded in shell holes or trenches, unable to get out. Seventeen tanks were hit during the attack. Seven were able to limp back while ten remained, more badly damaged, on the battlefield. Most of these were later recovered but a few were still there as partly dismantled, rusting hulks when the war ended. Casualties among the tank crews were surprisingly light which is all the more surprising since some commanders found that the armour of

their tanks was not even capable of keeping out machine-gun fire.

Events such as this, the very first tank attack, are bound to generate myths. Many concern the state of mind of those German troops who had to confront tanks for the first time. Reports filtering back to Britain, and nurtured by the press had the enemy fleeing from the field, uttering improbable Germanic oaths. Bearing in mind that the front-line troops had no idea that such things as tanks existed the majority appear to have stood up to them, or even attacked them, very well. There were instances of large groups surrendering when they failed to subdue the machines but the majority of German troops simply fell back and created new defensive lines. The German press was equally prone to exaggeration but from a different standpoint. They stigmatized the tanks as a cruel new weapon or suggested that the British must be desperate to resort to such devices.

Those on the British side who considered the tanks to be an overrated weapon declared that the trial had been a failure while those who believed in them complained that they had not been given a fair trial; that there were too few of them and that they had been used prematurely with poorly trained crews. Writing in 1920 Col J.F.C. Fuller, who joined the tanks in December 1916, agreed that this first attack was not a great success but went on to say that, considering the conditions under which they had been used they did at least show promise. Sir Douglas Haig appears to have been delighted with them. Encountering Albert Stern and Ernest Swinton at GHQ on Sunday the 17th, he was fulsome in his praise and when Stern got back to his office in London on the following Tuesday he learned that the Commander-in-Chief had placed an immediate order for 1,000 more tanks.

In the aftermath of this euphoria Stern was surprised to learn, on 10 October, that the Army Council had decided to cancel Haig's order. Stern immediately obtained an interview with Lloyd-George, pointing out that he had already started

Female tank C4, Chablis, 2nd Lt Campbell's tank abandoned in a wasteland of mud on the Somme.

to place orders for components for these tanks and any attempt to halt this would disrupt Britain's industry on an alarming scale. Lloyd-George summoned Sir William Robertson to his office and had Stern repeat his case; at this point Stern left but leaves his readers in no doubt that Lloyd-George, as Secretary of State for War, read the riot act to Robertson. The huge order for tanks was restored on the very next day.

Another tank attack had been mounted later in September with actions on the 25th and 26th. Two tanks were used to support an attack near Flers on 1 October and one tank was called upon to assist the 23rd Infantry Division on the 7th. Two tanks were again used on 19 October and 40 tanks, many from the newly arrived A Company took part in a battle on 13/14 November which enjoyed a modest success. Yet in all these subsequent actions, minimal as they were from the tank point of view, there had been a significant change in practice. In none of these actions did the tanks lead the attack, rather they were held in reserve and only called forward when the infantry were held up. In most cases this took so long to organize that there was very little they could do and, even where they did succeed, the infantry they had been sent to support were simply too exhausted to take advantage of the enemy's discomfort.

GERMAN REACTION TO THE TANKS

Little hard evidence filtered through at this time as to the German reaction to tanks. However a deserter, interrogated in December 1916, revealed that he had seen excavations taking place at strategically significant crossroads and other important locations behind the German lines that he understood to be anti-tank mines. This does not appear to be the later concept of a small explosive charge, set off by a tank driving over it, but a substantial excavation filled with explosives and detonated by an observer. The idea, presumably, was to disable tanks if they managed to break through in a major attack.

Although the proportion of mechanical breakdown, compared with other failures, was high in these early actions much of it could be attributed to the inexperience of newly trained crews in new machines. It is a tendency that has been repeated down the years. Even so there were serious failures. Philip Johnson who, from tank driver had risen to company workshops officer and technical adviser in a very short time, drew attention to a serious outbreak of track damage. He attributed this to the failure of weight-carrying rollers, which were of hollow construction. Summoned from Britain Tritton and Wilson

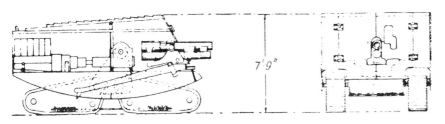

7'9"

Front View

Loaded 12 Tons – 110 H.P.

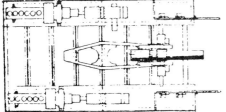

Plan – roof removed

Col Crompton's drawing of his third Emplacement Destroyer design, the ED3 that had twin engines and carried a single 4.5in howitzer.

studied the problem and blamed it on mud. Johnson scoffed at this explanation but failed to convince anybody until he took a collapsed roller and had it sectioned with a hacksaw to reveal the truth.

Most of Johnson's subsequent comments are more relevant to later developments but one might well be mentioned here. Commenting upon the original War Office requirement for the tank to deal with a 5ft high parapet, he suggested that this had been unnecessarily severe and proved to be rare in practice. He concluded that the tanks could have been lower at the front which might well have improved the view forward.

Both Johnson and Wilson were practical engineers but they also shared a dangerous inventive streak that was often at odds with the pragmatic approach of manufacturing engineers and soldiers. It is rarely a comfortable relationship; the demands of the military during wartime, no less than those of commercial people in peacetime, invariably require practical solutions immediately rather than the indefinite promise of something better. Crompton had already lost his place for this very reason yet he still carried on, producing drawings for impressive assault artillery that he called Emplacement Destroyers, none of which were ever built.

6 Full-Scale Production and Experiment

Haig's order for 1,000 more tanks appeared to have secured the future, although the Tank Supply Committee had a number of problems to consider. At the Wellington Foundry in Lincoln, Fosters had already added an extra bay to the boiler shop and had a new erecting shop under construction. Metropolitan had capacity to increase production at Birmingham but more companies would have to be brought on stream if the new tanks were to be completed in a reasonable time. Following discussions four more firms were added to the group. Armstrong-Whitworth in Newcastle-on-Tyne, Beardmores, Coventry Ordnance Works and Mirless Watson & Co. in Glasgow. Subcontractors included another Glasgow firm, Hurst Nelson. It is worth recording at this point that, despite what the

Commander-in-Chief may have wanted the actual production of Mark IV tanks ran to 1,015 fighting machines (produced on the basis of two female to one male) and 205 Tank Tenders or Supply Tanks. The grand total, therefore, stands at 1,220 and the last machines were not completed until May 1918.

If material resources were stretched by Haig's order, so too was manpower. One thousand tanks implied eight thousand trained crew men and the profligate use of Mark I tanks in France meant that there were hardly any left to train new crews on. So, in order to overcome this problem, one hundred more tanks were ordered from Fosters and Metropolitan. Some time later the entire personnel, officers, tank crews and supporting staff from three battalions under training were

Mark IV tanks under construction in the newly extended Foster's factory at Lincoln. Features to note are the skid rails, along the top run of the track frames, the stack of track lengths and the transmission components in the centre along with the stray tail wheel that seems to have been left over from Mark I production.

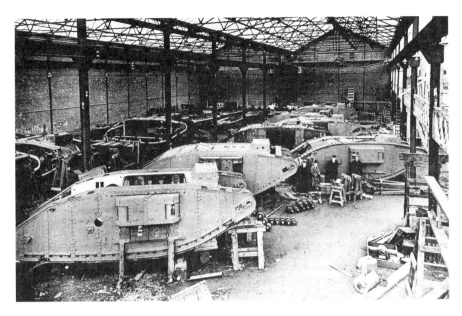

Female Mark IV tanks in various stages of construction at the Beardmore works in Glasgow. They range from track frames, laid on their sides in the far corner, to a complete machine on the right, ready to roll out.

sent to help out in the tank factories for a period of months.

Early in October the command in France changed again. Bradley was replaced by Lt Col H.J. Elles, the Royal Engineer officer who had been sent to Britain by Haig to investigate the tanks. Hugh Elles was highly regarded at GHQ in France and could therefore expect to get a better hearing for the tanks. His rank was elevated to full colonel and his staff expanded by four. Two of these men, the Brigade Major, Giffard Martel, and the Intelligence Officer, Frederick Hotblack, were particularly significant appointments. Headquarters was moved from a small hut in the village of Beauquesne to a large chateau at Bermicourt near St Pol. Shortly afterwards the War Office announced that, as the new tanks were delivered, the new companies created to operate them would be grouped into battalions, four of which would be created in France and five more in Britain.

This, in turn, suggested that the area allocated to tank training in Norfolk would not be adequate so Swinton organized a search for somewhere better. The chosen site was a vast area of unproductive heathland, north of the village of Wool in Dorset. It had been a military rifle range before

the war and was then being used mainly by Australian infantry training for the front in France. It was a bleak enough spot supporting a few farms and scattered cottages but its very

Brig Gen Hugh Elles, photographed with the King in France in 1918. Notice the tank arm badge on the General's right sleeve.

A male Mark III tank being tested over trenches on Wool Heath with the mixture of wooden huts and canvas hangars that constituted Bovington Camp in 1917.

isolation was ideal for the tanks. There was rail access over the London & South Western Railway at Wool station, just two miles south of the chosen site, and plenty of room to expand. It also solved the gunnery problem for a few miles south of Wool for on the rugged coast near the famous geological feature known as Lulworth Cove, was an area of sheep pasture that made an ideal gunnery range. The tanks could fire against a hill and if they overshot the rounds would drop harmlessly into the sea. The transfer from Elveden did not happen immediately. In the first place suitable accommodation had to be created for new men and tanks, both of which in any case would not arrive all at once. In fact the fifteen Mark I tanks which came down from Norfolk to commence the training programme were in such a bad way that they had to be sent back, five at a time, to be reconditioned at Fosters. At the same time those still fitted with tails had them removed.

Another change, ordained in November 1916, was from the Heavy Section to the Heavy Branch, Machine Gun Corps. This, presumably, reflected the increasing importance of the new arm although the War Office was clearly reluctant, at this stage, to create a new corps and it is interesting to note that the term 'tank' was still being studiously avoided. Yet, as a headline in *The Motorcycle* magazine announced on 22 September

ber 'The Secret is Out'. It went on to quote a recent communiqué to the effect that 'In this attack we employed for the first time a new type of heavy armoured car, which proved of considerable value.' Even so the public had to rely upon artists' impressions, most of which were dreadfully inaccurate, until the *Daily Mirror* printed a full-page photograph on the front of its issue for 22 November 1916. The paper actually used the word Tank at this time.

In fact, by the time that that picture had appeared in the *Mirror* (Capt A.M. Inglis's male tank C5 *Crème-de-Menthe*) most of the tanks had lost their wheeled tails. In practice they had proved completely useless over rough and muddy ground except as a platform to carry things on. The original crews were learning how to handle their machines and in some instances this conflicted with their written instructions. For example one method which had been recommended for steering, that of placing the secondary gears at different ratios, did nothing but damage the countershafts so it was dropped. On the other hand the instruction to use the differential lock as often as possible, except when the tank was steering on its brakes, was found to be very good advice. On soft ground, and most especially on slopes, if the differential was not locked until the tank started to slip the odds were that it would refuse to lock at all, leaving the tank and its crew struggling.

All of these matters and many others were considered when improvements were discussed for the new tanks and the designers took advantage of the order to build 100 training tanks in order to try some of them out. Among the more general improvements incorporated on the basis of combat experience were the removal of teeth from the front idler wheel, an increased ability to adjust the same wheel and the need for wider tracks in order to reduce ground pressure.

That first factor, the removal of teeth from the idlers, was due to the fact that the track itself stretched with use. Once this happened it would not be able to mesh with teeth at both ends of the frame. It seems reasonable to assume that the tracks stretched more than anyone had imagined and that would account for the need to increase idler adjustment. It gave the tracks a somewhat longer life before a link had to be removed in order to shorten them. Wider tracks were a bigger problem since it might take time to manufacture them. The existing tracks were 20½in (52cm) wide and the new type would be 26½in (67cm) wide. In order to accommodate them all tanks built after the Mark I had slightly narrower driver's cabs to provide clearance although the wider tracks did not in fact appear until 1918. One of the original tanks, the Metropolitan built female number 555 was adapted to test out most of these modifications and the majority were incorporated on the next batch of fifty machines.

These tanks, designated Mark II, were built by Fosters and Metropolitan; the former constructed the twenty-five male machines. They all lacked tails. They had the narrower cab, smooth idlers and extended track adjusting capacity and in place of the circular roof hatch they featured a wedge-shaped structure with a rectangular lid which permitted a crew member to peer out in relative safety. These details aside, the real difference between the Mark II and the original tanks that now naturally became the Mark I, was invisible. It concerned the plate from which the tank was

built. The Mark I, being intended for combat had, as we have seen, been built from bullet-proof plate. This was created by heating up the plates, once they had been cut to size and shape, and then cooling them rapidly in a water-cooled press. This hardened the surface of the plate without warping it. Since the Mark II was only intended for training it was decided not to give this plate the final hardening process so it was not bullet-proof. Even so, with a view to improving protection some thought had been given to thickening the side armour on these tanks which, if it worked, would then be applied with proper armour to the new production model. Extra holes were drilled in the side panels which would serve as rivet holes when an extra layer of armour was fitted but in practice this was never done.

Rather the next batch of fifty tanks, all of which were built by Metropolitan, had thicker plate along each side (12mm instead of 8mm) although again it was not heat-treated. Otherwise they were virtually identical to the Mark II and, in fact, one can only tell Mark II and Mark III tanks apart by examining the front plate of the cab where the arrangement of vision slits is different. However production of the Mark III

Naval personnel of 20 Squadron RNAS pose with a Mark II tank, probably one of the Oldbury Trials machines seen here without sponsons or such cab fittings as visor flaps or machine-gun mounting.

version embraced another change which was introduced over the winter of 1916–17. When the decision had been made to expand the original companies into battalions it was also agreed that they should be paired into brigades and 1st Tank Brigade, which consisted of C and D Battalions, was to be commanded by Lt Col C. Baker-Carr. Now Baker-Carr was believed to be a machine-gun expert and he is credited, or blamed, for persuading the War Office that American Lewis guns would be more suitable for tanks than the Hotchkiss.

There was, indeed, little wrong with the Lewis gun as a weapon. It was reliable and effective if rather bulky when compared with the Hotchkiss due to a metal sleeve which surrounded the air-cooled barrel. As it turned out, on this advice, the Lewis not only replaced the Hotchkiss in all tanks, it was also used to replace the Vickers heavy machine-guns in female tanks. Existing tanks simply had a new collar fitted into the machine-gun mounting in order to accept the larger barrel but some of the female Mark III machines, which had not been completed when the change-over was ordered, underwent a more drastic change. The Lewis gun is a good deal lighter than the water-cooled Vickers and it does not require such a heavy mounting. Thus it proved possible to redesign the original style of the female sponson and, in doing so, overcome one of its worst problems.

In order to create the widest possible arc of fire along each side of the original female tanks the sponson door, which was quite large on the male machines, was positively tiny on the females – closer to the size of a dog kennel entrance. It was therefore much more difficult for men to get in and out, and in an emergency, when the tank might be on fire, it often resulted in men becoming trapped and burned to death when they might otherwise have escaped. The new female sponson for Lewis guns was tiny compared with the Vickers type. It still gave the same arc of fire but the protruding part, like a small bay window, only occupied the upper half of the sponson

A Mark III male tank, running with empty sponsons during training at Bovington. It is using torpedo spuds, chained to the tracks, and odd branches to help in the difficult climb. The little hole, under the nose of the tank, was a pistol port that enabled the commander to shoot downwards when passing over a trench.

opening. The lower half was covered by a pair of hinged flaps, opening outwards from the centre and hinged at the sides and these could be kicked open in an emergency giving the crew a much better chance to duck down and roll out onto the ground.

From early 1917 onwards most of the training tanks at Bovington were of the Mark II and Mark III types. They now had sponsons but, when employed for driver training they generally operated without weapons. Bovington itself was expanding rapidly and on the sandy heathland around the camp various obstacles were being created such as shell holes and steps. The tanks were also permitted to use a complex arrangement of replica trenches laid out by Australian infantry who had trained there in 1915. Drivers were not only trained to negotiate these obstacles but were even encouraged to drive badly and get their tanks stuck, both to drive home the lesson and to provide experience of getting them out again. Around Bovington, satellite camps were springing up at the nearby towns of Wareham and Swanage where new intakes underwent instruction.

Officers were given more difficult tasks; their curriculum included exploration of the countryside and mapping, particularly with a view to noting how they might get their tanks across streams and other natural obstacles. Another part of the course involved a visit to Poole railway station where they had to examine the facilities for shunting tank trains and loading the machines, all work which would fall to them once they joined their battalions in France.

Other courses for all ranks included communications and the care of carrier pigeons, use of the revolver, which was the tank man's personal weapon and, of course, mechanical maintenance. This last was, however, a highly specialized trade and the average tank man could only be expected to do a certain amount of this. There would always be a requirement for trained mechanics with salvaging skills for whom workshop facilities would have to be provided. While they were at Elveden, maintenance was carried out by a small team of men who had an Albion workshop lorry. Each company that went out to France had its own travelling workshop consisting of two trailers, complete with power tools such as lathes and drills, towed behind a Foster-Daimler tractor which, of course, provided the power for tools. A more substantial, permanent workshop was established at Bovington whereas in France, now that headquarters was firmly based at Bermicourt, a huge base began to grow in the villages around that included workshops, stores and tank parks, of which more later.

Maj Wilson, as one might expect, remained critical of much of the engineering. He had gone along with the crude arrangements of the first tanks in order to meet the demand but he was aware of the need to improve things. In particular he disliked the laborious steering system which was wasteful of both power and personnel. Shortly after the first actions, in September 1916, he explained to Albert Stern the need for something better and suggested a system based upon epicyclic, or planetary, gears which he was convinced would improve matters. Stern understood the need for improvement but he was not an engineer and Wilson's explanations appear to have made little impression. While they were in France, in September, Stern and Wilson with other officers had been invited to see what the French were doing with their tanks. One place they visited was the company Forges et Aciéries de la Marine et D'Homécourt de St Chamond where they inspected a prototype heavy tank that would become known as the St Chamond. The feature that appealed to Stern was the drive train which involved a petrol electric system. To the uninitiated this appears to be ideal. The petrol engine generates electricity and all the driver has to do is to control the flow of current to a pair of electric motors in order to drive and steer the tank. There are no gears to change and acceleration is as smooth as the action of the controller; there are no complicated mechanical steering gears and no differential apparatus.

An engineer might see it differently. To begin with there was the problem of finding electric motors with sufficient horsepower to drive the tank and, indeed, a suitable power source to drive the motors. Even if these problems were solved the addition of two generators and two electric motors to the original petrol engine would make greater demands on the available space and probably increase weight to a prohibitive level. But Stern was more impressed with what he could see than with abstruse technical explanations so he was not prepared to trust Wilson's word. Rather he decided to open up the subject of tank transmission to competition. Ever since the first tanks had hit the headlines they had attracted the attention of engineers who reckoned that they could improve them. Stern therefore extracted five Mark II tanks from the production line and offered them

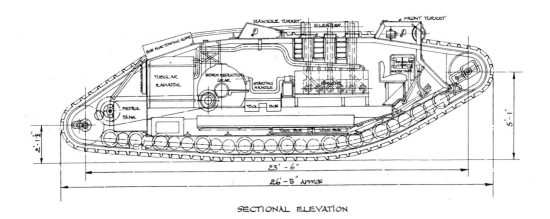

SECTIONAL ELEVATION

GENERAL ARRANGEMENT OF MACHINE MK IV

to various firms who should have their machine finished and ready for trials by the following March. Even so, Stern was so convinced of the advantage of the petrol-electric system that he offered the original tank *Mother* to the Daimler Company who agreed to develop something for him ahead of the others.

Production of the new service model, to be designated Mark IV, seems to have commenced early in 1917 but it was not an easy transition. For firms like Metropolitan who were to build the lion's share of these tanks, and even Fosters who now had more workshop space, it may have been relatively easy but for the new firms a massive amount of experience had to be gained very quickly. Likewise the increased demand for raw materials and components placed an additional strain on British industry and numerous bottle-necks occurred in the supply chain which conspired to slow down production.

To the average onlooker, and indeed to the crew, there were not many obvious changes in the Mark IV from previous designs but from an engineering point of view they were considerable. Many of these features had been foreshadowed in Marks II and III. To begin with the entire system of fuel storage and supply had been altered, partly to increase the range but primarily in the interests of

Mark IV Tank	
Data for a male machine	
Crew:	8
Weight:	28 tons
Length:	26ft 5in (8.06m)
Width:	12ft 9in (3.89m)
Height:	8ft 2in (2.49m)
Armour:	14mm (½in) max.
Speed:	3.7mph (6km/h) max.

safety. The new fuel tank, with a capacity of 70gal (318l) was located outside the tank at the rear, where the wheeled tail had once been, and encased in armour. This quantity of petrol gave the tank a theoretical range of 35 miles (56km) at the consumption rate of half a mile to the gallon (0.8km to 4.5ltr) although the combat range, which includes the distance out and back, effectively reduced this to 17 miles (27km). In practice, on typical battlefield terrain where one had to drive through glutinous mud and negotiate all kinds of obstacles the actual distance covered before fuel ran short was a lot less. Even so it was a great advantage and the safety factor should not be overlooked. The front-mounted petrol tanks of the Mark I were extremely vulnerable and come to

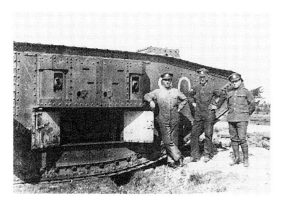

A female Mark IV showing the new style sponson with the large escape doors underneath.

that, difficult and dangerous to fill. This new arrangement required a revised fuel feed system since gravity alone would no longer work. Having tried various ideas the designers settled on a type known as the Autovac which, as its name implies, sucked fuel from the tank to the carburettor.

More significant still the design of the sponsons had been modified. That of the female machines has already been described since it was fitted to some Mark III machines but in the Mark IV there was an additional refinement. Each machine-gun sponson was split vertically at its centre line and hinged at each end so that, for rail travel, they could be folded into the hull thus reducing the width to suit the loading gauge. The male sponson could also be made to slide inwards but it incorporated two other changes. To begin with each sponson was redesigned as to its basic shape in order to make it slightly more streamlined. This was done in part to make it easier to push into the hull but, by shaving off the front lower corners, it was not so prone to dig into the ground and hinder the movement of the tank.

The other fundamental change involved the 6-pounder guns of the male tanks. The original weapons proved to be something of a liability because of their length; either striking against obstacles such as trees or buildings or even digging their muzzles into the soil as the tank ran

over rough ground. It should also be borne in mind that the long guns were only firing rounds with reduced charges, so they were not being used to their full potential. Whatever the reason the new version, known as the Ordnance, Quick-Firing Hotchkiss 6-pounder, 6cwt, had a shorter barrel, 23 calibres instead of 40 calibres long which in normal terms meant a reduction of some 47in (119cm). In fact the difference in performance was not great. The new weapon had a maximum effective range of some 7,300yd (6,675m) as against 7,500yd (6,858m) for the old gun. The difference in muzzle velocity was more marked, the short gun was rated at 1,350ft (411m) per second and the longer weapon 1,818ft (554m) per second although one must remember that in the tanks these guns fired a reduced charge.

The real advantage of the new gun was that, by running the barrel tube back on its mounting, it was possible to push it inside the tank along with the sponson and this is probably the main reason for adopting it. This is not to suggest that the task of retracting the sponson was easy, at least not on the male tanks. There were no guide rails or rollers to assist in the process; first the rear door had to be removed, then the gun run back and the entire sponson shoved bodily into the tank until rings on the sponson matched up with rings on the engine support plates and pins were dropped through to lock them into place. When tanks had been running for a while and hulls been twisted out of shape on rough ground, or when a sponson might have sustained a blow which caused it to distort, it was more than the average crew could manage to push it in themselves. The temptation to help it on its way by pushing with another tank must have been great but so were the dangers, especially to anyone inside the tank who was trying to guide the thing.

Albert Stern had set the date of 3 March 1917 for the competitive trial of rival transmission systems although it was more demonstration than genuine trial; that would have to be subject to the consideration of professional engineers. The event was to take place at the Oldbury Testing Ground

The engine and transmission unit that was standard for all tanks Marks I to IV showing the relative positions of the Daimler engine, gearbox, differential and radiator.

in Birmingham. A special course was laid out which included trenches and shell holes and over one hundred observers had been invited including a large contingent from France. The programme, which was printed in English and French, listed eight machines that were to take part although others, which had hoped to compete, did not appear.

The eight participants were;

1. A conventional Mark IV fresh from the factory.
2. The Tritton Chaser, a new lightweight design.
3. A Mark II with Williams-Janney hydraulic drive.
4. A Mark II fitted with Wilson's own design for a planetary, or epicyclic final drive.
5. The original prototype *Mother* with the Daimler petrol-electric drive.
6. A Mark II with a British Westinghouse petrol-electric drive.
7. A Mark II with a multiple clutch transmission by Wilkins.
8. The prototype Gun Carrier.

Number 1 may in fact have been a modified Mark I (tank number 555) which had been adapted virtually to Mark IV standard. Of the others number 5, the Daimler, had already effectively written itself out of the competition. It had been completed by December 1916 and had failed its initial trials but it still merits description. The programme describes it as being powered by a 125hp engine running at 1,400rpm and this would appear to have been a version of the 105hp Daimler which had been modified by a young Naval officer, a certain W.O. Bentley. He improved the power output by increasing the compression ratio, fitting aluminium pistons, twin Zenith carburettors and a lighter flywheel. The engine drove a master dynamo which supplied power to a pair of electric motors but, instead of using conventional controllers to alter the power this was done by adjusting the brushes on the commutator of the dynamo and both motors. Steering was achieved by moving the brushes on the two electric motors. In practice this did not produce ideal results. To deal with an obstacle the action was so violent that the tank moved in a series of fierce jerks which must have punished the electrical and mechanical components.

The Williams-Janney tank had a conventional 105hp engine which drove a pair of hydraulic pumps through a four to one reduction gearbox. These were connected by pipes to a pair of hydraulic motors in the track frames that were linked to the drive sprockets by means of bevel gears. Speed was infinitely variable up to about 4mph and was achieved by altering the angle of the swash plates in the pumps. Steering was effected by altering the stroke of the two pumps

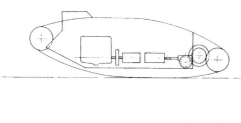

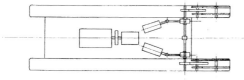

DAIMLER PETROL ELECTRIC.

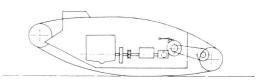

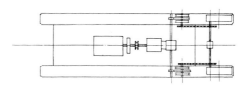

WILSONS EPICYCLIC TRANSMISSIONS.

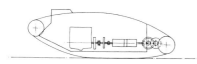

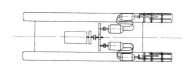

WILLIAMS JANNEY HYDRAULIC GEAR.   MARK V

Schematic drawings of the transmission layouts of the Oldbury Trials tanks.

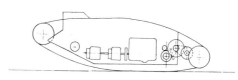

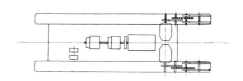

BRITISH WESTINGHOUSE PETROL ELECTRIC.

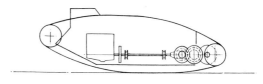

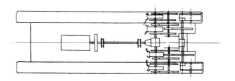

WILKINS CLUTCH GEAR.

71

A rear view of the Williams-Janney machine showing the ramshackle mixture of old radiators and oil tanks needed to cool the hydraulic oil.

relative to one another. In theory it appeared to be ideal but in practice the amount of heat generated by the pumps was excessive. In an effort to keep it within limits the tank had a conglomeration of old radiators situated between the rear horns, which not only looked vulnerable and untidy but must have been impossible to accommodate within the body of the tank without a major redesign, and even then the internal temperature would have been unbearable.

Wilson's epicyclic system also used the 105hp engine which in this instance drove through a clutch to a conventional four-speed and reverse gearbox and then through a bevel gearbox and cross shafts to simple epicyclics in the track frames. These gears were linked to brake levers under the control of the driver who simply applied the brake to the side he wished to turn, causing that epicyclic to idle while the other drove the opposite track, causing the tank to swing. Chains carried the drive from the epicyclics to the sprockets but these were linked by another cross-shaft at the back which had a dog clutch at its centre that provided the differential effect. Presumably the idea was that both tracks could be locked when the tank attacked a difficult obstacle,

just as the crews had learned to do with the original transmission.

British Westinghouse employed a six-cylinder Daimler engine which ran at 1,200rpm and developed 115hp; probably another Bentley conversion. The engine had been modified to drive through the front end of the block and it was located further back in the tank than was normal. The two generating dynamos were situated in line, in front of it. They were linked by heavy-duty cables to a pair of electric motors situated crosswise, at the rear of the tank, which drove the sprockets by double reduction gears and chain. The crude diagram, supplied with the programme to the trial, suggests that in this tank the driver sat on the left. He controlled the current from the generators by means of rheostats, which were in fact tramcar controllers, and they gave infinitely variable acceleration up to 4mph. The electric motors could be reversed independently by means of switches and steering was achieved by switching out one motor or the other as required.

The Wilkins system looks like a gear designer's nightmare. Drive from the standard 105hp Daimler engine passed via the flywheel and two flexible couplings to a bevel gearbox at the rear.

A view of the Westinghouse tank at Dollis Hill. The relocated Daimler engine can be seen inside.

Cross-shafts from here fed into a pair of three-speed and reverse gearboxes which employed multiple clutches to ensure that only one gear on each side could be engaged at a time. Drive then passed through spur gears on countershafts to final drive gears on a cross-shaft which meshed with gears on the sprocket shafts. Once again a dog clutch was employed on the cross shaft to create a locked differential effect. The three speeds could be selected by changing both gearboxes at the same time while steering was achieved by selecting different ratios in each box or even by reversing the drive on one side or the other. It was possible to change gear on the move but one gets the impression that it was an exceedingly complicated business which must have demanded highly skilled driving techniques. It had also proved necessary to extend the floor of this tank which, according to some experts, increased the risk of bellying on rough ground.

The competing tanks, which were identified by broad, coloured stripes along each side, first lined up in front of the viewing stand for inspection before moving up to one end of the field. Here they turned and lined up once again before setting off, simultaneously, down the course and over the trenches. Then they returned to the starting point. According to the programme some tanks (which ones were not specified) would also navigate a

large shell hole in front of the stand before returning to the starting line. One assumes that the option on the shell hole was permitted to favour the Daimler petrol-electric machine which had serious difficulties with such obstacles. The Wilkins multiple clutch tank failed to start on the day and did not take part in the driving demonstration.

Before looking at the two other entrants, mention must be made of others that did not appear. One Mark II hull appears to have been despatched to the St Chamond factory in France to be fitted with their version of the petrol-electric drive. Evidence suggests that this was not completed in time. The same is true of another hydraulic system, entered by the Compayne Company to the design of Professor Hele-Shaw of Manchester University. Wilson appears to have been quite impressed with this design although it is said to have used up every square inch of available space inside the tank. Other designs had been submitted by a company known as Elmo, by a Mr Chitty and by two RNAS officers, Shaw and Thornycroft, none of which were ever built. There were two others; a petrol-electric system offered by the Tilling-Stevens Company that was best known for its range of petrol-electric lorries and buses, and by the Thomas Company. This last is described as electro-mechanical and appears to

One of the Oldbury Trials tanks photographed at Richborough, later in the war, probably en route to France. The broad, coloured stripe is still visible on the side of the hull.

Tritton's prototype Chaser machine, photographed in a later guise with front mounted fuel tank and angular fighting cab.

have used direct drive from the engine for straight running with an epicyclic reduction, activating dynamos and electric motors, for climbing and steering.

The reason for painting coloured stripes along the sides of the tanks competing at Oldbury was clearly in order to enable onlookers to tell them apart at a glance. This would have been essential in the case of the various rhomboid-shaped machines but why it was considered necessary for Sir William Tritton's (he had been knighted in February) new design, the Tritton Chaser, is not clear. It was so entirely different from any of the others as to make it instantly recognizable. The design appears to have stemmed from discussions between Stern and Tritton in October 1916 and the intention seems to have been to construct a smaller, more manoeuvrable tank, armed only with machine-guns, which could be driven by one man. In effect a tracked armoured car. It may well have been inspired by the little French Renault tank, the design for which Stern may have seen when he visited Paris in September. Stern

announced the new design during a meeting at GHQ in France and obtained approval for its construction.

The extent to which Tritton had a free hand in the design is not clear but one may assume that it was almost total. Bearing in mind that the new tank would not be required to tackle the sort of trenches for which the heavy machines had been designed, Tritton elected to use lower track frames and he may have based these, to some extent, upon the design of *Little Willie*. In the drawing which was included in the Oldbury trials programme it is shown as having a box-shaped body, square at the front but with an angled driver's cab on the right. To the left of this cab is a small, drum-shaped turret said to have been the same as that fitted to the Austin armoured car and this turret would be equipped with a single Lewis gun. This layout suggests a crew of two.

Tritton came up with a form of drive that was capable of being operated by one man but only with some difficulty since it involved controlling two separate engines and gearboxes at the same time. It has been suggested that this rather crude arrangement was Tritton's simplistic answer to Wilson's epicyclic design but it must be remembered that Tritton was also working on the huge *Flying Elephant* machine at this time and that this also employed twin engines and gearboxes. The engines were four-cylinder, water-cooled units by the Tylor company and they were located side by side in front of the driver's cab and turret. Each engine drove through its own clutch to a four-speed and reverse gearbox and then via a bevel box to each track so that the right hand engine drove the right-track and its mate the left track.

The Chaser had the additional refinement, which it shared with the heavy tanks, of a cross shaft between the two bevel boxes, connected by a dog clutch, to achieve differential lock effect over difficult ground. The risk here was, that with two engines driving a locked shaft something dreadful might happen if one developed more power than the other. For this reason a device was incorporated into the clutch which caused it to

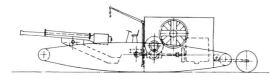

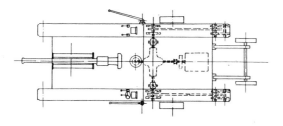

A schematic diagram of the prototype Gun Carrier Machine as printed in the programme for the Oldbury Trials.

release when the difference in power output between the two engines exceeded 12hp. By using the clutch a driver could also, just about, bring his tank home on one engine if the other failed. With maximum armour thickness of 9mm and weight calculated at 12t (12,192kg) a top speed of 7.5mph (12km/h) was estimated. Such evidence as there is suggests that the body of the tank may have been modified from the programme design with the turret replaced by an enlarged cab which included machine-gun mountings on all faces; however this cannot be confirmed.

The final participant at Oldbury was of an even more striking and unusual design than the Chaser and it certainly did not need any coloured stripe to distinguish it. This was the first prototype of the big gun-carrying machine which Stern had first mentioned in April 1916. Detailed design work had been carried out by Maj Gregg of Metropolitan and once again we only have a crude drawing from the Oldbury programme to base a description upon. Like the Chaser drawing this differs in many details from the final production model and may well be no more than a schematic representation. What it shows is a tank, with a large box-shaped body at the rear, resting upon a pair of low-profile track frames, virtually oval in elevation. This box contains the inevitable Daimler engine and Mark I style transmission system but arranged back to front so that the engine drives forwards through the primary gearbox into the differential, outboard to the secondary gearboxes and then back to the sprockets via very long loops of chain. According to the programme notes the drive sprockets were wider and stronger that those used in the tank so that the tracks were also wider. Again, like the tanks, a steering tail was fitted at the back.

Ahead of the superstructure the driver and gearsmen occupied seats on each track frame with their controls in front of them. They would have been woefully exposed in action. Between the track frames an open well occupied the space at the front and this contained a sliding cradle, capable of supporting a heavy artillery piece; the programme specifies the 60-pounder (5in) gun and 6in howitzer. With the gun in place, the wheels would have been suspended on the sides of the body and a pair of small davits were provided to handle these. Stowage would be provided for 64 rounds of ammunition for either gun and a large, horizontal pulley wheel is shown near the differential which was clearly needed to haul the gun aboard.

The results of the Oldbury Trial do not appear to have been conclusive. Wilson's own epicyclic system did not perform well since the engine was failing and Wilson himself claims that the regular tank, which he describes as a Mark IV, put up the best performance of all, possibly due to the experience of the crew managing a system which they knew well. That aside, and notwithstanding the fact that the War Office was committed to the Mark IV in the immediate future, Wilson's epicyclic system was selected as the transmission to be used for the next model with an option on the Williams–Janney hydraulic system for a more distant project. Tritton's Chaser, which also put up a good performance at Oldbury, was noted but not scheduled for immediate development while the Gun Carrier design was ordered. What Stern thought of all this is not clear; shortly before Christmas 1916 he had ordered 600 sets of equipment for the Daimler petrol-electric machine, even before it had been tested. It was typical of Stern's impulsive approach which, on a later occasion, proved highly successful. At this time, however, he was overruled by his engineers, led by Wilson, who managed to convince the authorities that it could not work.

If, as has been suggested, the standard Mark IV tank at Oldbury was, in fact, a heavily modified Mark I then it suggests that none of the new tanks were completed by early March 1917, at least not to the state where they would be suitable to take part in an official trial. Certainly we know that none were in France by April in time to take part in the next battle. Optimistic forecasts at the end of 1916 promised over 200 tanks for the proposed British spring offensive of 1917 but this figure decreased on a monthly basis, until by March it became clear that none of the new machines would be ready.

Heavy Branch headquarters in France could muster just fifteen of the surviving Mark I machines, all now shorn of their tails, and this figure was brought up to sixty with nineteen Mark II training tanks already in France and by bringing over twenty-six more from Bovington. This was a desperate measure by any standards since, as already explained, these tanks had been built from untreated plate which was not bullet proof. Photographic evidence from this time indicates that some efforts were made to remedy this situation since some of the Mark II female machines can be seen to have camouflaged sponsons, suggesting that these had been obtained from redundant female Mark I tanks.

The elaborate paint schemes applied to the first tanks in England and France had proved to be a complete waste of time and effort. Mud, carried round by the tracks, streamed down the sides of the hull and obliterated the camouflage. The training tanks, Marks II and III, would not require camouflage anyway and they were painted an all-over shade of earth brown that was also applied

A Mark II female tank abandoned on the Arras battlefield with a broken track. It is fitted with camouflaged Mark I female sponsons, converted to take Lewis guns.

to the surviving tanks in France. Presumably, therefore, the camouflaged female sponson seen on Mark II tanks in France had been removed from tanks that were no longer fit for service and that nobody had bothered to repaint. It must have been a rush job in any case since all of these female sponsons would need to be modified to accept Lewis guns in place of the original Vickers weapons.

THE BATTLE OF ARRAS

As first conceived, towards the end of 1916, the new British offensive was to take place north of the old Somme battlefield in an area between Arras and Vimy Ridge. It was modified to some extent to conform with the new plans of the French General Nivelle, who replaced Joffre, and later by the Germans who withdrew their troops on the Somme to new positions further east while they systematically devastated the abandoned ground. Known to the Allies as the Hindenburg Line, but called the Siegfried Line by the Germans, this was a superb defensive complex, intended to hold the Allies on the Somme while German troops were released to strengthen other parts of the front. The Hindenburg Line actually ended in the region of Arras but in order to bolster their original trench system, where it ran north from there, the Germans created another defensive position, known as the Drocourt-Quéant Switch Line, some 5 miles (8km) further east and it was this that seriously upset British plans. Finally an original British scheme to limit the preliminary artillery barrage to 48 hours was expanded to four days while for seventeen days prior to that the guns would be used to cut the German wire; and give notice precisely where the attack would fall.

Preparations for the battle were extremely thorough. The Heavy Branch had reconnaissance officers operating in the area from January, examining the ground and selecting starting points and routes. As the plans for the battle became more clearly defined, rallying points were identified where the tanks could meet up after the first stage of the fighting in order to prepare for further attacks. At these rallying points they would find replacement stocks of fuel and ammunition. However a clause in Third Army's instructions for 3 April to the tanks read; 'If for any reason, such as unfavourable weather or impassable ground, Tank detachments are unable to carry out their allotted tasks, they will come into Corps reserve and must not be used again without reference to Army Headquarters.' Unfavourable weather and impassable ground would plague virtually every tank at Arras but they would not go into reserve; they would try their utmost and suffer for it. It is worth noting too that armoured cars, operating under the auspices of the Machine Gun Corps were also ordered to Arras, presumably to exploit the advance if the opportunity arose. There is no evidence to suggest that any plans were drawn up to co-ordinate their actions with the tanks.

The main thrust of the attack on 9 April, supported by forty tanks, would be due east of the city of Arras but there would be supporting actions to the north and south which also involved tanks. To the north the objective was high ground overlooking the town of Vimy which was allocated to the Canadian Army with some British (mainly Scottish) support. Eight tanks had been designated to support 2nd Canadian Division whose primary objective was the village of Thélus. The unfavourable weather manifested itself at once; sleet steadily turned to snow, reducing visibility and creating the sort of impassable ground that the tanks had been warned to avoid. All eight tanks succumbed to the conditions and bogged down in the mud before they could play any useful part in the action. Vimy Ridge is regarded as the ultimate coming of age of the Canadian Army and the fact that they managed to capture it, in atrocious conditions and without the aid of tanks only enhances the achievement.

The British High Command never saw tanks as a key feature of the Arras battle and tended to play down their significance even more at the planning stage. We have seen the instructions issued to the Heavy Branch but the infantry were instructed to proceed as if the tanks were not available and, as a consequence, no great effort was made to promote collective training between the troops and the tanks. Since the latter were not available in adequate numbers they were organized into small groups and directed to deal with features on the battlefield that might prove to be particularly difficult for the infantry. To this end the tanks were ordered to start from locations up to 1,000yd (914m) behind the infantry start line and to meet up with them on the objectives. The infantry, meanwhile, would be assisted by another innovation, the so-called creeping barrage of artillery which swept the ground ahead of them.

The combination of the long approach march and dreadful ground accounted for far too many of the tanks so those that survived could hardly expect to achieve very much. There were exceptions; notably the C Battalion male tank *Lusitania*, 2nd Lt Charles Weber. The citation for his Military Cross explains that while supporting 15th Division he assisted in the capture of Feuchy Redoubt and Feuchy Chapel and managed to keep his tank in action despite a series of mechanical problems. Ultimately running short of fuel he turned back to get a refill but, upon being asked

Lusitania, *2nd Lt Weber's tank, photographed in Arras. The big Cunard liner, after which it was named, was sunk about two years earlier, in May 1915.*

for help he brought *Lusitania* into action again well aware that he would never now bring her back. Other sources claim that, in addition to fuel problems his magneto failed and he was obliged to abandon his tank on the edge of an enemy trench where it was subsequently wrecked by shellfire. In the event, the initial attack in this sector was counted a great success, most objectives being taken without the aid of tanks.

South of Arras and brushing against the northern end of the Hindenburg Line, 4th Australian Division was preparing to attack, supported by the British 62nd Division on its left. Twelve tanks from number 11 Company of D Battalion were prepared for this action but it was delayed for 24 hours when Australian patrols discovered that their artillery had failed to cut the huge belt of wire, 400yd (365m) deep in places, that confronted them. The original scheme called for the tanks to operate in pairs, one male and one female, at intervals along the Australian front but the delay gave a pause for thought. Maj W.H.L. Watson, somehow managed to persuade the Australians, and Gen Gough himself, that there was a better way. By keeping all his tanks together and launching them ahead of the infantry he hoped to crush down a great swathe of the German wire and give the Aussies a clear run into

the German trenches. Indeed Gough took everyone's breath away by suggesting that the attack should be mounted the very next day. This presented the tanks with a major problem; they had a 4-mile (6.5km) run from the railhead to the British line and then had to make their way forwards to where the troops would be waiting at the jumping-off point. In order to avoid detection they would not be able to start this move until after dark and, even if everything went to plan, it was going to be a close-run thing.

In fact virtually everything conspired against them. The twelve tanks experienced difficulties just getting off their railway wagons and one broke down at this point, then it came on to sleet and snow, covering the ground, obscuring the route markers that the tanks were supposed to follow. Meanwhile the Australian troops moved out to their starting positions and lay down to wait. Few of them had even so much as seen a tank before and tended to regard them as a bit of a novelty rather than a useful aid in battle.

Their objectives were two villages; Bullecourt to the north, from which the battle got its name, was within the Hindenburg system while Riencourt, somewhat south and east of the first village was just beyond it. As the time for the attack drew near the waiting troops grew increasingly anxious because no tanks could be heard. In fact they were well behind time, still well out on the rolling downs and making their uncertain way more or less in the right direction. First the attack was delayed for an hour, due to the non-appearance of the tanks, and then postponed altogether when it became clear that they would be far too late to take part. Fortunately the Australians were able to withdraw with relatively light casualties but nobody had notified 62nd Division that put in its attack and was hit very hard.

Despite objections all round it was ordered at the highest level that they should try again on the 11th. There was a further attack in the centre on this day, which included a few surviving tanks but Bullecourt was undoubtedly the main feature. Once again the tanks were late in starting and a

A German photograph of a female Mark II, shattered by artillery at Bullecourt. Notice the abandoned British steel helmet in the foreground and a detached torpedo spud by the broken track.

number broke down or became bogged down but those that did take part did moderately well. There were too few of them to have any serious effect on the outcome of the battle and they got little credit from the Australians but it was not a complete fiasco. At about 0600, when the sun came up, observers on both sides could easily pick out the tanks, looking like black snails against the snow, and what the Germans could see they could shoot at. Australian infantry reported some tanks literally sparkling with the volume of machine-gun fire aimed at them and most were ultimately knocked out. For some time after the battle a popular rumour credited two tanks with breaking the Hindenburg Line and vanishing through Riencourt with accompanying infantry but this was an optical illusion caused by the atmospheric conditions; no tank ever got right through the German system. Even so one male tank (Mark II No. 799, Lt Davies) got slightly lost and wandered some 500yd away from its infantry to end in a death or glory ride entirely on its own.

Two significant factors resulted from this battle. In the first place the Australians came to the conclusion that tanks were seriously overrated and would have little to do with them over the next fourteen months. The Germans, on the other hand, became more impressed and, for the first time, had a couple of disabled tanks within their lines that they could examine closely. One was Lt Davies's Mark II male, the other a female of unknown type. From examination and trials the Germans learned that the armour of British tanks was vulnerable to their anti-tank ammunition and they were also able to locate the fuel tanks that were indicated to their troops on specially prepared charts as a vital aiming point. If this boosted German confidence it was to be short-lived; the Mark IV not only had thicker armour but the fuel tanks, as already described, had been relocated.

There were two subsequent actions in this sector on 23 April and 3 May. For each the Heavy Branch had to work very hard to get any machines running and some of these broke down soon afterwards. Twenty were mustered for the first action but only ten got properly into action and they only enjoyed local successes. For the May attack, known as Second Bullecourt, only thirteen tanks could be persuaded to run and it is noteworthy that of these, ten were offered to the Australians who believed that they could do better without them. It was not an auspicious start to the year as far as the tanks were concerned and it was soon going to get a lot worse.

7 The Mark IV Enters Service

Even as the tanks were fighting at Arras others were in action in a very different theatre. In December 1916 it was decided to send eight tanks to reinforce the Egyptian Expeditionary Force that was fighting its way northwards into Palestine. Regimental legend claims that Mark IV tanks had been selected but worn out Mark I training machines were sent by mistake. The date alone reveals that Mark IV tanks would not have been available and it was equally inevitable that any spare Mark Is would be more or less worn-out. Presumably Mark II tanks were ruled out on account of being unarmoured.

The tank detachment was manned by personnel from E Battalion under the command of Maj Norman Nutt. They landed in the Canal Zone in January 1917 and carried out initial trials over adjacent sand hills. Some sources claim that the tanks behaved well in the new conditions but others suggest that the use of grease on the track runners had to be discontinued since it attracted sand and produced an abrasive paste. Without grease, it is claimed, the sand just ran through the tracks. Even so it is difficult to believe that track rollers would have worked for very long without lubrication and in a later report Major Nutt blames track breakages on a build-up of sand and grease.

THE FIRST BATTLE OF GAZA

When the First Battle of Gaza began, towards the end of March, the tanks were not ready. The Turkish positions at Gaza were well built, intelli-

gently sited and courageously defended and the British attack was not successful. The attack was to be renewed in April and it is suggested that Sir Archibald Murray, the British commander, placed considerable faith in this handful of tanks to redress the situation. He had also received a large shipment of gas shells but appears to have been reluctant to use them. According to the Australians great efforts were made to have the tanks moved up to the front in secret but it is generally understood that the enemy's spy

Domestic duties in the desert. Dwarfed by the palms this Mark I female tank in Palestine is serviced by its crew. Notice that, like all tanks in the Middle East, it ran without a tail and appears to have the extra studs intended to hold burster plates.

network in the area was extremely efficient and, as the Australian Official History points out, 'tanks do not lend themselves to concealment'.

It is hardly possible to exaggerate Nutt's difficulties. With a detachment of less than 300 men and very limited workshop facilities he had to maintain eight worn-out tanks in a hostile environment and command them in battle under two men, Generals Dobell and Murray, who did not enjoy the confidence of many of their Australian or British subordinates. Inevitably these two elected to employ the tanks incorrectly, just as Haig's generals had done on the Western Front. Tanks were seconded in pairs to selected brigades at different parts of the front.

The Philistine settlement of Gaza, one of the oldest cities in the world, was close to the coast but surrounded by agricultural land. The landscape was almost featureless with few trees, except in the olive groves, but near to the city deeply scoured watercourses and thick cactus hedges made it close country by Middle East standards and the Turks were stubborn defenders. On the first day, 17 April, only two of the six tanks ordered up for action were employed. These were with the 163rd Infantry Brigade of 53rd (East Anglian) Division which was attacking east of Gaza, across the Beersheba Road. One of these tanks, named *Sir Archibald,* was struck three

The female tank HMLS Kia-Ora *on the beach. It is interesting to note that Mark I tanks at Gaza were not converted to carry Lewis guns.*

HMLS Pincher, *a male machine, plunges through desert grass and cactus. The crew have opened the sponson doors and the manhole hatch on the roof for ventilation.*

times by artillery shells and set on fire and its consort did not achieve a great deal.

Two days later the attack was resumed. The Australian Official History is full of praise for the skill and gallantry of the tank commanders but points out that it might have been wiser to concentrate all of them at one point instead of spreading the tanks in pairs all along the front. The remaining tank with 163rd Brigade (HMLS *Nutty*) did extremely well, leading the 5th Battalion, the Norfolk Regiment into a well-defended redoubt that was afterwards known as the Tank Redoubt since this is where the machine was subsequently knocked out. Of four tanks allocated to the 52nd Division HMLS *Otazel* became ditched while *War Baby* made two attempts to lead infantry onto Outpost Hill, which they could not hold due to Turkish artillery fire and on its second attempt this tank was also knocked out. *Kia-Ora* also fought its way onto Outpost Hill but, finding no one there came back while HMLS *Pincher*, the reserve tank, moved up only to be told that the attack was to be called off. Of the two tanks supporting 53rd Division HMLS *Tiger* managed to do some good work without infantry support and only retired when all of its crew were wounded while *Ole-Luk-Oie* broke down. This odd name, by the way, is a Danish pen name adopted, at the time of the Boer War, by Ernest Swinton.

Whether the tanks came as a surprise to the Turks is not clear but their infantry stood up well to their first taste of mechanized warfare. The Allied infantry learned that tanks attracted enemy fire and the temptation to shelter near them was extremely hazardous. It is worth remarking that, once again, armoured cars were employed on the flank, with the Desert Mounted Column, but never in conjunction with the tanks.

THE BATTLE OF MESSINES RIDGE

Mark IV tanks began to arrive in France in May and were issued at first to A and B Battalions. At this time C and D Battalions were recovering from Arras and they were soon joined by F and G Battalions which came out from Bovington, without tanks, to prepare for Haig's next campaign in Flanders. As an overture to this, Second Army was to participate in a novel attack against enemy positions on Messines Ridge where they would be supported by A and B Battalions. Each battalion now had 36 Mark IV tanks in three companies of twelve tanks plus two reserve tanks and six Supply Tanks issued on the basis of two per company. These latter were redundant Mark I and Mark II male machines from which the guns had been removed so that the sponsons could be used as store-carrying panniers, the gun apertures having been plated over.

It is often quite surprising, to those not directly connected with them, to learn how attached tank crews become to their machines. It is similar, in a modest way, to the affection a captain feels for his ship and no doubt results partly from the care they must lavish on the machine and the belief that it was their tank that kept them safe. Its loss was often mourned. This attachment manifested itself in various ways; the crew usually called their tank 'she' irrespective of its gender or referred to it as 'the old bus', 'the jalopy' or similar dated terms. They also christened their tank and this practice dates to the very first machines, indeed

the sailors were naming their armoured cars in 1915. Both C and D Companies, probably before they left for France, had named all their tanks and started the practice, which was almost universal, of selecting a name starting with the initial letter of the company. C Company, in fact, went one better and, as far as possible, chose names with cocktail lounge associations; *Crème-de-Menthe, Chablis, Chartreuse* and so on.

The tanks also carried official markings. The most enduring, as far as the tank itself was concerned, was its own census number, issued when it was built. This would invariably be of three or four digits and, in most cases, was painted in white on either side of the machine, in rear of the sponsons. It was also to be found on embossed plates inside the tank, near the sponson aperture. The tank also had a battalion, or crew number, which it retained as long as it was with a particular unit. This started with the company/battalion letter followed by a number which would reveal to initiates the tank's place in the scheme of things. Thus, for example, tanks E1 to E15 would be from the first company in E Battalion, E16 to E30 the second and E31 to E45 the third. This figure would normally appear, again in white, on either side, near the front, on the rear for the benefit of following troops and on top of the cab as an indication to aircraft flying contact patrols. Names and battalion numbers were transferable. Crews handed their tanks in at the end of a major action and drew new ones for the next. While they retained their place in the battalion's order of battle they would keep their own number and presumably, if it was their choice, the same name although this was sometimes further indicated by a number, as in the case of F Battalion's *Flirt II.* Some battalions also adopted a symbol; the famous 'Chinese Eye' of F Battalion probably being the best known since it has survived to this day.

Training tanks, by contrast, were hacks, often operated by more than one crew on a particular day. Such tanks rarely warranted a name, unless they went on a War Bond sales trip, but they were

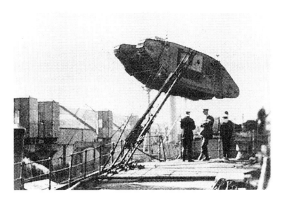

A poor but rare photograph showing a Mark IV male tank, probably being lifted off a ship at Le Havre. The picture emphasizes the problems of moving tanks from the factories in Britain to the front in France.

An excellent comparison between male and female Mark IV tanks as they race over a steeplechase course at Neuve Eglise, watched by King George V and Gen Elles in July 1917.

RIGHT: An artistic crewman sketches a large maple leaf on the front plate of the F Battalion tank Forage, which suggests that the commander was a Canadian. The artist appears to have a brass MGC shoulder title and other badges on his leather belt and his companion also wears the MGC cap badge.

LEFT: A new Mark IV tank with its crew at the Rollencourt tankodrome. The officer, in his smart leather overalls, is 2nd Lt Lyles of A Battalion who was to gain a Military Cross on 23 September 1917. Here, however, the men still sport the Machine Gun Corps cap badge which suggests a date before July.

Another 6th (F) Battalion tank shows its battalion number, F4, on the back of the petrol tank. This would assist following infantry and it would be repeated on the cab roof for the benefit of contact aircraft. From this angle we also get an excellent view of the unditching gear.

issued with a number, usually of three digits, painted very large on each side, presumably for administrative purposes; although why the tank's own number that was also retained, would not have done just as well is not clear. Tanks used for experimental work often carried a special number. The Lanchester gearbox tank, seen at Dollis Hill, was designated Ex. 251.

The central feature of the Messines battle was the explosion of a series of massive charges, which had been secreted in underground chambers beneath the German lines. The role of the tanks was to support the infantry who would move in after the mines had been detonated but in the event they had relatively little to do. The devastation, which followed the huge explosions, meant that opposition was relatively light and the infantry followed up quickly. A Battalion claim that their tanks were slowed down at the outset by the sticky ground and by the time they caught up with the infantry the enemy were on the run. The tanks gave chase as best they could but it was not in the nature of Mark IV tanks to chase anything and many broke down or became bogged down. Even this was not the disaster it might have been because the crews stayed with their tanks overnight and were instrumental in breaking up an enemy counter-attack on the following day, even though they could hardly move.

Mark IV tanks move forward during the Messines battle while artillery batters the ridge ahead of them. In the foreground a couple of British soldiers make their way to the rear with two German prisoners.

TANK ENGINES

Even as the factories in Britain got into their stride producing the Mark IV, experimental work and future planning went on. It would be wrong to imagine this as a process of rigid stages; rather it was a perpetual undercurrent to the entire theme of tank production. Take, for instance, the matter of tank engines. From the very first it had been appreciated that the 105hp Daimler was barely adequate to move a 28-ton (28,448kg) tank and experience in muddy conditions only served to drive this home. W.O. Bentley's efforts to improve the Daimler had not proved successful and the company that already had priority contracts with the Royal Flying Corps, did not wish to develop a better power unit for the tanks. Albert Stern's writing gives the impression that he discovered Harry Ricardo purely by chance, or maybe inspiration. By Ricardo's account he had been consulted on various matters concerning tank production since early 1916 and was drawn into the design of a new engine by the following October. Indeed he hardly mentions Stern and prefers to be seen as working for Tennyson D'Eyncourt, in conjunction with Tritton and Wilson on a brand new tank design. This, according to Ricardo, was to be the Mark V for which Tritton would produce a new hull design, Ricardo the engine and Wilson the transmission. He goes on to say that Lloyd-George vitalized the proceedings by ordering 1,400 of the new tanks, straight off the drawing board, at Christmas 1916.

There are various aspects of these stories that might not stand up to vigorous investigation but the essence is there. To begin with there is no doubting Ricardo's engineering genius that can easily be demonstrated by explaining the constraints under which he had to work. To begin with the aviation industry's preferential claim on light alloys (which might well have been another factor in the failure of Bentley's scheme) restricted Ricardo in the use of materials. Secondly whatever engine he designed it would have to fit into the existing type of tank and thirdly, at least

A Ricardo 150hp engine manufactured by Mirrlees, Bickerton and Day of Stockport. Points to note include the large flywheel at the rear, the magnetos and distributor at the front and the large, detachable panels in the crankcase.

ideally, it should not create great clouds of exhaust smoke, even when the tank was pitched at a steep angle from the horizontal. Finally, of course, there was the production problem. Every engine manufacturer worthy of the name, if not building engines for transport vehicles, was fully engaged in aero engine work.

Ricardo's solution to the production problem was quickly arranged. In the Manchester area in particular there were various old companies still producing what were known as gas engines; solid and slow revving machines which ran on domestic gas and were used as industrial, or even domestic power plants. These firms had been rejected for aviation work, probably because their products were regarded as too ponderous, but this was not a worry where tanks were concerned. The Manchester firms, Mirrlees, Bickerton and Day, Crossley Brothers and Browett-Lindley were joined by Hornsbys of Grantham, Peter Brotherhood of Peterborough and ultimately Gardners and the National Gas Engine Company. Not only did they appear eager to supply engines, they assisted Ricardo with draughtsmen and, in the case of Peter Brotherhood, rushed through the manufacture of a prototype for initial trials.

In the days before piston rings the problem of burning oil in the combustion chamber, and the resulting cloud of blue/grey exhaust smoke was simply accepted. In order to prevent this Ricardo adapted a principle from steam engine design, known as the crosshead piston, which solved that problem and others such as oil temperature and consumption. Ricardo believed that they should be aiming for a horsepower rating of about 200 at least but Wilson set the limit at 150hp on the grounds that his transmission would not be able to cope with more. Ricardo also designed the engine with large, removable panels in the crankcase so that a lot of maintenance could be carried out with the engine still inside the tank. Perhaps it should be emphasized here that, like the 105hp Daimler, Ricardo's engine was an internal combustion, or petrol engine, not a Diesel. Indeed in describing it Ricardo refers more than once to the poor quality petrol that was being supplied to the tanks and how he designed his engine to operate well on it.

Peter Brotherhood had an engine on the test bench by March 1917 and it was immediately successful, delivering 168hp at 1,200rpm and 200hp at 1,600rpm. It was in full-scale production by the early summer of 1917 and in theory could have been fitted into later production Mark IV tanks from then on; indeed Ricardo, in his autobiography* claims that it was. In fact there is no evidence for this although there are references to a Mark IVA tank and Philip Johnson, during a visit to London in the autumn of 1917, says that he drove a Mark IV with Ricardo engine and epicyclic gear that performed very well.

This may well be the tank Ricardo refers to when he claims that the first Mark V was completed in June 1917. The surviving official description of the Mark IVA mentions not only

*Ricardo, *Memories and Machines* (Constable and Co, 1968).

the Ricardo/Wilson combination but fuel tanks relocated at the front, within the frames but separated from the crew area by extra armour, of tracks that were one inch wider on the outside only and possibly a rear machine-gun position. It was discussed at a meeting held on 18 July 1917 when both Daimler and Ricardo engined tanks were examined.

MARKS V AND VI

In fact the Mark V which Ricardo mentions as being designed in 1916 and ordered by Lloyd-George that Christmas was not the Mark V that entered production in due course. Rather it was an alternative, and somewhat more radical design, drawings of which were dated 9 June 1917. A full size wooden mock-up of this tank, and another designated Mark VI, were rolled out from the Metropolitan works on 23 June 1917 and again on 13 July. The Mark V, which is described as requiring the Ricardo engine and Wilson transmission, was similar in profile to the Mark IV but somewhat longer at the rear end. The driver's cab was more prominent than on existing designs and the rear end of the body had been reshaped to

The full-size wooden mock-up of the original Mark V design rolled out from the Metropolitan works for its official photograph. Notice the improved mounting for the Hotchkiss machine-gun in the male sponson and the enlarged rear fighting cab.

The Mark VI mock-up was shown at the same time. One can see the forward-mounted 6-pounder, the little side sponson-cum-door and the combined driver's cab and superstructure. The wooden tank stands on a traverser, normally used to transfer railway rolling stock from one track to another.

provide a backwards firing machine-gun. In fact, although the male sponsons were of the usual pattern, all of the machine-gun mountings (which incidentally show Hotchkiss guns fitted) are more substantial than the types then in use.

The Mark VI was an even more striking departure from what had become the norm. The hull appears to be somewhat lower and shorter than the Mark V but this could be an optical illusion created by the central superstructure which is a lot higher than on any previous design. This structure incorporated a driver's hood and commander's lookout post with an extension to the rear that housed four machine gun mountings, one at each corner. In front of the driver and below him was a long extension of the hull which contained a six-pounder gun mounting. This was arranged to fire forwards, from between the track horns with flank machine-guns in miniature sponsons that doubled as exit doors, on each side.

The intention was obvious, to create a tank in which both the driver and commander could see what the gunner was shooting at and, indeed, direct him onto suitable targets by pointing the tank at them. From the driver's point of view this might have been a mixed blessing since the gun was a lot closer to his seat and firing it might seriously impair his view. On the other hand he would not need to account for the extra width of conventional sponsons when manoeuvring in tight corners, even though his view ahead would be spoiled to some extent by the fact that he was much higher up and further back on the tank than in a Mark IV.

From the gunner's point of view it would probably have been more comfortable to work at the front but he would need far greater co-operation from the driver since the traverse of the gun (the short, 23 calibre, six-pounder) was very limited and there was the additional risk of damage if the gun struck an obstacle or got plugged with mud when travelling across country. Mechanically, the Mark VI was like the proposed Mark V but for the fact that the engine was located off to one side in order to create more room inside the hull with the result that the drive train had to be rearranged around it in a rather complex way. For example both steering epicyclics were arranged in line, on the same side of the tank so that the drive shaft from one ran clear across the hull. The Mark VI would have had 14mm armour and much wider tracks (29½in (75cm)) than any so far developed.

Neither design was accepted for production despite the fact that the United States, having declared war on Germany on 6 April, placed an order for 600 of the Mark VI version. The most likely explanation of this cancellation was a matter of practicality. With mass production now getting into its stride there was a lot to be said for retaining at least the basic profile of the current heavy tank since many components could be ordered in bulk. Too many changes at this stage would inevitably lead to a dissipation of manufacturing effort and potential confusion, all of which must conspire to a slowdown in production.

Another change which occurred in July involved a new site in the London suburb of Dollis Hill. Presumably the Mechanical Warfare Department's experimental ground at Wembley Park was regarded as too small, and probably not secluded enough for the sort of work that was going on there. The new location included a large area of land behind a factory on the Edgware Road that belonged to the McCurd Lorry Manufacturing Company. The experimental section from Oldbury also moved here, bringing with it the survivors of the famous Oldbury Trials and the ground was soon as churned up as any part of the Western Front. The site was also referred to sometimes as Cricklewood but the boundaries between London boroughs have never been hard and fast as far as the public are concerned, never mind what local councillors might think.

So much for the big picture. At Bovington, trials were taking place of various types of machine-gun mounting involving both the Lewis and Hotchkiss weapons. Whether this was due to an early realization that the Lewis gun did not perform well in tanks, or an attempt to create a mounting adaptable to both is not clear but the former seems the more likely, based upon experience in France. Reliable as it was with the infantry the Lewis gun was a problem in tanks. The air-cooling jacket that surrounded the barrel was quite bulky and was easily damaged by enemy fire while the flow of cooling air, from breech to muzzle, was

reversed when fired from a tank with the engine running since the radiator fan was designed to draw air into the tank. Thus the Lewis gunner as he fired, had the additional pleasure of a stream of hot gas blown into his face.

Indeed this might be the place to record a number of other experiments initiated at Bovington around this time, proving that the camp had now settled down to a regular training programme and people had the time to indulge in a spot of inventing, and the workshop facilities to support it. At least three experiments were concerned with the problems of getting infantry over barbed wire entanglements in the wake of the tanks. The simplest was a sort of knife blade, beneath the tank's hull and close to one of its tracks, which was supposed to slice through the wire. Another saw a tank equipped with a roll of coir matting, suspended from the front, which unrolled and pressed down over the wire as it went. The prize, at least for title if not practicality, must go to Lt Col E.B. Matthew-Lannowe's Bomb, Bullet and Shrapnel Proof Box. This was described as an armoured compartment, fitted at the rear of a tank and designed to carry a party of Lewis gunners, not unlike one of the Landship Committee's Trench Storming Parties.

None of these ideas was ever developed. Neither was a proposal by Maj Knothe, one time commander of No. 711 Company ASC, to fit an extra set of tracks beneath the hull of a tank to help it over rough ground. It is very difficult to see how this might have worked, given the limited ground clearance of these tanks, but there is evidence to indicate that Metropolitan, in Birmingham, was asked to investigate the possibility. Fosters might have been a better proposition since they had been involved in the abortive *Flying Elephant* design which also had this feature.

8 The Flanders Campaign – Trial by Mud

At Central Workshops in France even more frantic work was going on. Over the winter 1916–17 many tank officers had been considering the problem of how to move tanks through the mud. Various ideas had been suggested and some adopted. These included track attachments, usually called spuds, which either spread the surface area of the track shoe or raised it to give extra bite. Many of the Mark II tanks used at Arras had a bolt-on track attachment, normally applied to every fourth or sixth link that extended the width of the plate and thus reduced overall ground pressure. This was a semi-permanent device whereas the torpedo spud was for use in real emergencies. This was a substantial piece of round timber, held within a collar that could be attached to the track by chain to provide additional leverage if the tank got stuck. It worked moderately well but that is the best that can be said for it.

Philip Johnson, who was now an engineering officer with special responsibility for experimentation at Heavy Branch HQ in France, came up with a much better idea, known as the underditching beam. This was a massive piece of oak, bound on two sides by iron plating, which could be chained to both tracks at the same time and then drawn round, underneath the hull, if the tank was slipping or stuck in a hole.

The problem was that this equipment was far too heavy to handle, even in good conditions, so a means had to be found of stowing it permanently on the tank in a way that would permit it to be used quickly and easily. Johnson solved this by designing a set of parallel rails that ran from the front to the back of the tank, going above the cab in the process, and upon which the underditching beam was chained when not in use. In theory, if the tank got stuck, all one had to do was release the beam, attach clamps to the track and let the beam find its way round until the tracks had something firm to bite upon. In practice, it was by no means as easy as that.

To begin with, once the tank was stuck it was probably perched at an alarming angle, half out

Drivers being trained in the use of torpedo spuds at Bovington. Notice how the tank has been so well ditched that the bottom of the hull has scraped the mud as it climbed out of its hole.

A classic view of a Mark IV male at Central Workshops demonstrating the unditching beam. Notice how it is shackled and chained to the track, a dangerous task when carried out under fire. Observe too how the support rails are mounted in such a way that they carry the beam over the cab.

of a shell hole. It would probably be plastered thick with mud and, on the battlefield, was inevitably the target of every enemy weapon that could be aimed at it. These incidental difficulties, notwithstanding, at least two members of the tank's crew would have to climb out of their vehicle, scramble up on top and then start fiddling about with nuts, bolts and chains with as much haste and care as they could muster. It was not a job for the faint-hearted yet it was performed, over and over again on the battlefield.

The problem for Central Workshops, having created a prototype, came when they tried to get the beam and its fittings manufactured in Britain. Nobody was prepared to do it, at least not in a hurry and certainly not without revising the design to the point where it would probably end up being more trouble than it was ever worth. Central Workshops therefore undertook to manufacture all of this equipment for every Mark IV tank delivered to France which was no mean achievement and it remains one fairly crude way of assessing whether a Mark IV, photographed later in the war, had seen service in France or not depending on whether it was fitted with unditching beam rails.

Of course much of the actual work fell to the personnel of the tank battalions in France. A Battalion, for example, record that most of their time between 6 and 17 July 1917 was spent handing in their old torpedo spuds and fitting the new unditching gear. The intention was to have the equipment fitted to all tanks that would be going into action at the end of the month. Incidentally B Battalion claim, at this time, that their crews were engaged in camouflage painting their tanks. This is difficult to explain since, as we have already seen, painting exotic patterns on tanks proved to be a complete waste of time once they became plastered in mud. It may well be that they are referring to another practice noted around the summer of 1917. This was an ingenious little subterfuge that involved painting straight black lines on any part of the tank where a vision slit was visible. These slits showed up black against the brown of the hull and made excellent aiming points for enemy gunners wishing to distract or even blind the crew. By extending a black line either side of every slit its precise location would be less obvious.

Although every battalion that came over from England was considered to be fully trained, it did

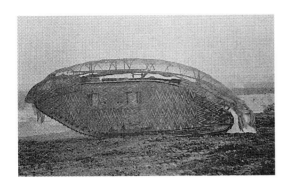

A startling exercise in camouflage that was probably conducted at Bovington. The intricate zig-zag pattern broke up the outline of the tank, at least in theory, while the flimsy cover was presumably carried to disguise the tank from the air. Quite how long any of this would have lasted on active service can only be imagined.

Tank F1 provides a good view of a Mark IV female sponson equipped with Lewis guns and also illustrates the practice of using stripes to disguise the location of vision slits. Notice the playing card symbols which were adopted by 6th Battalion.

not end there. F Battalion, for instance, which left Bovington in mid-May, was issued with training tanks when it arrived in France and spent some time practising over abandoned German trenches around Wailly. That done, each company spent a week on the Channel coast near Merlimont where a gunnery school had been established; and that was not all that was going on at Merlimont.

Before examining this remarkable subject it is well to remember that, at the time it was proposed, the tank, as a practical proposition, was little more than one year old and had only been employed in a few uninspiring battles. The plan, which became known as the *Hush* Operation, had first been mooted in 1916. The idea was to exploit the only open flank available to the British by putting a substantial force ashore on the Belgian Coast, somewhere north of Nieuport, which could encircle Ostend and establish itself behind the German lines. This had to be abandoned when it was agreed to fight that season's battles on the Somme but it was revived in 1917 and, this time, the attacking force would include tanks.

Without going into excessive detail over a scheme that never actually took place, suffice it to say that it involved putting nine tanks, with infantry, artillery and medical support, ashore from three gigantic barges, propelled by warships. Moving inland this force would meet up with other British troops who would fight their way along the coast from a salient north of Nieuport and act as a major threat to German troops already dealing with the main British attack at Ypres. The biggest problem, from the tank aspect, was a high sea wall, with an outward curving lip at the top that no tank, nor indeed any other vehicle, could hope to climb unaided.

The scheme was heavily promoted by Admiral Sir Reginald Bacon, now commanding the Dover Patrol, and a special tank detachment was formed under Capt the Hon. J.D.Y. Bingham working in conjunction with Frederick Hotblack and Philip Johnson whose task it was to overcome the technical problems. Johnson had some of the tanks equipped with special, power-operated winches and a short ramp that hung like a bowsprit from the nose of each machine. The tanks were further equipped with sharp metal teeth on their tracks that would cut through the green slime that coated the wall and bite into the concrete to provide a firm grip. As each tank came ashore from its barge it would push the ramp ahead of it, up the slope

A large crowd gathers to watch as a Mark IV male tank, pushing a wedge-shaped ramp ahead of it, tackles the replica sea wall at Merlimont in preparation for the Hush Operation. *Notice the screens, erected to shield the practice wall from view.*

of the wall, until it lodged beneath the lip. Then, having dropped the ramp, it would proceed to climb over it in a series of short, sharp jerks, until it came to rest on top. From here, those tanks equipped with winches would pay out a line and haul up other vehicles and equipment.

Special training ramps were created at Erin, and in the dunes at Merlimont upon which the tanks were tried while the naval element practised in Britain. Fuller poured scorn on the whole idea but there is no denying its originality and equally

One of the Mark IV female winching tanks designed for the Hush Operation *seen on a salvage operation at the end of the war. The winch drum is located behind the sponson, protected by an armoured shield.*

no doubt that all of the practical problems associated with it were solved. That it was never launched may have been due to a small German attack, early in July that eliminated the salient near Nieuport and to the subsequent sorry mess of the entire Ypres campaign of 1917. Even so the entire force, including the special tank detachment, was held in a high state of training and almost total isolation for some weeks and, indeed, Bingham's special tank force was not officially disbanded until October.

THE BIRTH OF THE TANK CORPS

A Royal Warrant, promulgated on 28 July 1917, declared that in future the Heavy Branch, Machine Gun Corps, would be known as the Tank Corps. In a world heavy with symbolism and tradition this carried a lot more meaning than a mere change of name might suggest. The establishment of the Corps, in its own right was an indication of maturity, a marker around which a whole new body of tradition could be created. Tank Corps personnel would wear their own badge, instead of that of another Corps and would have their own flag displaying three horizontal bands of brown, red and green. This new identity appeared to mark a new era and an indication of Royal approval that is the foundation of regimental pride. A pity then that it should have been conferred on the eve of a battle which, over the next few months, would bring the new Corps almost to its knees and to its lowest point in military esteem. Indeed there were those who suggested that those who disapproved of tanks had ordered them to be used here in the hope that they might fail and duly disappear.

FLANDERS CAMPAIGN

The Flanders campaign of 1917 has been studied in great detail and all that needs to be said here

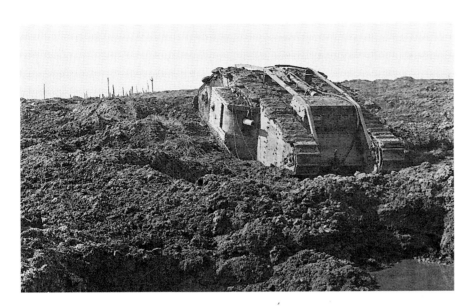

Pulverized landscape with tank; a Mark IV male in a vista of mud, water and blasted trees that was so typical of the Salient. The tank that has already lost its unditching beam, is probably stuck fast. The photograph was taken near Westhoek in September 1917.

is that it was one of Haig's pet schemes that with a bit more luck and a lot more sense, could have been made to work. If, as some claim, it was an attempt to defeat Germany before the Americans could get seriously involved and claim much of the credit, bearing in mind that the French Army at this time was in a parlous state, is not our concern here although a cynic would not dismiss it. What matters most is the fact that, despite having tanks and well-trained crews in relatively large numbers, the generals preferred to rely on tried and failed methods that in this instance, positively ruined any chance the tanks might have had to redeem the situation.

By insisting upon a preliminary bombardment of unprecedented proportions the high command not only turned a fragile area of reclaimed swampland into a prehistoric quagmire, they delayed the start of the offensive up to the very day when a forecast period of very wet weather began. This final factor created a landscape that would hardly support a human being, never mind a 28t (28,448kg) tank and the scale of misery thus engendered has probably never been equalled.

The Germans had been unable to extend the Hindenburg Line into Flanders, precisely because of the high water table. Instead they had begun,

in 1915, to create a chain of reinforced concrete pill boxes in which men could shelter during a bombardment and then improved this defensive network with massive blockhouses and machine-gun posts, all of exceptional strength and so arranged that they provided one another with mutual support all along their line.

Those battalions already in France; A, B, C, D, F and G would all take part with E Battalion, newly arrived from Bovington, in reserve. The battle, known as Third Ypres, would commence on 31 July. In the preceding weeks reconnaissance officers had walked all over the battlefield, checking bearings so that tanks could navigate by compass. Tank officers and drivers had been brought into the front line to look over the ground and the Royal Engineers and Pioneer Corps had been out night after night, creating routes, roadways across the mud made from railway sleepers and building causeways across waterways where the tanks were to go. Finally parties went out with rolls of white tape to mark out approach routes.

Two days before the battle the tanks began to move, although in fact they only did so at night. A Battalion camouflaged its tanks after each night move and then brought the men back to camp in lorries each day. In G Battalion the men stayed with their tanks, working beneath the camouflage on final maintenance and preparatory work such as filling the magazines of Lewis guns. Each move was a nightmare in itself. The sleeper roads were choked with traffic, animal and mechanical, and progress was painfully slow. Sergeant Allnatt, of G Battalion reckoned it once took him four and a half hours to travel just over a mile.

Before the battle began officers and men studied maps issued by GHQ. They were, in Allnatt's view, little more than works of fiction, or maybe art. They showed a civilized pattern of fields, roads, villages and streams, all orderly and neat. The reality was a sea of mud where roads were indistinguishable from fields and you only knew you were in a village by the stain of red brick dust in the mud. Streams were another matter. Alnatt, who was driving the tank *Grave-digger*, was told that the Steenbeek stream near St Julien was 10ft wide with banks 5ft high at either side. By the time he arrived the banks had gone and the stream, such as it was, extended some 40ft. Capt Douglas Browne of G Battalion was so irritated by the neat maps that he tried to create one of his own, based on what he could see, but he received no thanks for it. This kind of realism could so easily be portrayed as negative thinking.

The plan of attack required the tanks, yet again, to support the infantry by dealing with strongpoints on the assumption that the Germans had three regular lines of defence. The tanks would move forward in three distinct waves. The first would take the infantry to an initial objective, the second wave would then pass through to deal with the next stage and so on. This picture of machines, rolling forward in unbroken lines was very suggestive but in fact the German trenches were not arranged in this simplistic way and in any case many of the tanks plunged into the mud and remained fast. Allnatt, who reached his objective by very skilful driving, found himself entirely alone at one point, with no living thing in sight anywhere. Rolling back to the rallying point he passed another tank, standing still with all guns firing. Turning, they found the enemy mounting a counter-attack and Allnatt kept his tank cruising up and down while it fired. At the same time he was mentally urging the other tank to do the same but it just sat there, probably unaware that enemy guns were ranging on it and that shells were dropping all around. Allnatt looked away to check his route and when he looked back the other tank had simply vanished.

Tanks of A Battalion, directed to deal with enemy opposition from Inverness Copse, found the going so hard that it took some tanks 9½ hr to do 1¼ miles, only to discover on arrival that they were not required. On the way back they lost two tanks and one man. There were tanks that, having attached their unditching beams, simply left them in place and put up with a seriously uncomfortable ride in the hope that they could at least keep going. Douglas Browne, in G46, was heading for a strongpoint known as Bosche Castle. There was a road leading in this direction which could still be identified, amidst the mud, by the twisted remains of a light railway but he had been told to avoid it on the grounds that it was mined. Moving off the road his tank sunk to its belly and proceeded to push its way forwards, through liquid mud for some 200yd. Any attempt to steer proved impossible since the engine did not have the strength to swing the tank out of the rut it was creating for itself and they finally came to a permanent halt in a deep pool which flooded the tank, swamped the engine and soaked the clutch to the point that it ceased to work.

One can go on almost indefinitely with such stories but the point is surely made. There were successes of course, and many great acts of gallantry, but it is notable that of eighteen Military Crosses awarded to Tank Corps officers both tank commanders and section leaders, the majority went to men who dismounted and walked ahead of their tanks to assist them over the dreadful ground. Shortly after the battle Haig's headquarters apparently circulated a document which sought opinions on the value of tanks on such ground. It no doubt provided ammunition for the

Possibly one of the tanks from the Cockroft action, abandoned in the Steenbeek. The 6-pounder gun has been removed from the near side sponson and other fittings have also been salvaged, but one wonders how anyone could work in such conditions.

anti-tank faction but the Tank Corps had no choice, it was a question of continuing with this futile battle or voting for extinction; some might say that the result would be the same either way.

For the next two weeks work went on to salvage as many tanks as possible from the mire. Troops clearing Inverness Copse came across large quantities of German anti-tank ammunition, the so-called 'K' round, and this may have offered a crumb of comfort. The ammunition had been prepared as a result of examination of captured Mark I and II tanks so here was evidence of a sort that the thicker armour of the Mark IV could resist it.

Elimination of German Strongpoints at St Julien

On 19 August tanks were involved in a small action that was a model of its kind. Two days earlier twelve officers from G Battalion had been ordered to prepare tanks for action and it indicates how long it was taking to recover from Ypres that they had to create scratch crews and take any working tank from the park. The object of the operation was to assist the infantry in eliminating

a nest of strongpoints in and around the ruined village of St Julien. In the end eleven tanks went into action and the majority of them made it into the village and proceeded to eliminate the various pillboxes, one at a time, simply by halting outside and blasting away with every available weapon until the enemy gave up. Most of the tanks ended up stuck in the mud but nearly every objective was taken and the casualty list was so ridiculously small that it hardly sounds like a First World War battle at all.

The Arrival in France of Gun Carriers

By June 1917 production Gun Carriers were being delivered. They differed from the Oldbury prototype (at least as it had been drawn) in a number of details. To begin with the driving positions had been moved forwards into a pair of armoured cabs that straddled the track frames. The secondary gearsmen remained inside the hull and the design had been changed here to include a pair of winding drums on the output shafts of the differential which could be clutched in as

A Gun Carrier machine photographed at Dollis Hill. This example carries the big 60-pounder gun and still retains the tail wheels.

A Gun Carrier transporting a 6-inch howitzer in France. Notice the gun's wheel, suspended on the side of the hull and observe also that every possible hatch and door is wide open on each cab to provide as much air as possible.

required. This was part of the equipment used to mount the guns.

The Gun Carriers had been designed to carry either of two weapons; the 6in, 26cwt Howitzer Mark I or the 60-pounder Mark 2 Field Gun, a long barrelled 5in calibre piece. The former weighed over 3t (3,048kg), the latter around 5t (5,080kg). The gun was carried in the well between the track frames at the front, its wheels slung from brackets on the side. It was winched aboard the carrier on a trolley, running on a pivoting cradle. Once the weapon and its cradle had been pulled all the way back, and bolted securely to a cross member between the tracks it was virtually at its normal firing attitude. In theory either weapon could be fired from the carrier, which was the whole purpose of the design, but in practice it was only said to be possible with the howitzer. The reason given is that the Gun Carrier had been designed to handle the latest model of the 60-pounder, the Mark 2, but since none of these were available in 1917 they carried the Mark 1 version which could not be fired without dismounting.

Production of Gun Carriers was entrusted to Kitson and Co. of Leeds, a firm that normally specialized in railway locomotives. Fifty had been ordered but in fact forty-eight were completed as Gun Carriers, the other two as salvage tanks.

These machines had no forward cabs. Instead the driver and his mate were located in a raised cab at the front of the main superstructure, the area in front of which was decked over. Here was mounted a hand-operated crane with a 3t (3,048kg) lifting capability.

The first company of Gun Carriers had arrived in France in July and, for some strange reason, they still retained their wheeled tails. They were used on odd occasions throughout August and September but only to carry supplies over difficult ground. It was a role for which they proved ideal. Without a gun mounted the huge area at the front would take a considerable load and it was easier to get at than through the sponson doors of a supply tank. Even so it was not as exciting as transporting and firing artillery and one imagines that the crews continued to expect this kind of work.

All the remaining tank actions in Flanders were small-scale affairs and generally confined to what was left of the roads. On 22 August, during another attack near St Julien involving F Battalion, a tank named *Fray Bentos* became so firmly ditched inside the enemy lines that it remained there, in action, for some 72hr beating off repeated attacks by German infantry. An action involving

Tank F47 Foam knocked out during the fighting on 22 August 1917. By the time this photograph had been taken the tank had been robbed of many fittings, grass had started to reclaim the ground and the plank road, in the foreground, was falling into disuse.

A Battalion on the Menin Road on 20 September appears to have included a wireless tank that set itself up and maintained contact for some 24hr under fire. This was repeated six days later, only on this occasion the wireless station was manned for 36hr. The early experiments with tank wireless at Elveden have already been mentioned but nothing more appears to have been done until the summer of 1917. When Queen Mary visited the Tank Corps headquarters in France that summer she was shown a Mark I female tank modified to the wireless role. It had a Morse key-operated trench wireless set installed in one disarmed sponson while the other served as a cramped office. It also carried a tall mast that had to be erected above the cab to support the aerial wires when the set was being used. Thus one did not expect the tank to move around during a battle but to find itself a central location and remain there, acting as a focal point for messages and instructions to and from brigade or divisional headquarters. There were two separate actions on 4 October, one of which involved A Battalion and resulted in the first Victoria Cross being awarded to a tank officer. Inevitably, in the Salient, it was for leading tanks on foot, under fire, and equally inevitably

the award to Capt Clement Robertson was posthumous.

To extend the subject of tank communications briefly it should be recorded that tanks were provided with a selection of signalling devices such as flags, or coloured discs on poles which could be waved about to deliver various simple messages. Sometimes local arrangements were

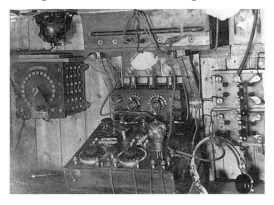

A typical trench wireless set installed in a tank. Notice how the interior has been lined with wood but one wonders how well this vulnerable equipment would stand up to the pounding of an unsprung tank on rough ground.

A detail view of the aerial arrangements and modified female sponson on a Mark I wireless tank.

Mark IV male training tank number 402 displays a pole aerial during trials involving wireless communication with aircraft at Biggin Hill aerodrome in Kent.

made. One universally recognized signal was a helmet raised up on a rifle, indicating the location of a wounded man who trusted that the tank would see him and not run him over. Douglas Browne records that, during the fighting at the Cockroft the signal for the infantry to come forward was an ordinary shovel, raised through the top hatch. He goes on to say that no notice was taken of this whatever and he ended up having to send a member of his crew back with a verbal message.

Runners, who regularly undertook these duties, were always wary of tanks. A Tank Corps section commander might have two or three men with him acting as runners but it was not much fun trying to attract the attention of a tank crew, especially when they were preoccupied in action. Those inside a tank tended to imagine that anyone outside, trying to get in, was an enemy so the first greeting often involved a revolver. Even so it was just as bad for the tank crew when they wished to send a message. While a tank was on the battlefield it was, invariably, the target for every gun that could bear on it so one approached at one's peril. Often the only way to attract a runner to take a message was to open a sponson door and wave a bottle of scotch.

THE THIRD BATTLE OF GAZA

On 1 November the Egyptian Expeditionary Force, now under the forceful command of Sir Edmund Allenby, had another go at Gaza. Maj Nutt's tank detachment had been brought up to strength with the arrival of three Mark IV tanks but the surviving Mark Is were still running, which is no mean achievement in itself. This Third Battle of Gaza, important as it was, is best seen as a holding action while a larger force outflanked the city through Beersheba and effectively cut it

War Baby II, *a Mark IV female tank that joined the Tank Detachment in Palestine. Notice that unditching beams were not fitted to these machines.*

off. As before tanks worked in pairs and on this occasion there appears to have been a greater incidence of tracks breaking. Only two tanks were seriously damaged, one from a round that plunged in through the top and the other, after it had been ditched, by an explosive device placed under the track. In his report on the action Maj Nutt announced that the first of these would soon be salvaged and repaired (despite the fact that a shell had exploded inside) while the other was so badly damaged that the best they could

hope to do was to patch it up and use it for training and supply carrying.

Despite their dedication the men of the Tank Detachment did not see action again in the Middle East although they remained there until March 1918. A request for Whippet tanks was turned down and indeed, as Allenby's victorious army swept on, it is difficult to see how they would have kept up, particularly if they had to operate far beyond the range of the existing railway system.

The fruits of experience. This amazing photograph shows another Mark IV in Palestine with its tracks removed. The crew appear to have used spare track plates to provide extra protection at the front; a practice that would be copied by tank crews in the Second World War and even as late as the 1991 Gulf War.

9 The Battle of Cambrai – a Taste of Victory

Under normal circumstances, such as they were in the First World War, few major campaigns were mounted in the winter months. If the fighting in Flanders was anything to go by then things were quite bad enough in the summer. Yet if the opportunity presented itself the Tank Corps felt duty bound to accept the challenge. There had always been opponents but the tanks had also lost many friends in 1917, starting with the Australians. Those who opposed tanks at GHQ had a concise argument. If tanks could not function in conditions such as prevailed at Ypres then they were of no use at all since such conditions could be found anywhere and it was not realistic to fight only where the ground was suitable.

Yet, down through history, commanders had sought to fight on ground of their own choosing and if tanks could be launched over terrain that suited them who knows what they might not achieve? Such, at least, was the argument put forward at Tank Corps headquarters and in the hope that it might prove agreeable they proceeded to plan.

THE BATTLE OF CAMBRAI

The origins of what became known as the Battle of Cambrai are complicated. The area, south-east of Arras, north-east of St Quentin and the Somme, had attracted the eyes of tacticians for the last two years yet it had seen little fighting. Realizing its importance the Germans had built part of the Hindenburg system through it but, by the autumn of 1917, it was regarded as a relatively quiet

The architects of Cambrai; Elles, centre left, with his staff at Bermicourt Chateau including J.F.C Fuller on the extreme left.

sector. J.F.C. Fuller, who had been looking for an alternative to the Flanders front ever since he arrived in the area, saw it as an ideal location for the employment of tanks and he suggested it to Elles who, in turn, placed it before Gen Byng and through him to Haig himself.

Fuller's motives were equally complex. He realized at once that the Ypres battle would be a washout and that this would reflect upon the tanks; he felt that there would be a desperate need for the Tank Corps to redeem itself as soon as possible and, appreciating that the British Army would not be able to sustain a second, major offensive, promoted it as a raid. Trench raids, involving anything from a handful of men to a battalion were a common feature of warfare on the Western Front but what Fuller had in mind

An aerial view of the Cambrai battlefield looking roughly eastwards along the Bapaume–Cambrai road. Bourlon Wood dominates on the left with Fontaine-Notre-Dame beyond.

was on a much larger scale. He reckoned that the two brigades of tanks (some 216 machines), supported by Gun Carriers, Royal Engineer demolition parties and dismounted cavalry could move into an area such as this, wreak havoc and then withdraw. There would be no attempt to hold any ground taken, nor to exploit the breakthrough, just a quick, clean strike and withdrawal. This would serve to show what the tanks could do and seriously unsettle the enemy.

The area west of Cambrai commended itself for a number of reasons. It was hemmed in to the east and west by canals which would serve as defensible flanks, Cambrai itself was a major communications centre for the Germans and the terrain was chalk downland, well drained and not much disturbed by artillery; perfect ground for tanks to operate over.

The plan was not well received when first put forward since all eyes were on Flanders and in any case tanks were not popular. However as the fighting died down it was studied again, and altered. The advantages of a raid did not appeal at GHQ where it was believed that something more tangible must result from such an attack; if it could be mounted as a battle, with specific

objectives, that was another matter. The objective, as finally agreed, was not Cambrai specifically, but the creation of a breakthrough, north-west of the city, which would enable a striking force to move through, into the valley of the river Sensée in the direction of Valenciennes; it was ambitious stuff, to put it mildly, particularly in view of what the British Army and its tanks had suffered through the summer.

If Fuller was disappointed by the change he was equally surprised to learn just how much GHQ was prepared to invest in the attack. It amounted to every tank battalion then in France, all nine of them shared between three brigades, and no less than six infantry divisions. Better still it was going to be the Tank Corps' battle. There would be no lengthy, preliminary bombardment by artillery and the tanks would lead, supported by the infantry. An element of fantasy crept into the plan at this point because the force would also include a cavalry corps, by no means dismounted that would take over where the tanks left off, ranging far and wide into enemy-held territory with the ultimate intention of bottling up the large German forces.

It is our purpose here to observe matters from the tank point of view and the problems facing them were daunting enough. To begin with they had to be withdrawn from Flanders, repaired and reconditioned. Since the decision to mount the attack was not taken until 20 October, and the battle was scheduled for 20 November this did not leave a lot of time. Next a series of training camps would have to be established behind the lines so that tanks and infantry could be taught how to work together and finally a system would have to be devised to help the tanks deal with the Hindenburg Line.

The training was, as much as anything else, an exercise in confidence building. Once the infantry had picked up the rudiments of what the tanks could, and could not do, they were invited to create defensive works of their own that would disable the tanks. As far as is known the tanks managed to defeat the best that the infantry could

An F Battalion tank tackles a mass of enemy wire during training at Wailly in October 1917. It could tear its way through the most complex entanglements that had even defeated artillery bombardments.

come up with and this was probably the most effective result of this period. Even so, the Hindenburg Line was an imposing obstacle comprising two parallel lines of trenches. In the area in question it ran roughly south-east to north-west, passing through the village of Havrincourt and later joined the Canal du Nord, a prodigious, unfinished earthwork in its own right. Wherever possible the Germans had sited the two main lines of trenches on the reverse slopes of any high ground that faced the British front and the whole system was protected by four belts of wire, together some 100yd (91m) deep.

The trenches were 12ft (3.5m) wide in some places, too wide for tanks, narrowing to about 3.5ft (1m) at the base and on average some 7ft (2m) deep. Ahead of the main trench system was an outpost line of isolated trenches and strongpoints, normally built into farms, arranged chequerboard fashion to give one another mutual support. Behind the main trench line was the support line which ran in roughly the same direction, crossing the Grand Ravine and the rear slopes of Flesquières Ridge and village before meeting the Canal du Nord near Moeuvres.

Further back still was another system that amounted to a duplicate Hindenburg Line that incorporated sections of the St Quentin Canal and

then ran across country to the thick, dark mass of Bourlon Wood. The Germans had been able to prepare this part of the system in relative peace, while the major battles took place elsewhere. They had clearly created it with tanks in mind and they also allowed for the usual massive British barrage by creating huge underground bunkers in which troops could shelter.

The Hindenburg Line presented the tank with two problems that might be described as practical and tactical. On the practical side there was the matter of getting a tank, designed to cross a trench 9ft (2.7m) wide, to tackle one that was 12ft (3.6m) wide. This was a workshops responsibility, solved by the use of fascines, of which more shortly. The tactical problem was Fuller's. Firstly he retained the wave technique adopted for Third Ypres by identifying two main objectives, the Hindenburg Line (known as the Blue Line) and its Support Line (the Brown Line). Typically a tank battalion would send two companies against the Blue Line and once that had been secured the third company would pass through, still carrying fascines, and tackle the Brown Line.

In more detail, sections of three tanks would follow a prepared drill to deal with a given section of the double trench. In the lead would be the advance tank, slightly nose down under the weight of its fascine. It would drive through the wire and up to the lip of the trench whereupon it would swing to the left and move along its allotted sector, firing into the trench and keeping heads down. A short distance behind would come the main body tanks, side by side, each leading two files of infantry. Passing through the wire in the wake of the advance tank, the left-side tank of this pair would deposit its fascine into the trench and pass over; it would then also turn left while its mate went straight on to place its fascine in the second line trench. Having cleared their sector the other two tanks would follow across the second trench and form up to await the infantry.

Having picked their way over the crushed wire the infantry would form into various groups with tasks such as trench clearing or trench stops; these parties would fortify the ends of their sector against enemy troops attacking along the trenches. Once all this was secure, the infantry would form up behind their tanks and move off towards the Brown Line. Meanwhile those tanks allotted to the Brown Line would move across the captured trenches and use their fascines on the Brown Line in the same way.

Writing at the time that he proposed the tank raid Fuller had identified three deadly sins; publicity, pusillanimity and pulverization. The first of these could be avoided so long as secrecy was paramount and the lengths that the planners went to maintain this state was impressive. Nothing must be done within the battle area to warn the Germans that anything unusual was taking place and this appears to have been achieved. Examples relating to tanks will be given as the narrative proceeds. Avoiding the second was more a matter of luck. It depended on everything going according to plan so that senior commanders need not interfere at the last minute and cause havoc. Again, in the early stages, this was achieved but there were exceptions and these reveal a curious fact about the British Army at this time. Fuller's plans, outlined above and endorsed by Elles and Haig's staff might appear to be sacrosanct but they were not. Notwithstanding the scale and novelty of the

forthcoming battle, divisional commanders were free to make changes to the plan as they saw fit, whether they were qualified to do so or not. The most glaring example was Maj Gen G.M. Harper's 51st (Highland) Division that, for reasons of its own, altered the plan. Clearly driven by Harper's own prejudices (although he was not quite the reactionary that is often portrayed) his men were trained to stay well clear of the tanks for fear of exposing themselves to concentrated fire and the tanks were organized in a different fashion as will be explained later.

Likewise 62nd (West Riding) Division under Maj Gen W.P. Braithwaite intended to introduce a somewhat looser formation since they did not believe that files of soldiers would be capable of identifying and sticking with particular tanks. These might well be regarded as details but it does seem strange that the success of such a grand scheme should be placed at risk in order to accommodate the wish of particular divisional commanders.

As for pulverization, this could be avoided if the attack was launched without a 3-week-long preliminary bombardment or, preferably, without any bombardment at all. Not that artillery should be excluded from the battle, it most certainly was not and up to 1,000 guns were assembled to cover the attack. However they would only begin their barrage a short time before zero hour and they would adopt the creeping barrage principle so that tanks and troops would advance across the entire battle zone behind a curtain of shellfire.

Although it has no direct bearing upon the tanks it is probably well, at this point, to comment upon the artillery arrangements. The science of firing against targets from identification on maps, as distinct from having observers watch for the fall of shot, had developed dramatically over the past two years. It involved trigonometry, meteorology and even calculations to allow for the variations between individual weapons so that guns from one, to any number of batteries, could be directed onto targets purely from an accurate map reference. Techniques such as flash ranging,

Double-headed tank trains prepare to move out from the Plateau railhead to carry the tanks, complete with their fascines, to the forward unloading points.

sound ranging and aerial photographic interpretation enabled the guns to locate enemy batteries and the first the enemy would know about it was when the shells began to fall around them. This technique would be used for the first time on a large scale at Cambrai and its only limiting factor was communications. This became obvious during the battle when tanks, running well ahead of the timetable, had to wait for the barrage to lift onto the next objective or run the risk of operating within it.

The logistics for the forthcoming battle were equally impressive but once again we only need concern ourselves here with the tanks. To begin with there was the matter of getting all of these tanks to the battle zone. There would be, in all, 378 fighting tanks, fifty-four supply tanks or gun carriers, nine wireless tanks, thirty-two wire-cutting tanks, two tanks carrying bridging equipment for the cavalry and one to transport telephone cable drums. This amounts to 476 and every one had first to be collected from the various divisional training camps and from Bermicourt itself, concentrated at a vast railway depot known as the Plateau and then dispersed to the final railheads.

Movement of tanks was in the hands of the Railway Operating Division which began moving them to Plateau from the training centres over the period 11 to 14 November, running nine trains a day each carrying twelve tanks. At Plateau the tanks would dismount from the trains to be fitted with their fascines, remount the trains and, over the next five days 15 to 19 November be carried to the final detraining stations. From here they would move up to their assembly points in the villages of Villers Guislain and Gouzeaucourt and in Dessart and Havrincourt woods. Here the tanks were given their final checks and camouflaged from air observation. Special tarpaulins, painted to resemble brick walls, had been provided for tanks which had to park in ruined villages.

The saga of the fascines is an epic in its own right. The idea is credited to Lt Col Frank Searle, the officer commanding Central Workshops. As an article of war the fascine, a bundle of sticks used to fill a ditch, is one of the oldest of all but it was hardly suitable to support a tank. Searle had some 22,000 ordinary fascines made and then rolled them up, seventy-five at a time, and bound them with chains into a sort of super fascine. Hundreds of members of the Chinese Labour Corps, attached to Central Workshops, virtually

The A Battalion female tank Auld Reekie *climbs onto its train and provides an excellent view of a fascine. Notice how the French railway wagon is literally bending under the weight of the tank.*

denuded the Forest of Crécy by removing 400t (406,400kg) of brushwood that they then made into fascines. These were bundled together in a cradle, chains wound around and two tanks made to pull in opposite directions until the whole thing was compressed as far as it would go. The result was a 54in (137cm) diameter bundle, some 10ft (3m) long and weighing over 4t (4,064kg). This was now rolled, through a sea of mud, to the nearest rail point and loaded onto a train. And it did not end there. Special harnesses had to be manufactured for each tank so that, when the fascine was perched on top of its cab it would be held firmly in place and a quick-release gear devised that would enable a tank driver to loose it at the appropriate moment. As if that were not enough Central Workshops also manufactured 110 sledges, to be towed behind supply tanks plus the towing and release gear for thirty-two wire-cutting grapnels. All of this, of course, in addition to the maintenance and repair of tanks for the great battle.

Books have been written about the Battle of Cambrai and elements of it have become regimental folklore but we can do no more than summarize events here. By 0600 on the morning of 20 November a line of tanks, each with a fascine on top of the cab, stood with their engines running and their noses pointing roughly north-east in pre-dawn darkness and a thin mist This line extended from the village of Gonnelieu in the south-east to a point some 5½ miles (8.8km) to the north-west where the Canal du Nord brushes against Havrincourt Wood. Close to the hamlet of Beaucamp, near the centre of the British line, stood the tanks of H Battalion and it was one of these, a male machine incongruously named *Hilda,* that General Elles had selected as his tank.

On the previous day Elles had issued an inspiring Special Order and he elected to continue in the spirit of Nelson by going into action with his tanks. At 0610 the tanks began to move, sweeping steadily down towards the British front line and then onwards. Ten minutes later the artillery opened fire, planting their barrage some 200yd (183m) ahead of the advancing tanks and moving it forwards in stages. Despite a scare, about an hour before dawn, it seemed as if the Germans were caught entirely unprepared and the tanks were soon through their outpost line and making for the first objective, the Blue Line.

At the first trench the appointed tank nosed over the edge and, once the driver judged it to be at the correct angle, the fascine was released by

G Battalion tanks pass a captured German battery in the vicinity of Graincourt. Notice how cans of petrol are carried on top of the nearest tank; a risky business at the best of times so close to the exhaust pipe, enhanced when a tank comes under fire.

moving a lever in the cab. This tumbled into the bottom of the trench and the tank began, carefully, to lower itself down, drive over the fascine and heave itself up the other side. While this was going on a crew member jumped out and placed a small flag on the edge of the trench to show following tanks where the fascine was. It was physically impossible to lift the fascine back out of the trench and in any case, after a few tanks had driven over it there was no point. Freed from this encumbrance the tank must have been somewhat easier to handle although quite a few were ditched at various times throughout the day.

Every battalion, indeed virtually every tank had a story to tell. On A Battalion's front tank A2, *Abou-Ben-Adam II* commanded by Lt Duncan was also carrying their section commander, Capt Richard Wain when it was struck by a shell and knocked out, killing most of the crew. Wain himself, although badly wounded, picked up a Lewis gun and rushed the nearest German strongpoint that he captured single-handedly. Wounded again he refused help and continued to fire a rifle at the retreating Germans until he collapsed and died, gaining another posthumous Victoria Cross for the Tank Corps.

One problem, created by the rigid artillery timetable, was that tanks running ahead of schedule after capturing the first objective had to hang around, sometimes for more than half-an-hour, before they could move on to tackle stage two. Tanks of F Battalion had broken through the Blue Line by 0800 and the Brown Line some two hours later when they were ordered to their rallying point. The waiting proved too much for Maj Philip Hammond who, with a volunteer and a captured rifle, made it on foot to the battalion's third objective, the town of Masnières on L'Escaut Canal where he attempted to capture a bridge single-handedly. Unfortunately the Germans blew up the bridge in his face although it seemed to settle on its original foundations.

When tanks began to arrive F22 *Flying Fox II* was ordered to try and cross the bridge but it collapsed under the weight, taking the tank with

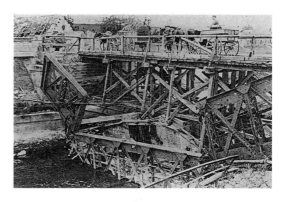

Tank F22, Flying Fox, *in the canal at Masnières on the remains of the old bridge. By this time the Germans had rebuilt the bridge, using the hull of the tank as a pier.*

it into the canal. Enveloped in a cloud of steam from the hot engine the crew scrambled out through the top hatch and escaped. Sometime later a party of what Hammond described as our medieval cavalry galloped up and, despite warnings, rode right down to the canal and came under fire. Disdaining to reconnoitre for another crossing place they then retired.

The fact that the medieval cavalry even got as far as Masnières was only thanks to the foresight of the Tank Corps. Tanks could crush down wire sufficiently for two columns of infantry to double through without serious difficulty but it was nowhere near good enough for horses. Cavalry needed wide gaps in the wire so that they could pass through in a body and it could require a massive amount of labour to clear such a gap in belts of wire so deep. The Tank Corps solution was simple, brutal and immensely effective.

Ten or so tanks from each brigade were fitted with large, four-pronged grapnels which were carried on the back of each tank and attached to it by a long cable. Upon entering the entanglement the wire cutting tank released its grapnel and towed it along behind. The grapnel turned as it was pulled and each fluke gathered up wire, twisting it into an enormous and lethal cable as

2nd Lt Lyles (see Chapter 7) commanded Antigone at Cambrai and was knocked out while engaging enemy positions across the canal at Masnières.

it went. Once clear of the wire a pair of tanks would turn left and right, ripping away huge swathes of it, pickets and all. Following a demonstration for the sceptical Cavalry Corps, shortly before the battle, Fuller said that it looked as if the area had been swept clean by a giant vacuum cleaner.

Other tanks of A Battalion reached Marcoing by way of Welsh Ridge with orders to cross the canal. The only feasible route was by way of the main railway bridge, a single track, plate girder affair with high sides which was, apparently, only wide enough to allow a female tank through. At least four got across, one of which was knocked out in the village of Rumilly while the other, A55 (2nd Lt Lipscomb) came to grief beyond a location known as Flot Farm. It is claimed that this tank got closer to Cambrai during the battle than any other.

It was tanks from D and E Battalions that were destined to support Harper's 51st Division onto their objectives. Fuller, who had every reason to be biased, said that Harper would countenance no new idea that he had not thought up for himself.

Fuller points out that while Harper's principal change to his (Fuller's) plans brought about the disaster on Flesquières Ridge, the General's innate stubbornness was proven by his insistence that the tanks, upon reaching the German trenches, should turn right, simply because Fuller wished them to turn left! In fact, Fuller says, it didn't matter which way they turned just so long as they all turned in the same direction.

Harper's plan, which it has to be said, was approved by the commander of 1st Tank Brigade (Baker-Carr) involved a leading section of tanks dedicated to wire crushing and other sections providing the main body of fighting tanks. The wire crushing tanks moved off four minutes before the rest and these, in turn, were followed at a respectful distance by the infantry dressed in ranks, rather than files, the leading platoons keeping 150yd (137m) in rear of the rearmost tanks. On arrival at the first trench line the wire crushing, or advanced tanks dropped their fascines and turned right. When the fighting tanks came through, two would use their fascines, if necessary, to cross either side of an advanced tank while the third would use the advanced tank's fascine and then drive straight for the second line.

This procedure led to trouble but it was not obvious to begin with. Even before they reached the first line the two battalions had been warned to be prepared for difficulties from a feature known locally as le Grand Ravin. Whether this was an example of French understatement, or a Gasconade is not entirely clear but as ravines go it left a lot to be desired and many tanks hardly noticed it. From here it was a steady climb, up towards Flesquières. Trouble began at the wire. The tanks crashed their way through but the infantry, being so far behind, apparently had difficulty finding the gaps in the wire. Why they simply could not follow the marks the tanks must have made on the ground is not clear but it seems that on the way to the Brown Line, they dropped even further behind. Topping the ridge, with D Battalion on the left, and E Battalion on the right of Flesquières, the tanks ran into German artillery batteries that had been pushed forward from their dugouts in readiness.

Obviously the tanks had no idea what was waiting for them over the crest. Had they done so they might well have formed up and come over in a body and overwhelmed the defenders. As it was they trundled over one after another and were picked off in the same way. Many have argued that if the infantry had been up with them, as Fuller would have wished, they could have picked off the gun crews but even this would be difficult to prove. Rather, one suspects, they came up against some particularly well-handled batteries, trained in anti-tank work and presented with a sequence of near ideal targets. Between them, D and E Battalions lost thirty-two tanks to shellfire on Flesquières Ridge, some of which were still burning the next day.

The 62nd Division employed similar tactics to the 51st but did not encounter similar problems. The early stages of their attack took them through Havrincourt and then virtually north, with the Canal du Nord on their left, towards Graincourt where they overran and captured two German 77mm guns. A gunner from a G Battalion tank that had already been knocked out, brought down a German aircraft with his Lewis gun and 2nd Lt McElroy, of the same battalion, qualified for a Military Cross having defended his burning tank single-handedly while his crew was being evacuated.

Supply Tanks

Finally, in this survey of the first day of Cambrai, some mention must be made of the work of the supply tanks. Dumps had been established for each brigade from which ammunition, petrol and grease would be drawn. Supply tanks hauled trains of supply sledges but there is no evidence that the Gun Carriers did so; they probably had enough carrying capacity in their own right. In passing, it is worth mentioning that a photograph taken at Plateau railhead shows one of the two

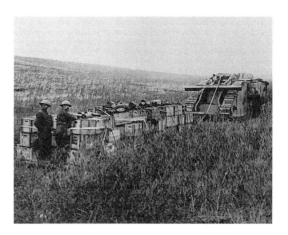

A tank with supply sledges. They are attached by ropes to a towing position on the upper, rear hull and must have provided the tank's crew with considerable handling difficulties.

Gun Carriers that had been completed as salvage tanks, on a railway wagon. What it was doing there is not recorded although it would have been extremely useful in lifting and fitting fascines.

When Sir Douglas Haig was first shown a map of the Cambrai area it is said that he placed his forefinger on the image of Bourlon Wood, identifying it as the biggest problem. No matter where one stands on the Cambrai battlefield it is almost always visible as a dark mass of trees, on a slight rise, away to the north. Led by the tanks, British forces had broken through the German lines, and formidable lines they were, on a front of about 6 miles (9.6km) and to a depth, in some sectors, of 4 or 5 miles (6.5 or 8km). As a victory it was deemed good enough to warrant the ringing of church bells in Britain, a signal more properly reserved at that time to denote invasion. Yet some of the objectives set for the first day had not been met and the high ground around Bourlon was one of them.

The other was the third objective, the Red Line, that, although incomplete, was being built on the same scale as the original Hindenburg system. Thus, on the second day of the battle efforts were made to deal with this unfinished business. To the north-west, G Battalion captured the village of

Anneux, *en route* for Bourlon while H Battalion struck out for Fontaine-Notre-Dame. Writing after the war, Fuller berates himself for not preventing tanks from attacking villages. His view was that the tanks, taking advantage of their mobility and relative immunity, should outflank these settlements and cut them off, since fighting in built-up areas against troops under cover and with the tanks' ability to manoeuvre restricted, they became vulnerable. This is all very well but it misses another point. These villages were precisely the places that the enemy defended most strongly and if they were not taken they remained, to dominate the battlefield with their machine-guns and hold up the infantry who were supposed to be supporting the tanks.

This is the case with Fontaine-Notre-Dame. Two tanks from H Battalion entered the village on the 21st and shot the place up but the infantry at first found it difficult to follow because of machine-gun fire from Bourlon Wood to the north and Cantaing to the south-east. However Fontaine and Cantaing were in British hands by the end of the day. Meanwhile there had been further action on the other side of l'Escaut Canal. Using the railway station as their rallying point, tanks of A and F Battalions worked towards Flot Farm and around Rumilly but the area was so dominated by higher ground to the east that machine-gun fire could not be eliminated.

At the end of the second day it was time to take stock. Almost anyone on the ground would have recognized that the battle had gone about as far as it could go. The troops were tired, the surviving tanks in need of maintenance and the Germans, with forty-eight hours to get their act together, would now be rushing up reinforcements. Yet, predictably, the British high command elected to make one more effort where prudence might have dictated otherwise. Even so some respite was essential and the only tank action on the 22nd was in the very south-east corner of the battlefield, near a bend in the canal opposite Crèvecoeur which achieved nothing because the supporting infantry did not show up.

On the other hand the Germans did. Attacking fiercely out of Bourlon Wood and from Raillencourt in the north-east they recaptured Fontaine-Notre-Dame. It was a dramatic demonstration of how quickly the Germans could react but it made no change to British plans. Far from going onto the defensive a major attack was projected for the following day, the 23rd.

The events of the 23rd, at least as far as the tanks are concerned, can be seen as three independent operations but they were all focused on that one area – Bourlon Wood, the high ground it stood on and, of course, Fontaine-Notre-Dame. In all some 90 tanks were available and three infantry divisions although co-operation between the two was never anything like as smooth as on the 20th. Tanks were operating in composite companies with improvised crews and the infantry battalions now being committed had not been trained to work closely with them. What is more the time available for planning and the opportunities for reconnaissance were limited. This is particularly true of Bourlon Wood itself which was a complete mystery to everyone.

Starting in the north-west, E Battalion was launched against the Hindenburg Support Line trenches to the north of the Bapaume to Cambrai road and lost eight out of eleven tanks. D and G Battalions were directed against Bourlon Wood and the village of the same name on the high round beyond it. But those working within the wood appear to have suffered heavily; like village streets the forest rides were no place for tanks in combat.

A composite battalion created from elements of B, C and H Battalions was directed to retake Fontaine-Notre-Dame. While some tanks attempted to deal with machine-gun positions on the fringes of Bourlon Wood the main body of tanks came storming straight down the road, crashing through improvised barricades and making straight for the village. Inside it all hell let loose. In addition to concentrated machine-gun fire from ruined buildings that virtually shot-blasted some tanks silver, there were now mobile anti-aircraft

German soldiers gather around Black Arrow *in Fontaine-Notre-Dame with the body of a British soldier in the foreground.*

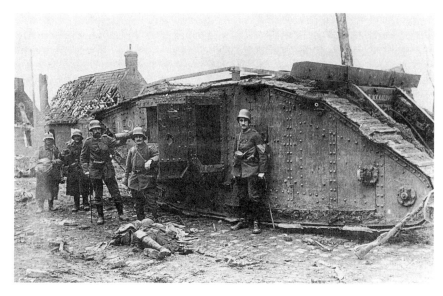

trucks, operating in the anti-tank role. The tanks did their best to subdue fire but it was never enough and the infantry could not get near the place. They even tried to carry soldiers inside the tanks but one after another the tanks were hit and burst into flames. In the end nearly half of the tanks committed were lost and Fontaine remained in German hands.

Bourlon village was attacked again on 24 November, just as it began to snow. Once again the Germans employed roadblocks, with anti-tank weapons sited nearby and picked off the tanks as they manoeuvred to get through. Then, after two more days of trying to reorganize a now doomed offensive, the usual practice of attempting to capitalize on failure, they had one last try on the 27th. Twenty tanks were mustered to go for Bourlon and thirteen for Fontaine which appears to have been entirely pointless since the cavalry, the only force that would be able to exploit the breakthrough, had already left the area.

The remains of Grasshopper *and another tank in one of the rides in Bourlon Wood. Both tanks appear to have suffered major internal explosions, possibly destroyed by their crews.*

After the battle, abandoned tanks could be found all over the battlefield. Hyena, *on the left was later recovered and used by the Germans.*

On 30 November the anticipated German counter-attack came in with such force that it drove the British back as far as Gouzeaucourt in the centre although they held on to Flesquières and Masnières for the time being. Such tanks as could be coaxed into action were used over the next couple of days to recapture Gouzeaucourt but in the end, all it achieved, was to litter the battlefield with even more tanks that nobody had the opportunity to recover. The amount of captured ground that was retained was a pathetic return for so much ingenuity, courage and sacrifice. On the other hand a point had been made, and it was a significant one, that if they were used sensibly and preferably in large numbers, tanks could change the face of modern warfare.

In the early stages of the battle, while the British had control of the battlefield, tank salvage and recovery could be undertaken. In an ideal situation, where the tank could be unditched, or repaired in the field, it could make its own way back to base and possibly take part in subsequent actions. For those tanks that required more substantial repairs it was always possible to tow them back to the railhead but those that had been seriously damaged were simply left where they lay. Even so these tanks would be visited by salvage parties who would inspect and remove any useful components.

In the latter days of the Cambrai battle, when tanks were sent out in ever smaller numbers to confront increasing resistance, there was little chance of recovery. Indeed many of them might

The British had already started to clear the battlefield when the Germans counter-attacked. Here tanks in various stages of destruction are assembled at the Marcoing railhead.

111

The best of the surviving tanks were taken back to a German workshop complex at Charleroi in Belgium, the remainder were stripped of spare parts to keep the survivors running.

just as well have been thrown away. As German forces moved back into the area they started to recover the more useful tanks and are believed, in the end, to have taken some fifty machines away.

Faced with a major problem of moving tanks in various stages of disrepair, the Germans quickly came up with some ingenious solutions. For example, they created trolleys, supported upon broad rollers that could be fitted beneath the tracks of a tank so that it could be taken away under tow by a steam traction engine. Massive, hand-operated jacks were produced, four of which could lift a tank high enough for the rollers to be pushed underneath or, indeed, so high that, with the tank straddling the line, a railway wagon could be shunted beneath it. The tanks were then taken by rail to workshops established at Charleroi in

Belgium where some thirty serviceable machines were completed from the fifty wrecks.

Meanwhile one tank, the male F41 *Fray Bentos* that had to be abandoned in Fontaine-Notre-Dame on the 27th, was repaired and taken to Berlin where it was inspected by the Kaiser on 19 December and subsequently driven to the Berlin Zoo where it went on exhibition with other items of war booty. The German Army had started serious work on tank design and construction early in 1917 but it was painfully slow and no doubt suffered, vicariously, from the British failures that summer. Cambrai not only changed the attitude in Germany, it also provided their army with a collection of serviceable tanks that outnumbered the home-designed product right through to the end of the war.

10 New Designs and Expanding Production

Two Mark IV tanks were invited to participate in the Lord Mayor's Show in the City of London in 1917. The two tanks, one male and one female, plodded along in line like elephants in a circus parade and they seem to have made quite an impression. They were certainly given considerable photographic coverage. These were the first tanks the majority of Londoners are likely to have seen as indeed would be true for most of the country. Tanks had appeared in the newspapers, in the various weekly war journals and, of course on cinema screens but one gets quite a different impression when seeing them close up for the first time.

The effect created by these tanks was not lost on the National War Savings Committee whose unenviable task it was to sell the war, quite literally, to the populace. By means of War Bonds and other investment schemes the public was encouraged to lend money for the prosecution of the war and this was a lot easier to arrange if they could be presented with a spectacle, something to identify with, and what better than a tank? In due course five or six machines were borrowed, along with skeleton crews, and shipped all around England, Wales and the industrialized regions of Scotland.

All but one of these tanks were training machines from Bovington, with large, three-digit numbers on the front for identification. But in order to personalize them for better public acceptability they were also named. Tank No. 130

A Mark IV male passing beneath the railway bridge at Ludgate Circus during the Lord Mayor's Show in London, November 1917.

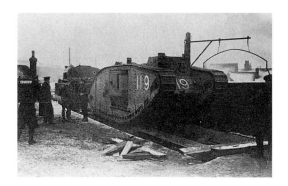

Tank 119 Julian *arrives at Nottingham. The railway loading gauge behind the tank reminds us why the male tank has to travel with its sponson folded in.*

The Mayor of Leicester, and other dignitaries assemble on top of Julian *to address the crowd and whip up enthusiasm for War Bond sales during Leicester's Tank Week.*

became *Nelson* and this was soon joined by *Julian, Iron Ration* and *Drake* among others. Then someone came up with the idea of introducing a genuine war veteran and *Egbert* was added to the travelling circus. Clearly an E Battalion tank *Egbert* had taken a fair amount of punishment at one time. There was a large hole in the hull just in front of the driver and one of the sponsons was equally well ventilated. Wearing his battle scars proudly *Egbert* became a particular favourite.

All of these touring tanks that inevitably became known as Tank Banks, were male machines, partly no doubt because they looked more warlike than females but also because a male sponson, with the door open, was just the place to have your War Bond certificate stamped by a man in uniform. Applicants also came away with a tiny paper tank flag to pin to the lapel and a patriotic paper napkin.

The tanks were transported all around Great Britain by rail. At each venue the crew would drive the tank off its wagon and reposition the sponsons in the station yard. Then, when everything was ready and often escorted by a band, local citizens and the inevitable small boys, the tank would make its way to the town centre or city square. Here it would not only serve as an office for the sale of War Bonds but as a platform from which civic dignitaries and even theatrical

persons would deliver patriotic speeches encouraging the population to spend even more. Indeed in many major cities an element of competition was introduced by comparing the amount raised with neighbouring communities.

An album, rather like a large autograph book, survives from *Nelson* in which purchasers recorded their names and the amount invested. Bearing in mind that the book covers a period when *Nelson* was in Yorkshire, a county not normally associated with a careless attitude

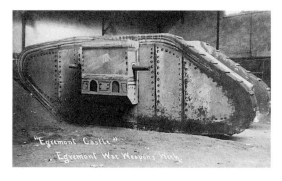

If real tanks were not available, dummies were created by local enthusiasts. The Egremont here is assumed to be the Wallasey suburb on Merseyside. The sponson seems to have been designed as a sales booth for War Bonds.

This Mark IV, HMLS Britannia, *toured the United States on the same errand. Here it demonstrates its climbing skills, overlooked by the Statue of Liberty.*

Tank crews working on new machines at Rollencourt in July 1917 show the typical appearance of a tankodrome. Notice the workshop lorry and canvas hangar in the background.

towards money, some of the amounts pledged are amazing, even when judged by today's standards. Many people appear to have been able to find four-figure sums which, after three years of war, does seem surprising.

Meanwhile back in France the battalions that fought at Cambrai were still trying to sort themselves out and new ones were arriving from Britain. This placed a lot of extra pressure on the available accommodation and some of the veteran battalions spent most of December getting their new premises into shape, rather than training. December and January 1917–18 were remembered for the bad weather, bitter cold and snow. Not ideal conditions to be training but there was some relief for men sent up to the coast, to the Gunnery School at Merlimont where it may have been a bit warmer and was certainly more relaxed. Training, however, was the order of the day virtually every day and this carried on until the end of February 1918 although it was more interesting for some than others.

WHIPPETS, MEDIUM MARK A

F Battalion, for example, was inspected by Gen Elles on 6 December and then moved its tanks to a new Tankodrome on the 13th. The best it could muster was eighteen machines, fifty per cent of its pre-battle strength. The rest, according to its history, were either 'derelict or behind the enemy's lines, or too near the German lines to enable them to be repaired'. However this did not matter so much for F Battalion since they were about to undergo a change. They learned that they would be converted to a Whippet tank battalion and on 14 December two Whippets were issued from Central Workshops so that training could begin.

In June 1917, following the demonstration of the Tritton Chaser in March, Fosters received an order for 200 Tanks, Medium Mark A. As already mentioned, there is a possibility that when Tritton's prototype appeared at the Oldbury Trials it sported an Austin armoured car turret but whether it did or not, it was soon altered. In this new form the turret had gone, to be replaced by an angular structure, a sort of extension of the driver's cab, with machine-gun mountings on all four main faces. The only other important difference was the transfer of the main fuel tank from the back to the front.

Dexterity and good co-ordination were required of the would-be Whippet driver. Sitting in his seat the controls arrayed in front of him

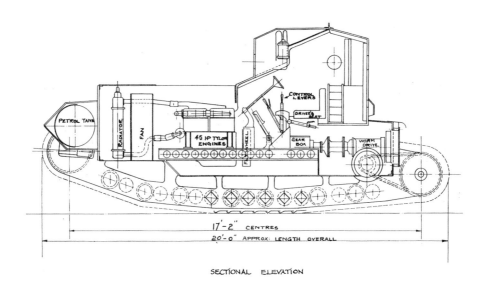

SECTIONAL ELEVATION

GENERAL ARRANGEMENT OF MACHINE MED. Mᴷ A

Medium A Whippet Tank

Crew:	3 or 4
Weight:	14 tons
Length:	20ft (6.1m)
Width:	8ft 7in (2.62m)
Height:	9ft (2.75m)
Armour:	14mm (½in) max.
Speed:	8.3mph (13.4km/h) max.

were: a steering wheel, upon the column of which were the magneto controls and throttle, two clutch pedals, two handbrake levers and two complete gear change levers offering four forwards speeds and reverse. When driving straight the hand throttle was set and gears changed in succession, double de-clutching up and down the box. For a gentle turn the steering wheel was employed. Being linked to both engine carburettors it slowed down one engine and speeded up the other but it would not work when the main throttle was at its minimum or maximum settings. Furthermore unless it was done with care this action could easily stall one engine.

For a more positive turn one selected a different gear ratio in each box and in order to spin the tank around it was possible to have one track driving forwards and the other in reverse. Then again one could depress the clutch on one side (or put the gearbox in neutral) and apply the track brake. It was possible to crank-start one engine from inside the cab but it was more easily done by dismounting and fixing a crank handle at the back. Small fans on the engine drive shaft helped to maintain air pressure in the cab and, to some extent keep it free from fumes.

As originally specified the crew consisted of a driver, commander and two machine-gunners but in the confined space it proved very difficult to work effectively and in practice just the one gunner was carried. The top speed was 8mph (12.9km/h), twice as fast as a heavy tank, but even this is relative. There is a short piece of film showing heavy tanks driving across a field. They are soon overtaken by a Whippet which appears to leave them standing but when the Whippet turns out of the field, onto the road, it is immediately passed by a horse-drawn wagon which swings out and overtakes it!

116

Whippet tanks Flip Flap *and* Flapper *of 6th (F) Battalion with crew members. Seen together these two tanks provide an excellent view of the complex shape of the cab.*

Trying to train an entire battalion on just two tanks, bearing in mind that training involves driving and maintenance, was inevitably going to be a long job but well before it was complete there was a serious hiatus, as will be related. On the subject of maintenance there were complaints about the extra time it took to work on two engines and keep them matched in terms of tuning. In action, crews were less than delighted with the fact that one had to dismount in order to work on the engines. Unless the tank could limp to somewhere relatively safe on one engine it was a matter of climbing up onto the tracks, lifting the heavy armoured engine covers and poking around inside.

Sometime late in 1917, but probably before Cambrai, Maj Philip Johnson went over to Britain on a quick tour of inspection. At Lincoln he took a close look at the prototype Whippet and pronounced himself impressed. Indeed he said that it came closer to his own ideas, promoted a year earlier, before he had even heard of Tritton's design, than anything else produced so far. At this time the tank had clocked up 870 miles (1400km), mainly in the hands of Tank Corps officers and, as Johnson understood it, had made no involuntary stops. In London he was shown drawings for the Whippet's successor, Walter Wilson's design

known as the Medium B and again he thought it was very promising.

In Birmingham he was particularly interested in work being carried out by Maj Buddicom on improvements to unditching beams. The original type, believed to be Johnson's own design, had certainly proved itself but two main problems had been identified. One was the security of the beam when stowed. Given the intense machine-gun fire directed at tanks in action it was not unknown for chains and shackles to be shot away, causing the beam to fall off the tank or, worse still, jam itself

An unditching beam experiment that Philip Johnson did not report upon. Parallel loops of Renolds chain, passing over driven gears at the back and a free roller system at the front, to launch the beam mechanically.

somewhere inconvenient. Johnson did not think a mechanical clip would work and advocated creating a dip in the unditching beam support rails.

Worse still was the problem of attaching the beam to the tracks under fire which could easily prove fatal bearing in mind that one or two men would be working on top of the tank in full view of the enemy. It is interesting to note that these men soon got into the habit of carrying three or four of the correct size of spanner each when doing this job. Having to pass one spanner back and forth, in an emergency and under fire, was above and beyond the call of duty and even two spanners were only any good until one of them was dropped.

Buddicom had various ideas to offer. The simplest was to attach short loops of chain to some of the track links which could be reached through small hatches in the tank roof and shackled to chains from the beam in relative safety. Johnson thought that chains permanently fixed to track links would not last very long and preferred a powerful spring clip which could be worked in the same way. In the end, however, both men seem to have agreed that the ideal method would be to create an extra cab, further back along the top of the tank, with side flaps that could be opened while the beam was secured.

EVOLUTION OF THE MARK V

Johnson does not mention the Mark V in his paper although, as already noted, he did get to drive the modified Mark IV with Ricardo engine and Wilson transmission and thought well of it. Even so, work must have been quite advanced at the time he was in Britain because the first production Mark V was completed in December 1917. Of course it incorporated the rear cab, for handling the unditching beam, which Buddicom designed and had a spring clip system for retaining the beam when not in use. Since this,

Mark V was really little more than a slightly improved Mark IV, and nothing like the wooden Mark V design seen in June at Birmingham. Johnson may not have attached much importance to it.

Apart from the work done by Ricardo, Wilson and Buddicom, it is probably more correct to say that the Mark V evolved, as distinct from being a design in its own right. In terms of basic shape, internal layout and even the type of sponsons it was hardly different from the Mark IV at all. Seen from the side one would notice the second cab and round at the back there were extra hatches and a rear machine-gun position. This had been demanded because there had been instances of Germans hiding as tanks went by, only to spring up and take on the British infantry who were following. Even if they were out in the open enemy soldiers were relatively safe from a tank if they lay still, and were not lying directly in its path. It was probably considered more trouble than it was worth to go through all the evolutions of swinging a Mark IV to deal with a few individuals who might already be dead.

So with a man placed at the back of the Mark V with his own machine-gun there was at least a chance of dealing with such tactics and, of course, since the new tank was a lot easier to drive, those who lay nearby, playing dead, were more vulnerable. The other great improvement to the fighting potential of the Mark V resulted from placing all the driving controls in the hands of one man. By retaining an eight-man crew it was possible to keep all the weapons manned while the commander could leave the front seat when necessary and observe all around from the rear cab. To this end he was provided with a somewhat dubious semaphore signalling device and cable-operated indicators that were used to direct gunners onto targets.

If there was a flaw in the Mark V's design then it was the ventilation system. In all previous heavy tanks air for the radiator had been drawn through the body of the tank; it could hardly be described as fresh air but at least it kept moving. In the Mark

V the designers had installed grilles in the hull sides at the back so that air was drawn in from outside and directed along steel ducts, via the fan and radiator, before being expelled on the opposite side. This worked perfectly well as far as the radiator was concerned but conditions for the crew quickly became unbearable.

When the engine had been running for any length of time the exhaust manifolds started to glow red, heating up the air and presenting an immediate danger to the crew. Worse still, once the metal got hot enough it would expand and, upon cooling, shrink to the detriment of adjacent joints in the exhaust system. Next time the engine was started clouds of carbon monoxide would billow from these spoiled joints and before long members of the crew could be rendered quite ill, if not unconscious. The problem was partially cured later by fitting a shutter into the air ducting but even that was not an ideal solution.

Johnson also failed to mention a modification of the Mark V which was also under consideration at this time. The problem of passing tanks across wider German trenches had hardly been solved by the fascine since it was a crude, labour-intensive and unrepeatable solution. Various alternatives had been suggested and the most promising was devised by Central Workshops in France, in the summer of 1917. A spare Mark IV tank, assuming there was such a thing, was cut in half just behind the sponson aperture and then lengthened with additional extra panels so that the body of the tank was extended by 6ft (1.8m). It was relatively easy to do and the only mechanical modification was to extend the main drive shaft, but there was one disadvantage.

Tank design was still in its rudimentary stage; it had not yet become a science, and some basic laws of physics, as they applied to tracklaying vehicles, were not properly understood. The law that applied in this case is now known as the L over C ratio where L is the Length of track in touch with the ground and C the distance between track Centres; the longer the track in touch with the ground, the wider must be the gap between track centres, otherwise the tank will be difficult to steer. One assumes that the original designers had come upon the correct proportions more or less by accident when they designed the Mark I, although Tritton was getting close to it when he modified the long Bullock tracks on *Little Willie,* but the stretched Mark IV broke the rules. Not that they could do much about it because width was still dictated by the British railway loading gauge but in adapting an existing design it was inevitable that this would happen.

An original diagram comparing the Mark IV Tadpole Tail arrangement with the lengthened Mark V* and conventional tanks of both types.

119

The Mark IV Tadpole Tail tank is shown here towing two supply sledges over a mud churned testing ground.

Even so it was agreed that the advantages outweighed potential steering problems and there was one other asset. The extra space created inside the tank, with a hull that was six feet longer than normal, could be used to carry extra personnel or even stores. Thus it was decided that once production of Mark V tanks, of which 400 had been ordered, was complete a stretched version, to be known as the Mark V* (Star) would follow down the production lines.

The prototype Newton Tractor gives a demonstration of its climbing powers revealing its farm tractor origins and the load-carrying tray at the front.

While on the subject of crossing wider trenches it is interesting to compare Central Workshops' solution to one conjured up by Fosters in Lincoln which was known as the Tadpole Tail. This also involved extending the tank's track frames but not its hull since the extension was added to the rear track horns. In this form the tank was capable of getting across a 13ft (4m) wide trench but it lacked the inherent rigidity of the Central Workshops version and, despite the fact that dozens of these Tadpole Tail attachments were made and shipped out to France, there is no evidence that they were ever used, except experimentally on a couple of Mark V tanks later on.

There were two other projects in the pipeline at this time, of which Johnson, in his brief tour, may not have been aware. One was the Mark VII which would incorporate the Williams–Janney hydraulic transmission, the other the Mark VIII, an extensively redesigned heavy tank, both of which will be studied later.

There is one other reference in Johnson's report that is a bit obscure but worth following up at this point. During a visit to Leeds Johnson says that he was shown a design for a tracked machine that had started out as a fighting machine but was now a lorry. It is not altogether clear what he is referring to but the location may be a clue. Before the war Johnson had worked for John Fowler & Co. of the Steam Plough Works in Leeds and they are believed to have been the designers of a tracked lorry, using Pedrail style tracks that was prepared in 1917. The reference to a fighting machine is even more obscure but it may be connected with the original Pedrail Landship of 1915. During later trials of this machine, when it had been rejected as a tank, someone noticed how the action of the Pedrail tracks tended to consolidate the ground it passed over rather than tearing it up. A suggestion was put forward that if it could be fitted with a tipper body, capable of carrying road metal, it might prove useful to road-mending crews in France. Here you would have a machine that could not only carry and unload road stone, it would also be able to tamp it down, being delivery vehicle and road roller all in one. Fowler's design may well have been produced in answer to this requirement yet, as far as is known, such a machine was never built, at least not by Fowlers. Something very much like it, but known as the Roller Track Wagon, was built by an obscure company known as the Humphrey Pump Co. and tested in War Department markings around 1917 but it elicited no orders. Fowlers built a much larger version of the same thing, for commercial use, some years after the war.

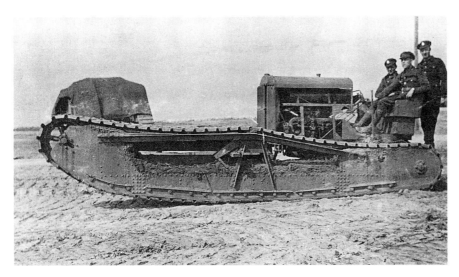

A production Newton Tractor, manufactured in the United States, shown with a Tank Corps crew at Bovington shortly after the war.

Not that this was the only design of its kind in the pipeline. A Col Henry Newton, described as a member of the Trench Warfare Committee, submitted a design of his own to the Ministry of Munitions which, when compared with the Roller Track Wagon, was simplicity itself. In fact it consisted of little more than an open tray, with narrow tracks at each side and with the engine, transmission and seat of a farm tractor in the back. A prototype was built by his firm, Newton Brothers of Derby and fitted with a Ford T car engine. It was vulnerable of course and no doubt considered expendable but large numbers of them, each capable of handling 3t (3,048kg) of supplies, might well prove very useful since they should be able to follow the tanks. The Ministry therefore placed huge orders with various American manufacturers including Buick and Studebaker but deliveries did not begin until the war was virtually over and further production was cancelled.

A more conventional solution to the supply problem was to design a tank specifically for that purpose, rather than convert redundant machines. Work began on this project in September 1917 but this will be dealt with later.

TRANSMISSIONS

Early in 1918 the matter of transmissions was revived although it is not entirely clear why. The work is attributed to 20 Squadron RNAS but factual information on it is limited. It is simply known as the Lanchester Gearbox Machine or as Experimental Machine K. The Lanchester Motor Company built high quality cars that were particularly renowned for their three-speed epicyclic gearboxes which worked on the constant mesh principle and therefore made for smooth and easy gear changing on the move. What is not clear is whether standard car transmissions were used for the tank or special heavy-duty versions created but, under the circumstances, the former seems more likely.

It is not even clear how the Lanchester transmission was used although two alternatives suggest themselves. In a tank already equipped with Wilson epicyclic transmission a single Lanchester gearbox, in place of the conventional four-speed Wrigley unit as fitted to the Mark V, would have improved gear changing. It would be simple to change gear on the move, which was almost impossible with the conventional box, and this would improve the performance of the tank in action. Doubt has been cast on the ability of a standard car gearbox to stand up to the stress of moving a 28t (28,448kg) tank, but if it was only being used to demonstrate the principle, with a view to designing something more substantial for production machines it may have been sufficient.

On the other hand, if two gearboxes were used for speed changing and steering this might have given the tank more flexibility than Wilson's simple epicyclic system but at the expense of much greater complication. The tank was photographed at Dollis Hill later in the war but the pictures do not give much away. It is clearly a Mark II and almost certainly one of the redundant Oldbury Trials machines. Since we know that the Williams-Janney tank and the two petrol electric machines survived the war, bearing in mind the questions raised above, then it may have been the Wilson epicyclic tank if just one gearbox was used or the Wilkins multiple clutch tank in the case of two gearboxes.

11   Tanks on the Defensive

The existence of Tank Corps' Central Workshops in France has been mentioned in previous chapters. It had been approved in November 1916 and work began on construction in January 1917. The site chosen was in the Pas de Calais, in the valley of the River Ternoise, centred on the village of Erin. It covered some 24 acres and included the usual wooden huts for accommodation along with canvas hangars donated by the Royal Flying Corps for workshops. Adjacent to Central Workshops was Central Stores which distributed everything from a pair of boots to a compete tank and the whole camp was commanded by Maj J.G. Brockbank with Lt Col Frank Searle, a celebrated designer of London's buses, as technical advisor. Part of the site was also given over to training and long rows of sheds, referred to as Tank Stables, were constructed nearby.

The site at Erin was close to a line of the Nord Railway, so tanks could be delivered direct from Le Havre into a network of sidings and to make communications even better the main road passing the camp was a Route Nationale. New tanks, arriving from Britain, all had to go through a preparation procedure at Erin which included many modifications demanded by the Tank Corps. At the same time existing tanks had to be serviced and battered wrecks, hauled back from the battlefields, were virtually rebuilt. We have already seen that Central Workshops also carried out a lot of experimental work and all of this placed a great deal of stress on the existing manpower. This was eased, to some extent, by the arrival of a company of the Chinese Labour Corps in the summer of 1917. In due course some 700 Chinese labourers were employed there, many of whom graduated from basic labouring tasks to skilled mechanical work and the staff at Central Workshops always spoke highly of their work.

Starting in November 1917 work began on a new site for Central Workshops at Teneur, about one mile down the valley from Erin, in order to

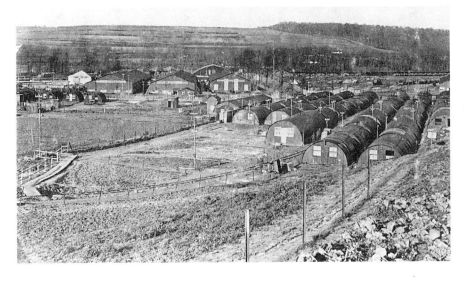

A general view of Central Workshops in France. The main railway line is away to the left but a light, narrow gauge line can be seen in the foreground, leading between the rows of huts.

At times the whole area became a sea of mud, aggravated by the tanks. In this view Whippet and Mark IV tanks can be seen, with Chinese workers on the railway and some redundant Tadpole Tail attachments on the right.

cater for the increasing number of tanks. Erin then became an expanded Central Stores. By this stage the number of specialist workshops attached to the base could carry out all kinds of mechanical work and the establishment was virtually self-sufficient.

Each company that went to France in 1916 had its own workshops and these naturally expanded into battalion workshops. However there were those who criticized the practice of having skilled men dispersed in this way so, from the summer of 1917, the workshops were brigaded. The object of these changes, besides the conservation of manpower, was to increase the ability of tank crews to service their own machines. Indeed a distinct line was drawn between maintenance, that was tank crew work, and repair, that was seen as a workshop function. It was argued that, as crews expanded their maintenance skills they would naturally take better care of their tanks. For one thing a well-maintained tank was less likely to let its crew down in battle and in any case, if a tank was kept in good condition maintenance became easier, more routine, leaving the crew with more free time. Salvage companies had also been created in 1916, charged with the task of recovering damaged or broken-down tanks from the

battlefield. Fighting battalions believed that it was bad for morale for tank crews to remove the bodies of their comrades from wrecked tanks and left all this to the salvage companies. When tanks had been burned out this was very grim work. It was rigorous in other respects as well. Transport could rarely get close enough to abandoned tanks with the necessary tools and there is a case on record of a party of men struggling over a considerable distance, carrying a complete new set of tracks for a tank and the special lifting jacks required to fit them. Salvage companies were subsequently renamed Tank Field Companies in recognition of the fact that their role on the battlefield was more than just dragging back abandoned hulks. Later some tanks were equipped with a light lifting jib, known as a Portable Tank Crane that could be erected on the nose of the tank that could, of course, go anywhere.

Much of the work undertaken by Central Workshop will be recorded in context elsewhere but an example of their work that might be dealt with here concerns supply tanks. Early examples had been cobbled together from redundant Mark I and Mark II tanks in the summer of 1917 and greater numbers had been prepared in time for Cambrai. Up to this time supply tanks were issued

A Mark IV female, fitted with a portable jib, lifts part of the differential housing from another machine that is in the process of being scrapped.

Here one of the two Gun Carrier Crane machines is shown upon the same work. Notice the raised crew cab and the platform, over the gun well, that supports the hand-operated crane.

to battalions but in February 1918 it was decided to form independent tank supply companies. There were five of these companies, each consisting of four sections of six tanks. The men were trained at Bovington but the tanks were converted at Central Workshops and this increased the workload considerably. Each Mark IV tank had its original sponsons removed and replaced by larger

sponsons in mild steel. Mesh frames were then fitted inside to prevent stores from falling against the engine.

The men from these five companies, according to Fuller, were drawn from the infantry and Royal Engineers, but these supply tanks, which were also known as tank tenders, or baggage tanks, served exclusively with the Tank Corps. By

During the Royal visit to Neuve Eglise in July 1917 Queen Mary was shown a newly converted Mark II Supply Tank. The empty male sponson has been planked off with steel plates to create storage space.

contrast the two Gun Carrier Companies, which also reverted to the supply role, were manned mainly by Tank Corps crews but were employed to carry stores for artillery, infantry and the engineers. Their work, particularly in the great Battle of Amiens will be described later.

The location of Central Workshops had been chosen for more than its proximity to good communications, it was also situated far enough back from the fighting line to be safe from attack, or so it was fondly hoped. It suffered air raids of course but for the two months March/April 1918 there was the risk of a German breakthrough. During this period extensive schemes were made to prepare the site for demolition, soldiers based there were formed into a scratch Lewis gun battalion and all the tanks kept fully armed. In the event it never came to that but it was close. Even so the commanding officer's report for this period explains that they were inundated by refugees, evicted from their homes by the German advance. He claims to have been amazed at the lengths that his men would go to in order to feed, clothe and even provide temporary accommodation for these unfortunate people.

The massive German attack of 21 March had been anticipated but it still took the Allies by surprise. The collapse of Russia reduced the German commitment on the eastern front and sufficient divisions were sent to the west to outnumber their opponents, at least until the United States Army increased its strength. Of course it was still a matter of guessing where the blow might fall and in this, to a certain extent, Haig got it wrong. The other problem was what to do with the tanks in such a battle. Fortunately a suggestion that they should be used as pillboxes was dropped in favour of a more sensible plan. This was to group the battalions into their brigades and hold them in three locations some ten miles behind the lines. Here they would form the core of reserve forces mounting counterattacks.

With a long winter of virtual inactivity behind them the tank battalions were mostly up to full strength in terms of personnel and machines. They had also undergone intensive training so they were in excellent form when they dispersed to their battle stations. The 4th Tank Brigade was ordered south; its battalions were now numbered,

Tanks of 6th (F) Battalion beneath camouflage nets in a wood. This picture probably dates from the summer of 1917 but it gives an impression of how the Savage Rabbits waited for action in March 1918.

rather than lettered so that A, D and E Battalions took the official designations 1st, 4th and 5th respectively. By way of contrast the practice of numbering companies consecutively throughout the Corps was changed for a system of letters whereby every battalion had its own A, B and C companies while the section that formed the companies were numbered successively.

The Savage Rabbits

The 4th Battalion detrained at Tincourt and set up a 'tankodrome' in Buire Woods in the second half of February 1918. In the middle of March four sections of tanks were moved closer to the front line and located in dispersed sites where they were carefully camouflaged. This scheme that was known at Tank Corps headquarters as the Savage Rabbit tactic, was intended to frustrate the Germans' infiltration tactics. The idea was to maintain the strictest camouflage up to the point when the German stormtroopers entered their area and then the tanks would strip away their camouflage and spring out to attack them, concentrating on the flanks and rear of the assault troops. Later,

when the direction of an attack had been identified the rest of the battalion would be mobilized at its tankodrome and take part in a more substantial counter-attack.

In practice it did not work out as planned. In the case of 4th Battalion the German advance that began on 21 March, was so rapid that crews of some of the Savage Rabbits were killed or wounded before they could even reach their tanks. Others did get into action and caused some havoc among the Germans but there were not enough to stem the flow. Most of the Savage Rabbits eventually ran out of fuel and had to be burned, those that survived fell back on Buire Woods but even then the Germans were too quick for them. For one thing, following their experiences on the first day, the Germans now made a point of avoiding tanks whenever they saw them. If tanks were encountered the attackers moved off, across country, so that the tanks, even if they spotted the manoeuvre, simply could not move quickly enough to intercept them.

The fate of 5th Battalion was, if anything, worse. They were separated from the 4th Battalion by the Cologne river, a tributary of the Somme.

The aftermath of the disaster at Brie with abandoned tanks, mostly pushed off the road, after their crews withdrew to safety.

A Tank Corps Lewis gun team brewing up. The officer and men look suspiciously clean although the cook is wearing a sheepskin cover for warmth.

The Prime Minister of Newfoundland, Sir Edward Morris, inspects a Whippet at Erin. This particular example sports the white/red/white markings adopted after the March action when the Germans began to operate British tanks.

Here they covered the infantry as they fell back in the face of the German attack but, when they in turn prepared to retreat, the bridge at Brie was blown up prematurely by an over-excited officer and they remained stranded on the wrong side of the river. Three tanks did manage to get back, but all of the remainder had to be destroyed.

Thus, within three days both battalions had lost the majority of their tanks although human casualties were minimal so the men were organized into Lewis gun teams and sent back into the line. Early in April, the 4th and other Tank Corps battalions were temporarily organized as Lewis gun battalions although skilled drivers were exempt. In this unfamiliar role the men gave an excellent account of themselves and the Tank Corps *Book of Honour* records many examples of gallantry. The 6th Battalion had most reason to be upset by these developments. They had been training on Whippets when the emergency arose and had to return to their Mark IVs. Even so they were never reduced to serving as a Lewis gun battalion and somehow contrived to have some men away on training courses, even at this difficult time, while others remained with the tanks.

If Mark IV tanks were too slow for this kind of work it was ideal for the Whippets. The first Whippet battalion to become operational in France was the Third, the erstwhile C Battalion. They were located at Bray-sur-Somme at the start of the German offensive and many of the new tanks were under repair. A number had to be destroyed but on 26 March two companies, comprising twelve tanks, were ordered to the village of Mailly-Maillet, then held by a small detachment of British infantry that was on the point of retreating.

Leaving some of the tanks to cover their flanks the remainder advanced and almost immediately ran into a large body of German infantry, some 300 men, advancing in close order. The tanks launched themselves at the troops and captured or killed a large number. The remainder made a rapid retreat, closely pursued by the tanks, as far as the village of Serre. This action, insignificant in itself, ruined German plans for a major attack and, to that extent, had a profound effect upon the entire campaign. For the Germans were learning what had become obvious to the British nearly two years before, on this same Somme battlefield; that an advance, unless carefully consolidated,

A group of German soldiers, looking well pleased with themselves, pose with the captured 10th Battalion tank J2, Jacob *which has track extension plates added in a random way. The photograph was taken at Hendecourt.*

would become less tenable the further it progressed.

The German achievement should not be underestimated. Without the aid of tanks or massed artillery they had broken through the British lines to a depth of 40 miles (64km) in places and initiated councils of deep despair among the Allies. But their leading infantry, designated Stormtroopers, were worn out and on the point of starvation since it proved impossible to get supplies and reinforcements across the old Somme battleground. To make matters worse the Germans now had to find men to cover the flanks of an enormous salient when those men were needed to support new attacks which they had planned further north.

Haig had always believed that the main German effort would be directed against Arras, which is where he had posted most of his strength, both tanks and men. Thus, when the Germans did launch an attack in this area on 28 March they came up against a well-prepared defence and were quickly stopped. Nearly two weeks later they tried again, in Flanders, in what became known as the battle of the Lys. Here, as on the Somme, they had the advantage of a heavy morning mist to cover the initial attack and once again it achieved remarkable results. Haig countered by shortening

his line and giving up a lot of hard-won ground in the process. No tanks were available but the Tank Corps supplied five Lewis gun battalions, rushed up by lorry from the south, and they made a significant contribution to the successful outcome of the battle, at least as far as the British were concerned.

It says much for the strength of the German Army, reinforced as it was by divisions released from the collapsed eastern front, that they were able to mount so many offensives in quick succession. In retrospect it may be seen as the Germans pursuing the unfortunate British practice of attempting to capitalize on failure with more of the same but, despite enormous losses, Ludendorff had one more attack up his sleeve.

GERMAN TANKS

The Germans first used tanks in action on 21 March supporting their infantry assault around the city of St Quentin. To the north five captured British Mark IV female tanks were employed while five of the new German-built A7V tanks operated further south. Although they were operating against British troops in the area, who had

German troops, some occupying training trenches, observe the performance of a captured Mark IV male tank at the St Armand training ground, north of Charleroi in occupied Belgium.

no tank support of their own, the presence of German tanks of any kind was not reported to the British high command at this time.

The Establishment in Germany appears to have been, if anything, even more resistant to the idea of the tank than were their counterparts in Britain. They ultimately authorized the construction of about twenty machines of a rather ponderous design, the first of which were ready for service by the spring of 1918. Mechanically sophisticated and well-armed, with a 57mm cannon and six machine-guns they were not suited to the conditions on the western front. They might be faster and much more manoeuvrable than the British type but their cross-country performance was pathetic and their propensity to tip over into shell holes or trenches quite alarming. The design certainly had some odd features. In order to get maximum effect from its weapons the A7V had a two-man cab, like a raised cupola, in the centre of the roof. It made it easier for the crew to drive the tank in either direction but their view of the ground, particularly close to the tank where it mattered, was very restricted which no doubt explains why they ran into trenches and shell holes. The driver and commander, on their elevated platform, sat directly above a pair of Daimler four-cylinder engines which were probably even worse than the engines in British tanks for raising heat, noise and pollution levels.

Imagine this in a tank that required a crew of eighteen and the vision is not pleasant.

Most of the Mark IV tanks in German service were captured at Cambrai. The German Army created a repair and maintenance workshop at Charleroi in Belgium where the machines were overhauled and prepared for service. The work entailed fitting new machine-guns of the German pattern and replacing the British 57mm guns with a similar weapon of their own. It was the slow delivery of these guns that limited the British tanks available on 21 March to female machines only. The biggest problem, from the German point of view, was the provision of spares which, inevitably, could only be salvaged from the battlefield.

During the first attack at St Quentin, the captured British tanks did not acquit themselves well. The very essence of the German offensive was speed and flexibility and neither adjective could be applied to a Mark IV. The infantry soon left them behind and some were knocked out by British artillery. Knowing that there were no British tanks in the area the gunners must have realized that the machines they were facing belonged to the enemy, despite their familiar outlines, so it is even more surprising that none of this was reported to higher echelons. Of the five German tanks only two finally made it into action. Being faster they were able to support the infantry and did good work dealing with troublesome British strongpoints but they were very sensitive to ground conditions and in the end both withdrew when things inside became unbearable. It is worth noting that, when German tanks confronted them for the first time, British infantry seem to have been every bit as fearful as the Germans had been in 1916.

The German High Command authorized an operation for 24 April 1918 around the town of Villers-Bretonneux, the main object of which was to straighten out the German front line in this area. The terrain was judged particularly suitable for the deployment of A7V tanks and in the event thirteen were ready to take part. This time, however, the British also had tanks in the area. A section of three Mark IV tanks, two female and one male, were acting the part of Savage Rabbits in the Bois de l'Abbé, a large wood to the west of the town.

In a thick morning mist that somewhat confused the German tanks but also sheltered them from view, the A7V tanks were extremely successful. Even the British Official History was forced to admit that infantry in the area, whether British or Australian, were daunted by the German machines. The main force of the German attack passed north of Villers-Bretonneux but one detachment of three machines was directed to the south, aiming to pass between the town and the nearby village of Cachy. With the German attack already underway Capt F.C. Brown, the commander of the section of 1st Battalion tanks, issued forth from the wood and headed east. There was still mist about and pockets of German gas filled the hollows but the infantry were still in their trenches and the tanks started to patrol. It seems that Allied infantry drew Brown's attention to the approaching German machines, two of which now seemed to peel off to the south, towards Cachy. Brown pointed the enemy tanks out to Lt Frank Mitchell, commanding the male tank of the trio who then started to manoeuvre to engage the nearest machine.

Up to this time the Germans do not seem to have been aware of the presence of the British

tanks and, once they were identified, began by opening fire on the two females. The Germans soon had the two British machines retreating from the arena, with large holes blown in their sides. It now came down to a two-tank duel. Frank Mitchell's tank No. 4066 and Wilhelm Biltz's A7V *Nixe*, No. 561. In theory the German tank should have had the edge. Its gunner must already have established the range of the British tank and, with its sprung suspension the gun was less likely to suffer from vibration.

Mitchell swung his tank around to bring the right hand gun to bear and his second-in-command, Sgt McKenzie, took charge of it. McKenzie's eyes were stinging from the gas but as the unsprung tank clattered across the ground, the vibration caused the image in the gun sight to jump around and thus ruin any chance he had of ranging on the A7V. Mitchell brought his tank to a halt and, now that he could see the target, McKenzie pumped three rounds into it, causing the crew to bail out.

To that extent it was a victory but, a few moments later a shell hit Mitchell's tank, breaking a track and effectively disabling it. At the same time Biltz persuaded his crew to climb back into *Nixe* since it had not blown up. Starting it up, they moved the tank gently out of action before it broke down. Yet this was not the end of the drama at Cachy. Even as Mitchell and his crew stood to their guns in the disabled Mark IV, in order to beat off further German attacks, they were inspired by the sight of seven Whippet tanks of 3rd Battalion, an improvised company commanded by Capt T.R. Price that came racing from the corner of the Bois de l'Abbé and passed them to the south.

Price and his tanks had been positioned near a corner of the wood when a message was dropped from a British aircraft reporting the presence of two German infantry battalions hidden by a fold in the ground just outside Cachy. The Germans were just preparing to attack when the seven light tanks appeared with machine-guns firing. Price led his tanks straight through the German troops,

The fields around Central Workshops are littered with damaged tanks, Whippets and Mark IVs. This picture was probably taken after the Amiens battle, later in the year, but it must have been typical of all times. Notice the engine, on a rail wagon at the extreme left.

swung around on the far side and drove back through them again. The number of dead and wounded was estimated at around 400 but, more to the immediate point, the survivors were quite incapable of attacking. Price lost one of his Whippets, probably to an A7V, and its crew of three were killed. The action was a striking example of the power that men under armour have against those who are unprotected.

It is a pity that no figures survive in Central Workshops records to indicate the number of tanks that passed through their hands at this period because the rate of attrition must have been staggering. Many, of course, would have fallen

into German hands and been received as a welcome source of spare parts for their small fleet of British machines. Clearly with both sides operating upon the battlefield with the same type of tank the potential for confusion and tragedy was ever present. The Germans had taken immediate steps to prevent this by decorating their machines with large black crosses; originally the traditional Maltese style, replaced later in the war by the simpler Balkan Cross. The Tank Corps responded, in due course by decorating the nose section of each tank with three broad, vertical stripes in the pattern white/red/white; an arrangement that was extended to cab tops on later models.

12 The Battle of Hamel – the Mark V in Action

THE MARK V'S ARRIVAL IN FRANCE

Central Workshops recorded the arrival of the first Mark V tank in France on 14 January 1918. The staff were already familiar with the Ricardo engine since they had taken delivery of a sample in the previous August and no doubt spent a lot of time getting used to its unusual features. The long gap between these two deliveries adds weight to the suggestion, found in various sources, that a plan existed to refit existing Mark IV tanks with the new engine and transmission, creating a type which was to be known as the Mark IVA.

That this was entirely practical is clear from the fact that Philip Johnson had test driven a Ricardo/Wilson Mark IV during his visit to Britain

Mark V Tank	
Data for a male machine	
Crew:	8
Weight:	29 tons
Length:	26ft 5in (8.06m)
Width:	12ft 9in (3.89m)
Height:	8ft 8in (2.64m)
Armour:	14mm (½in) max.
Speed:	4.6mph (7.4km/h) max.

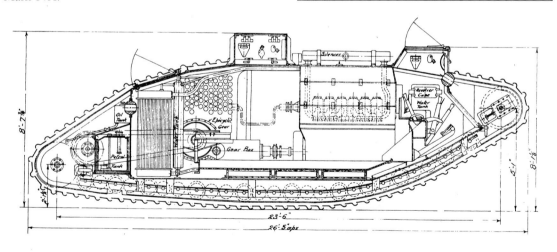

— Sectional Elevation —

GENERAL ARRANGEMENT OF MACHINE MK. V

and, of course, it was part of Harry Ricardo's brief that the new engine should fit into the mountings provided for the Daimler. Why it was not done is another matter but it may have been no more than a question of logistics. Presumably, since their workload was already enormous, Central Workshops would have balked at the idea of taking on the task in France and the extra work involved in shipping the tanks back to Britain for conversion was, one imagines, equally difficult to justify. In any case it could only have been done over the winter months when they were not required for operations, and this at a time when production facilities were stretched with the manufacture of new tanks.

The Mark V has already been described although it is probably fair to add, at this point, that these were the first new tanks to be supplied from Britain that came complete with unditching equipment. The delivery of Mark V tanks to France that could have started in March, was delayed by the emergency because the War Office and GHQ in France agreed that priority should be given to other warlike stores for the time being. This attitude hardened towards the end of April when it seemed, for a time, as if further expansion of the Tank Corps was to be halted and indeed a possible reduction in the Corps' strength considered. Clearly, in the light of the German attack, the authorities panicked and could see no further than the restoration of the infantry's strength at the expense of the tanks and other arms. Things hung in the balance throughout May and June before common sense prevailed and the original programme was restored, but it is instructive to note that when the chips were down, senior officers reverted to traditional resources and ignored the potential of the new weapon.

New Methods of Transporting the Mark V

Thus it was from May onwards that Mark V tanks started to arrive at Central Stores and they did so by a novel new route. Up to February 1918 tanks from Britain were moved by rail to Southampton

A Mark V male on the move. This one is fitted with the wider, 26½in tracks that reduced ground pressure.

docks, lifted onto conventional merchant ships by crane and carried across the Channel to Le Havre. Here they were craned off the ships and taken by rail to Teneur; it was a tiresome, labour-intensive and long-winded business. In February 1918 it all got a lot easier. Tanks could now be driven onto railway wagons at the factory and taken down to a new port complex at Richborough on the River

A trainload of sheeted down tanks, ready to board one of the special train ferries at the Richborough Military Port near Sandwich in Kent.

On the other side of the Channel the tanks are prepared for disembarkation from the ferry at Calais. These photographs were taken in August 1918.

A Mark V male tank Ecstatic *of 5th (E) Battalion photographed after the war. Crew members pose with their Hotchkiss guns that replaced the Lewis. Notice also the semaphore signalling device mounted just behind the rear cab.*

Stour near Sandwich in Kent. Richborough, the so-called mystery port, had been created out of nothing; at least nothing more than flat salt marsh and the winding, sluggish and muddy river. It now consisted of miles of railway sidings, extensive storage sheds, boat-building and ship-repair facilities with, best of all, a train ferry terminal.

Two large cross-channel steamers had been built that featured rails laid into the main deck. These craft could secure themselves to a pier head that rose and fell with the tide so that railway wagons could be shunted on board and taken off the other end at Calais to complete the journey. Thus nobody needed to touch the tanks between their loading onto a train at Birmingham and rolling off the other end at Teneur. It made a tremendous difference to the speed of delivery but seriously stretched the staff at Central Stores. Their Receiving, Testing and Despatching Section ,once recorded the arrival of forty-nine tanks in a single day and they soon came to regard the arrival of twenty tanks each day as perfectly normal.

Mark V tanks were first issued to 5th Tank Brigade but, before we examine their first action two other events should be recorded. On 3 January 1918 a new tank battalion, the 17th (Light) Battalion, was formed at Bovington Camp

under the command of Lt Col Edward Carter. The designation Light implies that it was going to be a Whippet battalion. It is interesting to note, in passing, that at one point the Duke of Westminster, one of the most dashing and successful armoured car commanders from 1914–15, had approached the War Office with a view to commanding a Whippet battalion. What became of this offer, or at least why it was rejected, is not known. In the event Carter was informed that, on 16 April, he would be commanding the 17th (Armoured Car) Battalion, Tank Corps.

ARMOURED CAR BATTALION

Armoured cars, at least British armoured cars, had vanished from the Western Front in the summer of 1917 and most of them had gone further abroad, to Africa, the Middle East or India. These would have been Rolls-Royces that had proved themselves to be an ideal design, but Carter would not be getting Rolls-Royces, only a handful of which would have been in Britain at this time.

Rather he was to be equipped with Austins, sixteen of which were then to be found at Cardiff Docks. The British Army had never operated Austin armoured cars. Up to the time of the October Revolution they had been supplied exclusively, by the manufacturer, to the Imperial Russian Government which, for some reason, had a very high opinion of them. The Revolution put paid to further business with Russia and the cars at Cardiff had probably been there for some time.

The Russians, however, had their own ideas on armoured car design which conflicted with British theories. The Russians preferred their armoured cars to have two turrets, either side by side or slightly staggered whereas the British, and most other users, felt that one turret was quite enough. The advantage, as far as the Russians were concerned, was that the car could fire in two directions at the same time or bring two guns to bear on a single target at certain angles. The drawback was that two turrets inevitably added weight and tended to make the cars top heavy.

Carter never recorded his reaction to this change but he went at it willingly enough. Neither is it clear where the idea to create an armoured car battalion came from; whether it was a logical extension of the Tank Corps' role, which it ought to have been, or the wish on someone's part that a stock of useable armoured cars should not go to waste. Whatever the cause the cars were driven from Cardiff to the Army Service Corps camp at Bulford on Salisbury Plain. Here the main task was to alter the turret machine-gun mountings to accept the Tank Corps' favourite Hotchkiss in place of the water-cooled Vickers guns for which they had been designed.

By the middle of June the battalion was in France, organized as follows. There was a battalion headquarters and two companies, A and B, each of four sections, there being two armoured cars to a section. Each car carried one officer, two gunners and two drivers. The second driver was not just insurance in the event of a casualty, he could also drive the car in reverse, in an emergency, from a rear-facing steering position so long

A well-decorated Austin armoured car of 17th Battalion. The paint scheme of pale blue over brown was supposed to disguise the vehicle against a skyline while the eye, painted around one of the machine-gun mountings, was clearly added by the crew.

as the first driver was in his place to operate the other controls. Following driving and gunnery training with the Tank Corps at Le Treport, the battalion was sent to the front on 4 June and subsequently attached to the French XXIInd Corps that was covering the junction between the French and British armies at Ravenel.

The 17th Battalion officers were impressed with the efficiency of French staff work which, from the very fact that they comment upon it, implies a contrast with British practice. Even so they suspected that the French had requested tanks, rather than armoured cars, because the attack they had planned was entirely unsuited to wheeled vehicles. The Austins could not get through to their objectives and did no more than fire into the villages that they had been directed to deal with. They lost one car to shellfire in the process.

On the night of 22/23 June five female tanks from C Company, 10th Battalion were sent out to raid the village of Bucquoy, south of Arras in conjunction with a company of 5th Battalion, King's Own Yorkshire Light Infantry. This would be the first full night of action involving British tanks and it is probably just as well that it was a limited objective. There is plenty of written evidence to suggest that it was difficult enough to get one's bearings from within a tank in broad daylight, never mind at night, so it is interesting to record that it was judged successful. To judge from citations for medals awarded for this action the officers mainly had to lead their tanks on foot and quickly lost contact with the infantry who soon got held up.

One tank broke down on the way back and was rapidly surrounded by the enemy. Using their machine-guns to keep the Germans at bay, and under heavy bombardment from trench mortars, the crew held on while the second driver worked hard for thirty minutes to get the tank running again. When the driver of another tank was blinded by a near miss one of the gunners took over his seat and managed to bring the tank home. Indeed all five tanks got back with one officer and three men wounded.

THE BATTLE OF HAMEL

The Battle of Hamel, on 4 July 1918, marked the combat debut of the Mark V tank and it was, in every respect, a model action. Tanks of 8th and 13th Battalions took part, supporting troops from 4th Australian Infantry Brigade. This would be the first time that the Australians had worked closely with tanks since the débâcle at Bullecourt in April 1917 and it was considered vital that their confidence in armour should be restored. This began with a long period of training during which companies of tanks worked closely with the battalions that they would be supporting in the battle and this resulted in a good deal of harmony and mutual understanding.

The objectives of the battle were limited and clearly defined and there is little doubt that much of its ultimate success was due to the excellent staff work normally associated with the Australian Army and their practice of making a plan and

sticking to it, rather than making pointless changes at the last minute. The infantry were to advance behind a creeping barrage, followed immediately by the tanks. Each fighting tank was to carry a supply of ammunition and drinking water for the infantry while four supply tanks brought up barbed wire and pickets so that they could establish sound defensive positions in the captured German trenches. Col J.F.C. Fuller calculated that the loads carried by these four tanks would, under the old system, have required 1,250 men. Air support was provided by No. 8 Squadron Royal Air Force, commanded by Maj Trafford Leigh-Mallory that had been allotted to the Tank Corps to learn how the two arms could co-operate. The airmen were taught in particular to look out for field guns being used against tanks and were directed to attack these as first priority.

The tanks, in their turn, were also trying out new tactics based upon the improved manoeuvrability of the Mark V. Up to this time German machine-gun crews, at least the hardier amongst them, had discovered that if they lay still when a tank was close by it would invariably ignore them. For one thing the tank crew, if they saw the machine-gunners, might suppose that they were already dead but, in any case, it was generally considered more trouble than it was worth to go through the various evolutions necessary in a Mark IV to swing the tank around and deal with the gun. In the Mark V, of course, it was simply a matter of hauling back gently on a lever so the tanks made it a practice to run over the machine-gun and its crew whenever one was discovered. They are said to have disposed of some 200 machine-guns in this way during the battle of Hamel.

The increased reliability of the Mark V was also evident since all the tanks made it to the start line at the right time. Those supporting the infantry were followed by a second wave of tanks as a mobile reserve. Despite their misgivings the Australians supported the tanks that, in the event, led the way throughout the attack. Not that it was easy by any means. The Germans, although clearly surprised, put up a tenacious defence and knocked out five tanks besides inflicting casualties on the infantry. In order to prevent them from falling into German hands in working order, all Mark V tanks were fitted with a small demolition charge, near the gearbox that would effectively wreck the tank if it had to be abandoned. Whether any of these were activated in the knocked-out tanks is not clear but all five of them had been recovered by the following day.

Among the many awards for gallantry that resulted from Hamel few can have been as hard-earned as the Military Cross given to 2nd Lt John Rawlinson of 13th Battalion. Returning from action, but still in an area swept by enemy artillery fire he discovered a tank that had been hit by a shell and was incapable of moving. Rawlinson attached a tow rope and began to drag the other tank back when he came upon yet another machine which had somehow rolled over onto its side. Detaching the disabled tank he now attached tow ropes to the new casualty and actually got it back onto its tracks. Seeing it safely on its way, under its own power, he again picked up the disabled tank and towed it home.

Another MC went to Acting Capt James Smith who was in charge of the four Gun Carrier supply tanks of 1st Gun Carrier Company. He led the machines on foot, under constant heavy fire, to within 400yd (370m) of the final objective where he supervised unloading. On the way back, on his own initiative, he picked up seventy wounded men who were taken, by the tanks, to a field dressing station. Among the other ranks, one might single out the Military Medal awarded to Cpl Terrington of No. 1 Tank Field Company. Finding a tank near Hamel with one track off, he and two fitters started to repair it under intermittent machine-gun fire. Finding the task too much for them Terrington collected a number of German prisoners and finished the job with their help. Having handed the prisoners over to the infantry he and his men drove the repaired tank back to the British lines.

The entire battle was virtually over by mid-morning and the tanks were able to withdraw. Some captured German troops apparently realized that they were up against an improved type of tank and claimed, as they often did after subsequent actions, that the Allies' success was due entirely to the use of tanks. Many blamed their own High Command for failing to produce sufficient tanks of their own although a few added, ominously, that the Germans would soon be fighting with a

A well-stowed Gun Carrier Supply machine on the move. The gun well, between the two driving cabs, provided plenty of space for stores but unloading, especially under fire, must have been hard work.

Lifting the engine out of a Mark V at Central Workshops while two other fitters work on the final drive chains through a hole in the side.

new design that had a much better performance, especially over trenches, than the original A7V. As for the Australians, it is said that they were so pleased with the results of Hamel that their infantry were even known, on occasions, to salute British officers if they were wearing the Tank Corps badge!

Reports from Central Workshops were not so complimentary about the Mark V as the troops had been. One tank that they had back for repair required an engine change and they found great difficulty in removing the upper hull plate to lift it out. Maj Wilson had already been warned of this failing when Central Workshops were testing the original machine and their experts had suggested a remedy which involved making the top plate in two parts and bolting it into place. This advice was ignored at the time and it was probably not remedied until the end of the war.

The staff at Central Workshops were also concerned about a tendency for the Mark V to catch fire when it was hit but, despite investigation, no obvious cause could be found. In due course the technical experts came to the conclusion that it was caused by the tremendous heat given off by the exhaust stacks of the Ricardo engine which would glow pink after a strenuous run. Measurements revealed an internal tempera-

ture of $120°F$ that, even if it did not cause fires, certainly debilitated the crew. By constructing an air-tight casing around the engine that reached from floor to roof and fitting fan blades to the flywheel, Central Workshops managed to bring the temperature down to $85°F$ which was at least bearable. The hot air was now expelled through louvres fitted in the tank's roof. Ever helpful the staff at Teneur prepared drawings and a description of this improvement, which was forwarded to the Design Department in Britain who turned it down without a trial. They also fitted a sliding shutter to the radiator ducting at the back of the tank so that excess heat could be drawn off that way if required.

Some two weeks after Hamel the 9th Tank Battalion, in 3rd Tank Brigade, was informed that it would be supporting 3rd French Infantry Division in an attack towards Moreuil. The history of the 9th Battalion up to this point is quite interesting. Having fought at Cambrai in the ubiquitous Mark IVs they were then earmarked for training on Whippets. A few were issued for training, although they appear to have been in very poor mechanical condition, but before this process had gone very far the German offensive began and the 9th, like most others, became a Lewis gun battalion. When they returned to tanks in May it was to Mark Vs which is what they took into action at Moreuil. We have already noted that both 3rd and 6th Battalions had been converted to Whippet battalions and that at one stage 17th Battalion was probably destined to go the same way. If we then add the 9th Battalion we come to a total of 144 Whippets; four battalions each with thirty-six tanks (three companies, each with three sections of four tanks). The total order for Whippets was 200 machines, which would have left a sufficient margin of safety for spare tanks on the understanding that new types of Medium Tank would have been available later in the year. Why no more than two Light Battalions were raised in the end is not clear. It may have had something to do with the vacillation at the War Office, recorded earlier, or greater losses of

Whippets in March and April than had been expected. Oddly, by August 1918, when the Tank Corps was preparing for the Battle of Amiens, the two Whippet battalions were increased to forty-eight tanks each by adding an extra section to each company.

ACTION AT MOREUIL

Returning to Moreuil the attack took place on 23 July 1918 and, considering the short time available for mutual training and the obvious language difficulty, it was quite successful. Once again the new tanks performed extremely well. Even before the battle they had to trek some 22 miles (35km) on their tracks, in addition to a rail journey, in just four days. Despite this punishing introduction only seven tanks fell by the wayside. The French infantry supported the tanks well and, like the Australians, seem to have developed a natural understanding about what the tanks could do and behaved accordingly. Even so casualties were high both in tank crews and the infantry, and German artillery, in the anti-tank role, proved very effective. There are those who claim that German machine-gun crews were not so effective as of old, a situation which seems to have its origins in the Hamel battle and one which got worse as the war progressed. As a result of this battle the French awarded the 9th Battalion the right to wear the badge of their 3rd La Genadière Division, known from its motto as *Qui s'y Frotte s'y Brule* (who I touch, I burn).

The battalion commander, Lt Col Hugh Woods, along with two company commanders, a section commander and the battalion reconnaissance officer were made knights of the Légion d'Honneur by the French and among the Military Crosses was one to Temporary Lt William Wilkins. His tank received a direct hit at one point that smashed a great hole in the side but, although this slowed him down, Wilkins kept his tank in action until another hit, just as he reached his final objective, knocked another hole in the tank. It was

still running so, with a great deal of care, he struggled to bring it all the way back to the French lines.

THE MARK V* (STAR)

Central Workshop's design for a longer tank was recorded in Chapter 10 with the experiment on a Mark IV which resulted in a design known as the Mark V*; expressed as Mark V Star. It should be stressed at this point that, apart from the original conversion of the Mark IV, all of the production tanks were built from new, they were not Mark V tanks which had been modified. Even so it is fair to say that, once the original order for 400 Mark V tanks had been completed (200 male and 200 female) by Metropolitan Carriage, Wagon & Finance in Birmingham no more were ordered. Instead Metropolitan received orders for 700 Mark V* in the ratio 200 female to 500 male, of which 579 had been completed by Armistice Day and another 66 subsequently.

The Mark V* was not simply a stretched Mark V. To begin with there was a full height door in each side of the tank, just abaft the sponsons and the rear cab was reshaped. That on the Mark V was a simple box shape while, on the Mark V*, it was sloped on the front and rear faces. Machine-gun ball mounts were located in each of these sloping faces and it is interesting to consider their purpose. The most obvious was that they would provide the tank's crew with some ability to shoot at enemy aircraft but one wonders if this was really possible. Visibility from inside a tank was minimal at the best of times and the chances of spotting an attacking aircraft under these circumstances would seem to be slim. Rather this design may have been the result of experience gained during the Cambrai battle when tanks entering villages often found themselves being attacked by infantry in the upper storeys of houses, against whom they had no adequate reply.

The preponderance of orders for male tanks at this time may well have been from fear of the risk of meeting enemy tanks although this would

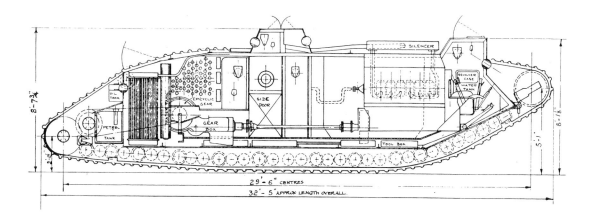

SECTIONAL ELEVATION.

GENERAL ARRANGEMENT OF MACHINE Mk V*

Mark V* Tank
Data for a male machine

Crew:	8
Weight:	33 tons
Length:	32ft 5in (9.89m)
Width:	12ft 9in (3.89m)
Height:	8ft 8in (2.64m)
Armour:	14mm (½in) max.
Speed:	4.6mph (7.4km/h) max.

Crossing a wide trench, a Mark V male training tank displays the new shape of the rear cab and the side door, with an extra machine-gun position in the upper part.*

LEFT: Mark V tanks under construction in Birmingham. An engine is being lowered in the foreground while beyond male sponsons can be seen, carried by travelling cranes.*

141

imply a rather shorter time scale than is normal in these circumstances. In fact one imagines that the order for Mark V* tanks, at least the initial order for 400, was placed before the first tank-versus-tank battle but this may well have influenced the subsequent order. Be that as it may, there is no doubt at all that some time in July Central Workshops were told by London to fit one male sponson to every female tank (and, one assumes, replaced female sponson to an equal number of male tanks) in order to produce what was known as a hermaphrodite; one exhibiting both male and female features.

Central Workshops, inevitably, complained about the extra workload but imply that they got on with it at once. This is difficult to verify. Surviving battle sheets for individual tanks from Hamel and subsequent battles still speak of male or female machines and photographic evidence is almost useless since it is virtually impossible to see both sponsons in one photograph. There is no doubt at all that, by the end of the war, most Mark V tanks had become hermaphrodites but there is no hard evidence to suggest it was done to Mark V* tanks, nor even retrospectively to Mark IVs. In fact there is photographic evidence to show that some Mark V* tanks were later converted to the Supply role, a fact that does not appear to have been recorded in writing anywhere.

Since the workload on Central Workshops was undoubtedly overwhelming, and likely to get a lot worse as the year wore on, it is interesting at this point to observe how manpower was being used for other purposes in the same area. One of the most interesting organizations was Number 3 Advanced Workshops that was formed at Erin in January 1918. Its function was purely experimental and its first commanding officer was the doyen of tank experimenters, Maj Philip Johnson. Within a week or two of this appointment Johnson was replaced; not that he was unsuitable for the job but because Gen Elles preferred to retain him at Tank Corps HQ on account of his peculiar expertise. Johnson was replaced at Erin by Maj M.E. Yorke Eliot, a Royal Engineer who transferred to the Tank Corps, but all the experiments they carried out were directed by Johnson.

These included tests to see what size of mine crater would stop a tank and a peculiar method of transporting fuel in a train of steel barrels towed by a tank. Work also commenced on a smoke-making device for tanks. Two or three different types were tested but the best was found to be that devised by Wg Cdr F.A. Brock, RAF from the famous firework manufacturers, who was killed during the Zeebrugge raid in April 1918. Other projects included a massive roller supply trailer for tanks, a prototype of which was eventually built by Ruston and Proctor in Lincoln.

Tank defence trials in the mud near Central Workshops, the Mark IV, fitted with special track spuds, appears to be digging itself even further into the hole. The officer with his back to the camera, the only one without a greatcoat, looks very much like Col Fuller.

A Mark V* taking part in smoke-generating trials, probably by squirting sulphonic acid into the exhaust gases.

The huge tank supply roller built by Ruston and Proctor; coupled behind a tank the roller rotates while the container, suspended from the axle shaft, remains upright.

13 Amiens and the Final Battles – Advance into Germany

THE BATTLE OF AMIENS

The Battle of Amiens, that began before dawn on 8 August 1918, was undoubtedly one of the most significant battles of the First World War. Tanks were destined to play a very important part and indeed, to some extent, the entire battle plan was woven around them. Yet it is well to bear in mind, that the date of this battle was just five weeks short of two years since the very first tank action. The comparison is made even more interesting by the fact that this new battle would take place not that far from Flers, where the first tank attack was launched. It is also well to notice that the 1918 battle took place several miles deeper into France than the 1916 action.

Since the basic shape, armour and armament of tanks had not changed a great deal in two years, nor their mobility improved very much, it must be agreed that the progress from those first, faltering steps by thirty odd tanks, to an all-out assault by several hundred must, in a large part, be due to the accumulated skills of Tank Corps personnel. We have seen this develop, not just at crew level but in every department from supply and repair, to planning and execution. It would be wrong to assign the success of Amiens and what followed entirely to the tanks. New techniques for target registration, first employed by the Royal Artillery, made a tremendous difference to the outcome of the battle, as did the actions of the infantry; and here one cannot but single out the Australians, Canadians and newly arrived Americans who, between them, contributed skill, fighting spirit and incredible enthusiasm at a time when Britain's own manpower was at a very low ebb.

The Battle of Amiens was largely about communications, in particular railways and certain major junctions such as Amiens itself or Chaulnes which were either in danger from German attack or still in German hands. It was precipitated by German troops drawing back in certain areas from their existing positions, many of which had become untenable since April. Marshal Foch was particularly keen to see the Germans pursued as precipitately as possible and passed control of French First Army to Haig, while Haig himself entrusted the task to Gen Rawlinson's Fourth Army, suitably reinforced. Rawlinson had started planning something, albeit on a smaller scale, straight after the Battle of Hamel once he realized how weak the Germans were in his area and how good the country, both for tanks and cavalry.

Rawlinson had, under his immediate command, one British Corps which included the American 33rd (Illinois) Division and the Canadian and Australian Corps, each of which included one British division, and the Cavalry Corps. The British Corps was supported by one Tank Corps battalion in Mark V tanks, the Canadians had three battalions of Mark Vs and one of Mark V* tanks while the Australians were the same but also had 17th (Armoured Car) Battalion. Both Whippet

Canadian infantry, training with the Tank Corps at Bony in June 1918. The Mark IV machine, advancing through the waist-high corn, sports the white/ red/white markings and unditching beam.

*BELOW:
A remarkable overhead photograph of tanks assembled near the ruins of a farm. Tank tracks are clearly visible on the ground, as are trenches, wriggling in all directions.*

A Mark V female tank demonstrates its powers to assembled troops before the Amiens battle. Whether it was wise to display its potential, rather than emphasizing its limitations, is an interesting question.

battalions were attached to the Cavalry Corps. One other tank Battalion, the 9th, was in reserve as it was still recovering from Moreuil.

Total strength was therefore some 600 tanks, including five companies of supply tanks and gun carriers. It was the largest tank force the world had yet seen and involved something like fifteen times the number of tanks that fought at Flers in September 1916. Training was intense but the time for preparation was limited. Some 2,000 guns had to be moved into the area and emplaced, vast supply dumps were created and, almost at the last minute, the tanks made their way into the area. All of this was done under cover of darkness wherever possible, in a strict code of silence and with maximum attention paid to camouflage.

Wrecked Gun Carrier supply machines in the orchard at Villers-Brettoneux on the eve of the Amiens battle. They show evidence of internal explosions caused by ammunition when the tanks caught fire.

American infantry assemble while tanks of 8th (H) Battalion move up in the background. The Mark Vs carry cribs while the Mark V*, second in line, does not need one.

Even so the whole game was nearly given away. On the evening of 7 August, the very eve of the battle, some random German shelling fell in an orchard near Villers-Bretonneux. Unfortunately this was where a number of Gun Carriers of No. 1 Gun Carrier Company, allotted to the Australian Corps, were all parked up fully loaded with mortar ammunition. Despite the courageous efforts of a few men who were on the scene a series of explosions ripped through the area, tearing some of the machines to pieces. That apart, preparations seem to have gone like clockwork. The enhanced reliability of the new tanks meant that all but a few were ready on the start line first thing next morning, enveloped in a welcome mist.

Wider German trenches still presented a problem but it was clear that something better than the fascines used at Cambrai would be desirable. The answer was developed by the inventive Number 3 Advanced Workshops and was known as the Crib. Roughly the same shape and size as the fascine, the crib was assembled from an angle iron framework with strong planks bolted to the

outer surfaces. The crib was carried on the cab roof of the tank and launched in the same way as the fascine but there were two significant differences. In the first place the crib was a lot lighter than the fascine, so it did not impair the performance of the tank. Further, unless it became

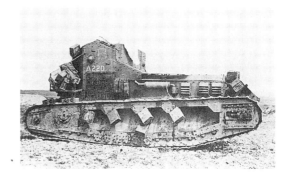

A Medium A Whippet, carrying dozens of spare petrol cans but no visible armament. Track spuds can be seen, attached to the hull side and clipped to the tracks but this tank lacks the canvas mudguards that were supposed to shield the flash of moving track links from enemy aircraft.

147

A line of 17th Battalion's Austin armoured cars, breaking free from the trench lines, speed along a typical tree-lined road, to exploit the success of Amiens.

damaged, the crib could be dismantled when it was finished with and used again. Of course, at the Amiens battle, cribs were only fitted to Mark Vs, the longer Mark V* tanks did not need them.

The Australians, with their recent experience of working with tanks at Hamel, continued to train at Vaux while the Canadians, for whom this was a more novel experience, did their training with elements of 9th Battalion at Cavillon. The Whippets do not appear to have done any specific training with the cavalry at all. Some weeks earlier, while located near an airfield, 6th Battalion had carried out a series of experiments in conjunction with the RAF whereby aircraft attempted to act as scouts for the tanks. The aircraft would seek out targets that the tanks could not see and then attempt to direct them in the correct direction. In practice it proved unworkable. It was difficult enough to see anything clearly from a Whippet tank and aircraft turned out to be the most elusive subjects. Even when the plane was spotted it was impossible to see what the observer was pointing at so the scheme was dropped. Similar training with the cavalry might have proved similarly impractical but this was not done. It would become clear in action.

Finally Lt Col Carter from the armoured cars was puzzling over how he could get his vehicles across the entrenched part of the battlefield and into the open country beyond. The answer came to him as he was driving past the Australian training ground on the evening of the 6th and trials began first thing the next day, within hours of the start of the battle. The scheme was for a section of tanks to be allocated to 17th Battalion, each tank to tow a pair of cars across the trenches. Where a trench might be unsuitable for armoured cars to cross the towing tanks would run back and forth over it a few times until an easier crossing point was created.

Long, straight military roads radiate from Amiens. To the north-east the road to Albert strikes away from the Somme valley and, in the area between, was British IIIrd Corps, supported by 10th Battalion Tank Corps. Their main purpose was to cover the northern flank of the attack; in particular the high ground north of the river Ancre. South of the Somme was the focal point. This area is divided by the Roman road to Brie, passing through Villers-Bretonneux. To the north of this road was the Australian sector, south of it the Canadian. A third road, aiming south-west through Le Quesnel to Roye, marked the southern boundary of the Canadian sector. South of this road one was entering the French sector and they also had the task of clearing high ground, south of the Avre river, which overlooked the main battle zone.

The early morning mist that shielded the tanks from the Germans, also served to separate and mislead some of them. In certain sectors the massive line of tanks and infantry that was supposed to sweep down upon the enemy in the immediate wake of the artillery barrage, broke up into small groups. Things went best of all in the centre and both Australians and Canadians co-operated intelligently with the tanks. At least this was true of the Mark V battalions, those equipped with Mark V* tanks – the 1st supporting the Canadians in the south and the 15th, with the Australians in the north – did not fare at all well. To begin with it had been decided to carry up machine-gun or Lewis gun teams in these tanks, in order to establish strong defensive points in captured trenches. The extra space, created in these longer machines, proved adequate to carry either two Vickers guns with ammunition, one officer and fourteen other ranks, or three Lewis guns with ammunition plus the same number of personnel. Further supplies of small arms ammunition were carried on a rack at the rear of each tank.

Infantry demonstrate debussing from a Mark V* female training tank. In reality these men would be giddy and sick after a journey shut up inside the machine.

Maybe it was the size of the tanks that made them less manoeuvrable than the Mark V, but more likely it was the fact that the Mark V* Battalions came up in the second wave when the mist had burned off. In both cases these battalions were working on the respective flanks of their Corps, well within range of enemy guns on the heights that decimated them. This may not have made a great deal of difference to the outcome of the battle since those machine-gun teams that survived, left their tanks feeling so ill from the fumes, heat and motion that they were unfit to take part in further action.

The true success of the battle must be attributed to the heavy tank battalions but the drama belongs to the Whippets and armoured cars. As already suggested the mix of tanks and mounted cavalry simply did not work. Over good ground, uninhibited by wire, the horsemen galloped away, leaving the tanks to clatter up in their wake. But when wire was discovered the cavalry had to wait for the tanks and, when machine-guns opened up they were forced to dismount and take cover from a hail of fire that the tanks could ignore. Thus, what should have been an impressive example of armoured exploitation, resolved itself into a series of little actions as the Whippet tanks tackled specific objectives of a local nature, in support of a mass of cavalry that, in the end, failed to gain any of its objectives. The promise of the Whippets was illustrated by the well known action of the tank *Musical Box*, commanded by Lt C.B. Arnold of 6th Battalion. Breaking away from the cavalry this tank roamed the German rear areas all day, creating untold havoc. Just three men, in a tank armed with three machine-guns, moving across country at will and taking targets of opportunity until it was finally stopped and burned out.

Armoured Cars

Yet even Arnold's achievement that in any case did not come to light until the end of the war, was eclipsed by the success of Carter's armoured cars. Again there are some excellent tales but the exploits of Lt E.J. Rollings captured the public imagination. The tanks that towed them across the trench lines remained on hand to drag fallen trees off the road to clear their way and then the cars were off. Often picking up different targets from each turret they penetrated well behind the German lines and proved almost impossible to stop. Rollings' memorable achievement was to take his section into the village of Framerville and empty a German Corps HQ before nailing the Australian flag, from his Corps Commander's staff car, to the front door. This escapade, according to one contemporary writer, drove the cavalry into a museum.

Faced with what promised to become a disaster, the Germans responded swiftly. New divisions were hurried into the line and built up defensive positions on the old Somme battlefield of 1916 that was still a maze of crumbling trenches and rusty wire. Allied efforts to dislodge them on the 9th were hampered by the fact that the infantry was weary and the tank force depleted. Of 415 combat tanks to set off on the 8th only 145 were fit for action on the following day. It was a repeat of Cambrai in more than one respect. Not that the disabled tanks were out of it forever. Salvage units in the field worked desper-

ately to free as many as possible and even the experimental No. 3 Advanced Workshops stopped what it was doing to join in. Central Workshops also stretched itself to repair machines but they were soon suffering from a serious lack of spare parts for the Mark Vs due to a shortfall in deliveries from Britain. Some tanks had to be cannibalized to keep others running and there is no more demoralizing sight for a soldier than tanks which could be easing his lot in battle, standing idle with parts missing.

On the 10th it was just sixty-seven tanks and on the 11th only about thirty. Here was another uncomfortable but inevitable lesson concerning tank warfare. Put simply it is that, the more tanks one puts into the field, the fewer the tank casualties. As the number of tanks diminished on subsequent days the percentage knocked out increased. That said there is no doubt that the German Army in France had received a major shock and would not recover easily. It was now up to the Allies to learn their lessons.

Whippets

One was clearly that the Whippet tanks could have achieved a lot more if they had been free of the

The Canadian Minister Sir Edward Kemp, inspects a Mark V* male tank smashed by enemy artillery fire near Le Quesnel on 24 August 1918.

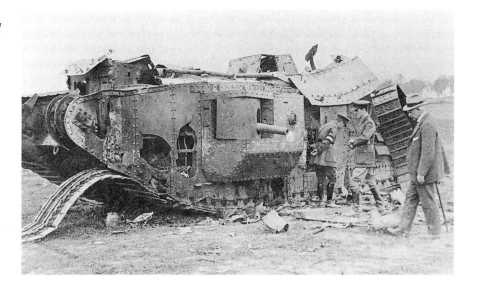

cavalry. Taking the lone example of *Musical Box* and multiplying it by ninety-six would have made a massive difference. At the same time it became clear that losses in heavy tanks would have been a good deal less than they were if tanks and infantry had been able to co-operate more closely at all times. As it was, by the very nature of the battle, men and tanks drew apart and it was at such times that the tanks became vulnerable to enemy guns. It simply drove home the lesson that Fuller had preached before, that these heavy machines were there to break trench systems, not to go roaming around the countryside looking for action. There were exceptions of course. An American serving with 10th Battalion, Lt James McGuire, got lost in the morning fog on the 8th and became separated from his infantry. Partly on orders and largely using his own initiative McGuire kept his tank *Ju-Ju* in action for two days, clearing up machine-gun posts, engaging enemy artillery batteries and rounding up prisoners, all of which earned him a well-deserved Military Cross.

Supply Tanks

Fuller also commented upon the activities of supply tanks during this battle, pointing out that on mobile operations such as these old Mark IV tanks were really too slow for the work. He advocated large numbers of smaller machines (such as the Newton tractors then in production) as a more sensible alternative. His views were echoed by Maj W.H.L. Watson, a section commander with three supply tanks under his charge. He pointed out that the road network, once one was clear of the British lines, was good enough to sustain ordinary lorry traffic that would have been faster and a lot more practical. Watson, incidentally, claims that some of his tanks were expected to tow supply sledges in the early stages of the Amiens battle but these were so badly designed that they would not tow accurately. He says that the towing lines were forever chafing and breaking so that, in the end he overloaded his tanks and left the

sledges behind. It was a Supply Tank from Watson's section that, being in the right place at the right time, led a party of Australian infantry against a German position since nothing better was available. Bearing in mind that each Supply Tank was armed with a single machine-gun, at the front, it is evident that tanks of this era were often as effective by their very presence as they were with their weapons.

Despite an increase in troops, released from the Eastern Front, the German Army in the west was still stretched. When it reinforced the line towards the end of the Amiens battle those troops had to come from somewhere and the British High Command, having discovered where that somewhere was, determined to attack there next. It proved to be further north, around Bapaume, west of Cambrai in Third Army sector. The attack was scheduled to begin on 21 August. Not that it was a simple matter, switching an attack in this way, even for the Allies. Men, artillery, tanks and supplies all had to be moved although some, in each case, were fresh.

In this connection it is worth noting that two tank battalions, the 7th and 12th were equipped for this battle with Mark IV machines. This is particularly interesting in the case of 12th Battalion that, in the summer of 1918, was also preparing to convert into a Whippet battalion. In the event, having taken delivery of a few Whippets and commenced training, they were ordered to change again into heavy tanks. They naturally expected to receive Mark Vs, only to learn that these were now in such short supply that they would have to return to Mark IVs, some of which certain members of the battalion swore they remembered from the summer of 1917.

Bapaume is interesting, from the tank point of view, for the variety of machines that took part. In addition to two battalions of Mark IV there were eight of Mark V, three of Mark V*, two of Whippets and the 17th, with their Austin armoured cars. The Mark IV tanks led the attack, probably as some sort of mechanical forlorn hope, followed up by the Mark Vs and Whippets. Once again the initial wave, the Mark IVs, took advantage of an early morning mist. They broke through the thinly held outpost line and moved on to the second objective where the Mark V and V* tanks took over. By now the sun had burned off the mist and the Germans, who had strengthened their rear lines at the expense of their front, offered far greater resistance. Pushing on as far as the Arras to Albert railway line the heavy tanks then made way for the Whippets.

Taken by surprise again the Germans had at least prepared a strong defensive system yet the tanks discovered that enemy infantry were becoming ever more ready to surrender at the very approach of a tank. It was a strong indication of something that the German High Command already knew, that the morale of their troops in the field was failing. On the following day, an attack mounted further south as part of the unfinished business of Amiens, saw the capture of Albert. Very early on the morning of the 24th some Mark IV machines from 7th and 12th Battalions took part in a battle by moonlight, supporting among others the New Zealand Division. German machine-guns that had been firing throughout the night, proved difficult to locate in the poor light but they fell silent as the

tanks approached so the Allied infantry could advance safely.

On 26 August British First Army struck further north, around Arras supported by 3rd Tank Brigade. The flexibility that these frequent changes imply were new and refreshing tactics as far as the Allies were concerned but it suggests reserves of transport, artillery and tanks that are sometimes difficult to reconcile with the catalogue of damage and mechanical failures that battalion histories retail. Figures for tank deliveries from Britain over this period are not available but they must have been adequate and it also argues a tremendous amount of work on the part of Central Workshops and its satellite units.

The German Army was now under such pressure that it started to withdraw, once again, towards the Hindenburg Line. This move was given even more impetus by 3rd Tank Brigade's attack on an intermediate defensive position known as the Drocourt-Quéant Switch Line that ran south, from a point east of Vimy Ridge, across the Scarpe and Sensée valleys to join the Hindenburg Line south-east of Bullecourt. Once this position was compromised the Germans had no option but to pull back and establish themselves within the Hindenburg system.

Mark IV tanks waiting in the dry bed of the Canal du Nord. The brick, revetted walls presented no serious obstacle to the tanks.

This was a particularly dangerous situation for the Allies. Tank strengths were dropping and the infantry were becoming weary but it was vital that they maintained the offensive in order to prevent the Germans from establishing themselves in these strong defences. According to one source, dummy tanks were used, in conjunction with the real thing, during an action mounted on 18 September to clear the approaches to the Hindenburg Line, the attack upon which was due to begin on 27 September. By this time the Tank Corps had been strengthened by the arrival of the 16th Battalion and the American 301st, the only American unit to employ British tanks in action that became a part of 4th Tank Brigade. The 301st, which had done its training at Bovington, was equipped with Mark V and Mark V* tanks plus one French Renault FT-17. It is worth noting, at this point, that under the orders of Marshal Foch an Inter-Allied Tank Tactical School was created at Recloses, near Fontainebleau, to which the Tank Corps contributed five Mark V, ten Mark V* and two Whippet tanks.

By a curious twist of fate the new attack that was mounted on a broad, 16-mile (26km) front, centred upon the old Cambrai battlefield. The front line, of course, had moved a good deal further to the west since then so that now the Germans could rely, to some extent, upon the massive earthworks of the dry Canal du Nord as an anti-tank obstacle. Indeed in a long a stretch near Moeuvres they had made the sides of the cutting almost vertical in the apparent hope of trapping tanks. The Tank Corps selected three locations somewhat north of Moeuvres but these still presented the tanks with problems. At one point the entry into the canal involved a 9ft (2.7m) drop from the west bank and was only overcome with some difficulty. At another crossing point the tanks were faced with a vertical brick wall, at the exit point. The tanks approached the wall at a point where it was covered in soil and all managed to scramble out with surprising ease. A few of the tanks at each crossing were fitted with cribs. These were Mark IV tanks of 7th Battalion that,

with poetic justice, moved on in support of the Canadian Corps to capture Bourlon Village and clear the sombre depths of Bourlon Wood that had given them so much trouble almost a year earlier.

At the southern end of the battlefield the St Quentin Canal presented a similar obstacle, but this was overcome by aiming the attack for a higher stretch of land where the canal passed through a tunnel. It was here, on 29 September, that the US 301st Battalion lost a number of its tanks on a minefield and, to make matters worse, it turned out to be one that the British had laid a year before and forgotten. It cost the Americans a quarter of their tank strength and many men because the mines, adapted from old two-inch mortar bombs, literally blew in the bottom plates of the tanks and wrecked them. A report, issued in mid-October, claimed that these mines had proved far more effective than any German mines so far encountered.

This is not to say that the Germans had not also considered mines as an antidote to tanks. By the summer of 1918 they had a wooden box mine, equipped with a leather carrying handle that could be laid in the path of a tank or, if the soldier was courageous enough, literally thrown beneath its tracks. The 7½lb (3.4kg) of explosive it contained was more than adequate to break a track and that, at least for a while, effectively disabled any tank. By late September British intelligence reports were describing buried anti-tank mines, made from 20cm shells that were laid in pairs, joined by a plank stretched across the road that set them off when a tank drove over one.

This emphasis, by the Germans, on anti-tank defence was becoming ever more obvious and it seems to have marked a change in their thinking. Certainly, by the summer of 1918, they had some new tank designs in the pipeline but these, with maybe one exception, appear to have been no more than sidelines. One was the type A7V-U in which Joseph Vollmer attempted to ape British ideas with all-round tracks and side-mounted gun sponsons. Only one example was built. Likewise two smaller, faster tanks, based loosely upon the

New Zealand soldiers take a look at the damaged German A7V tank Schnuck near Frémicourt. The tank is facing left, so the 57mm cannon is hidden. This machine has additional armour around the driving cab.

design of the British Whippet were being tested although they also came to nothing. Meanwhile, in a factory near Berlin two enormous tanks, each weighing around 148t (150,368kg) were taking shape. Designated K-Wagen, and again largely to Vollmer's design, they were an impressive final throw although still incomplete at the end of the war.

During the whole period August–September 1918 the Germans only mounted one tank foray, against New Zealand positions around Frémicourt, just west of Cambrai on 31 August 1918. Five A7V tanks took part, two of which seem to have been caught in the village of Beugney when a house they were passing fell down, apparently shaken by vibration from the tanks. Of the three other machines two, turning back to search for their own infantry, were mistaken for British machines and fired upon by their own side. Both tanks were then abandoned by their crews.

Clearly the German government had realized at a much earlier stage that they were never going to be able to compete with the Allies when it came to tank production and decided, instead, to develop their anti-tank strength. New weapons included a huge, 13mm calibre bolt-action rifle; a single-shot weapon well capable of penetrating

the armour of a tank assuming one had the courage to risk a broken collar bone by firing it. Not only that, the rifle could hardly be expected to knock out a tank with one shot. It would probably take four, five or more shots to seriously disable a machine or its crew and that required remarkable nerve, bearing in mind that it was only effective at around 250yd (229m) range. Another was a 57mm gun, virtually the A7V tank weapon, mounted on a motor lorry. Some of these were encountered in August near Montdidier. But their key defence, created in the same spirit that gave rise to the Hindenburg Line, was the Tank Fort. This was an earthwork of variable size, arranged with others in an interlocking defensive pattern, in support of the defensive line. A typical Tank Fort was armed with two field guns, three or four mortars on flat trajectory carriages, two or three machine-guns, three or four anti-tank rifles and a pair of small searchlights. Assuming that tanks were unable to bypass them, and could be separated from their infantry, it seems safe to assume that they would have worked quite well. However they must have been readily identified from the air and were just as vulnerable to an artillery barrage as any other emplacement. Certainly there is no evidence to suggest that they had an appre-

A German 13mm anti-tank rifle, captured by New Zealand troops at Cain on 22 July 1918, posed for a photograph in a farmyard.

ciable effect upon the outcome of any of the later battles.

Statistics for Amiens and the subsequent battles up to the end of September are instructive. Central Workshops had accepted 819 tanks for salvage over this period and Tank Corps casualties amounted to something over one-third of all personnel involved. The vigour with which these actions were conducted tends to conflict with the modern impression of war-weariness and one could also point to the fact that gallantry awards, as recorded in The Tank Corps' *Book of Honour,* do not diminish. Indeed awards issued to officers and men from 8 August 1918 probably equal all those issued up to that date. Two examples might suffice, both issued to young officers in action on 1 October.

Percy Boult, a 2nd Lt with 9th Battalion, mislaid his entire crew during the attack on Joncourt. While his tank was halted in heavy shellfire Boult decided to throw out a smoke bomb to hide his machine. Unfortunately the thing went off inside the tank and everyone bailed out of the Mark V. When the smoke cleared away Boult climbed back inside but could not locate the rest of his crew, all of whom had taken shelter in a shell hole. Undeterred, Boult set off by himself, picking up an officer and two men from 2nd Battalion the Manchester Regiment on the way. Since these men were unable to clear stoppages on the Hotchkiss machine-guns, Boult had to stop the tank at regular intervals and do it for them. After a spell of action Boult spotted another tank of his battalion, signalling that it was out of action and under heavy fire. Boult drew his tank up alongside, took off the crew of the damaged machine and carried on, releasing his infantry volunteers at the same time.

The 9th was a tried and tested battalion while the 16th had only just arrived in France but it had clearly absorbed the traditions of the Corps. Second Lt Robert Needham, who also commanded a Mark V at Joncourt, lost his entire crew from carbon monoxide poisoning and also elected to take his tank into action alone. Firing the front machine-gun from the driver's seat Needham supported the infantry onto their objective and then assisted with the capture of the village of Estrées before driving his tank back to the rallying point. Both officers were awarded the Military Cross.

Needham's experience proves that problems with exhaust fumes inside the Mark V had still not been resolved. Claims, by some sources, that more men died from asphyxiation in tanks than were killed by the enemy is denied by the evidence. A report, printed in October 1918, revealed that unconsciousness was quite common, particularly in Mark V and Mark V* tanks, but that men soon recovered when exposed to fresh air. In the earlier tanks it seems that fresh air was the main culprit. Crews seemed able to manage all day inside the tank, only to be smitten by sickness and blinding headaches when they got out at the end of the day.

Maj L.R. Broster, a Royal Army Medical Corps officer attached to the Tank Corps, conducted a series of tests in September 1918 to check working temperatures and carbon monoxide density. Generally speaking the latter never reached serious levels in the sample tanks although temperatures, at times, reached 120°F. Other results of these conditions were heart palpitations, a form of dermatitis and mental

A gruesome picture that brings home the horror of fire in tanks. The crew have tried to escape through the doors beneath the sponson of a Mark IV female but without success.

confusion, described by Broster thus: 'Men sit and stare in front of them and merely repeat orders without putting them into execution' while 'in another case a man ran about, shouting and cursing in an aimless manner'. Carbon monoxide poisoning reputedly gave crews of Whippets and Mark V* tanks a red complexion but Broster recorded that a pallid, or ashen grey effect was more common.

On the subject of battle wounds Broster is also interesting. In general, he calculated, casualties had been light and wounds were either very slight or severe. Among the latter, burns were the most common while minor wounds were mainly from bullet splash. The effect of mines or large shells exploding close to the tank caused concussion

with men complaining of swollen joints, around ankles and knees. In one tank an exploding mine caused all the men's bootlaces to break and buttons to burst off. Each tank carried a First Aid Bag but, looking ahead, Broster could see the need for Medical Tanks that he believed, could be converted from Mark V* or the new Mark IX machines.

Broster reckoned that there was enough room inside either tank to carry twenty sitting cases or a dozen lying down in stretchers or hammocks, arranged in tiers along each side of the tank. He even visualized a table, behind the engine, upon which wounds could be dressed, likening it to the sick bay in a battleship or as a mobile advanced dressing station. Of more immediate use Broster's main suggestions concerned the tanks themselves. He stressed that every effort should be made to check the tanks before going into action, to ensure that exhaust leaks were minimized. He further suggested that hatches should be left open for as long as possible on an approach march to battle and drivers changed at regular intervals. The key, in every case, was ventilation.

On 8 October the Germans mounted an attack with four captured British tanks at Niergnies, south-east of Cambrai. One was knocked out by a British tank while another was hit by a round from a captured German field gun, taken over by a Tank Corps officer; the others retreated. The recaptured female, the one taken out by the field gun, was found to contain three Lewis guns and one 13mm anti-tank rifle in its sponson mountings. There were a few more instances of attacks by German tanks but they never encountered their Allied counterparts again and their effect was negligible. Rather, captured German documents revealed that their High Command now advised the use of water as a means of defence.

Front-line troops were advised to fill any ditch with water if tanks were expected, since water would stop the engine, but the document also explained that concrete blocks could be used to halt tanks, if they were tall enough and dug in adequately to prevent the tanks from uprooting

Fifth (E) Battalion Mark Vs on the flooded Ignacourt–Cayeux Road, 9 August 1918. The tank on the left is ditched, the other gets ready to tow it out. Water, even shallow water, could soon halt a tank if it got inside and splashed over the engine.

them. This reliance on water became obvious when British tanks resumed the offensive against positions on the Selle river on 17 October. The tanks, however, employed cribs to help them across and three days later the Royal Engineers installed an underwater bridge over the Scheldt Canal which formed another part of the German line.

Tanks were used in small numbers during the attack on Maubeuge on 2 November and the Tank Corps managed to muster thirty-seven machines for the Battle of Mormal Forest two days later, an action described as the last set-piece attack involving tanks during the war. Here four Supply Tanks again took on a martial role to assist infantry in an attack near Landrecies. On the following day, the 5th, six Whippets from 6th

Battalion assisted the Guards around Bermeries and, although a few tanks were held in readiness for further action, none were required. Thus that brief action on 5 November 1918 was the last British tank battle of the Great War.

The armoured cars of 17th Battalion had been in action throughout this period and would carry on to the very end. Col Carter had established the principle that they should always work in pairs, so that one could cover the other if it got into trouble. This became even more vital as the cars began to succumb to an inherent weakness; recurrent failure of rear axles. This is hardly to be wondered at. These cars had been built for sedate civilian use yet here they were, carrying some 4t (4,064kg) of armour over atrocious roads. It was bound to affect their reliability.

An Austin armoured car of 17th Battalion passes a pair of trams in occupied Cologne.

It remains a mystery how the battalion managed to keep its cars on the road. Certainly spare axles could be obtained but some of the Austins were so seriously damaged that it is difficult to believe that they would ever fight again. Others came off the road of their own accord. For some reason the designers had only incorporated a single slit in the front visor plate so, when it was closed down in action, if the car commander wished to see where they were going he had to push the driver aside, often with unfortunate results. Sadly there is not enough evidence to say whether more spare cars were available in Britain, whether more were built or, as seems most likely, the battalion operated an ever-diminishing number of vehicles.

Numbers notwithstanding it fell to the armoured cars to continue the advance after the Armistice. While the tanks sorted themselves out in France the 17th Battalion followed the retreating Germans through Belgium, policing potential trouble spots, organizing prisoners of war and often bringing the first news of liberation to many communities. Under the terms of the armistice the

Germans had to withdraw all their forces east of the Rhine and then clear certain bridgeheads, on the right bank that the Allies would occupy. In the case of British and Dominion troops this bridgehead centred upon Cologne, extending to a 10 miles (16km) radius from that city.

Eight armoured cars of 17th Battalion, attached to 2nd Cavalry Brigade, crossed the Rhine by the Hohenzollern Bridge and entered Cologne on 6 December. Following negotiations with the civil authorities an official entry into the city was organized for the 12th when Gen Plumer took the salute. The armoured cars took part in this parade, one Austin carrying the Tank Corps flag that soon afterwards, it took to the boundary of the British area of occupation. In December the battalion was recalled, at very short notice, and rushed to Dublin.

Germany was in a state of utter turmoil as the various political factions vied for power and, while they had the chance, disbanded members of the German Army, known as the Freikorps, managed to create a small tank force in Berlin in December 1918. The unit ran one Whippet, until

A Mark IV, in German hands, crushing a barricade, during the internal struggles that tore Germany apart in the immediate post-war period.

it broke down, two Mark IVs and a modified A7V that were used during fighting in Berlin and Leipzig until May 1919. Another Mark IV appeared briefly in Stuttgart at about the same time but they were all broken up when the war ended, officially, in June 1919.

January 1919 saw the creation of the British Army of the Rhine (BAR) that included seven Tank Corps battalions, organized in two brigades under Brig Gen E.B. Hankey. Generally speaking, British soldiers appear to have been well received by the defeated populace and there was not a great deal of trouble. Even so there was a lot of pressure on the troops. To begin with the Dominion troops, each of whom had a sector within the Cologne perimeter, started to return home, headed by the Canadians. The French, who saw the future in starker terms, wanted the British occupation force to be as large as possible but they reckoned without the British press that agitated for the men to be brought home, and the British Government that wanted to reduce the Army as speedily as possible for economic reasons.

The need for tanks, with what was then known as the Army of Occupation, caught Central Work-

shops in the process of winding up. In February 1919 the men were dismayed to learn that they would need to refurbish a batch of Mark V tanks before they could go home. Starting on 17 February they completed their 89th, and last, tank on 20 May with due celebration.

Although Allied troops now had a strong grip upon Germany it was only under the terms of an armistice. Security would only come when a full peace treaty was signed and the German Government was not working quickly enough towards this end to suit the Allies. Thus, by May 1919, elements of the BAR were being prepared for a further advance into Germany in the event of hostilities being resumed. Under pressure from this threat the Germans signed the Treaty of Peace at Versailles on 28 June 1919.

By March 1920 the Tank Corps in Germany comprised the rump of 12th Battalion at Solingen and a composite company in Cologne. This last was replaced by B Company, 5th Battalion in April. The tanks serving in Germany were all of the Mark V type and, so far as one can tell, all Hermaphrodites with one male and one female sponson. Four tanks went up to Düsseldorf by rail,

159

Led by a British officer, a Mark V hermaphrodite tank of 11th (L) Battalion advances along the road with the bulk of Cologne cathedral looming in the background.

early in March when it was decided to occupy that city. Some tanks were required to parade in Cologne on 13 March when a party headed by one Wolfgang Kapp, tacitly supported by many senior German officers, tried to seize power in Berlin. His plot brought out the virulent anti-Communist Spartacists, some of whom were rounded up by the Inniskilling Dragoons and some tanks in Solingen. Later that month there was more rioting in Cologne that ended when a lone British tank trundled into the Domplatz.

The next trouble spot was Upper Silesia, on the German/Polish border where Nationalist groups were raiding across the border in both directions. A section of tanks from 5th Battalion went there in April and joined a force that gradually worked its way to the border, sorting out the opposing factions as it went. The tanks put on a show of force to subdue a hostile crowd in the village of Brobeck in June and again, to deal with a gang of Polish bandits in Antonienhutte in April 1922. British forces left this area in July of that year but they did not leave Germany entirely until 1929, by which time the Nazi Party was well established.

Tanks of 5th (E) Battalion parked up inside the vacated Zeppelin hangar near Cologne.

14 New Tanks for 1919

There is evidence to show that in 1918 the British government considered raising a new Tank Corps battalion from the New Zealand Army in France. This would have been a British tank battalion manned entirely by New Zealanders and not the first element in the creation of a New Zealand Tank Corps. The authorities in Wellington appear to have been quite enthusiastic but when news of it reached New Zealand Army Headquarters in France the suggestion was rejected out of hand.

The Canadians, by contrast, decided to raise their own tank force and the 1st Canadian Tank Battalion was formed, in Canada, in March 1918. It sailed for Britain in June and after some six weeks in Surrey, moved down to Bovington to commence serious training. This was still going on when the war ended but the Canadians remained in Dorset until May 1919 when they sailed home to be disbanded.

The Mark V*

The last new tank to see active service during the First World War was the decidedly unpopular Mark V*. Although, as already established, the Mark V* was a new construction and not a regular Mark V, chopped in half and lengthened,

Mark V** Tank	
Data for a male machine	
Crew:	8
Weight:	35 tons
Length:	32ft 5in (9.89m)
Width:	12ft 9in (3.89m)
Height:	9ft (2.75m)
Armour:	14mm (½m) max.
Speed:	5.2mph (8.37km/h) max.

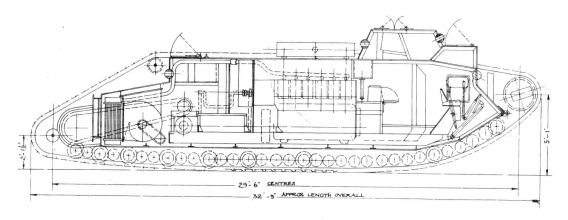

SECTIONAL ELEVATION

GENERAL ARRANGEMENT OF MACHINE MK V**

it was just that in terms of design. What this meant was that a perfectly good tank had been compromised in at least two ways. Firstly, by being stretched, the Mark V* was too long for its width and that, in tank design terms, made it difficult to steer. Secondly the extra armour plate and track links increased the weight of the tank, over a regular Mark V at 29t (29,464kg) to 33t (33,528kg). Since it still retained the same engine, the Mark V* was underpowered.

The Mark V**

Even so the need for a longer tank had already been established and in May 1918 W. G. Wilson began work on a new design which would be known as the Mark V**; the first star indicated an improvement on the Mark V, the second, a further improvement on the V*. The V** was the same length as the V* but the contour of the track frames was changed so that the length of track actually in contact with the ground was reduced, making it easier to swing, at least on a hard surface. Wilson also altered the centre of gravity by moving the engine further back, creating more space at the front. This in turn permitted the commander to work directly behind the driver while the rear cab that had featured on the Marks V and V* was now built further forward and amalgamated with the front cab.

The engine was still the Ricardo straight six, but now uprated to 225hp in order to cope with a tank that weighed 35t (35,560kg) in its male configuration. One assumes that Wilson must have beefed up his transmission in order to cope with the extra power although no written evidence to this effect has yet been found. All that may be said for sure is that the final drive arrangements were altered so that the chains were on the inner face of the inside track frames instead of between them. The fuel tanks were installed within the frames at this point instead. In most other respects, in terms of sponsons, armament and so on, the Mark V** was similar to earlier models.

*Mark V** tanks under construction in Birmingham. The superimposed commander's cab shows up well on the nearest machine, as does the towing gear, behind the exhaust silencer. Male sponsons, complete with gun mountings, can be seen lying between the rows of tanks.*

Substantial orders for 900 of these tanks, 750 of which would be male machines, were placed with Metropolitan Carriage, Wagon & Finance in Birmingham but the first was not delivered until November 1918, too late to see service, so the order was drastically cut. Even so, the Mark V** went on to create a significant place for itself in tank history as will be shown.

THE MARK VII

Harking back to the Oldbury Trials in March 1917 it will be recalled that the tank equipped with a Williams–Janney hydraulic drive system failed mainly on account of the heat, generated by the oil pumps and motors. Yet this did not deter the designers for whom, in theory at least, hydraulic drive and steering appeared to be so attractive. In October 1917 the Edinburgh firm Brown Brothers was awarded a contract to develop a tank along these lines that became known as the Mark VII. To all outward appearances it was a Mark V somewhat lengthened at the back, not as long as a tadpole tail but certainly similar.

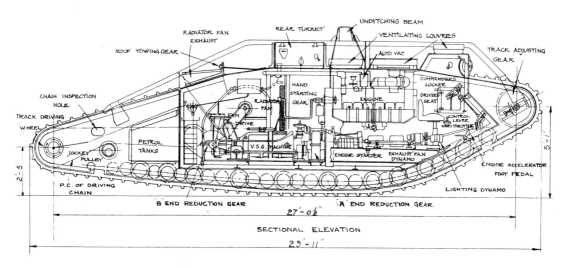

GENERAL ARRANGEMENT
OF MACHINE MARK VII

MARK VII

Mark VII Tank
Data for male machine

Crew:	8
Weight:	33 tons
Length:	29ft 11in (9.12m)
Width:	12ft 9in (3.89m)
Height:	8ft 7in (2.62m)
Armour:	14mm (½in) max.
Speed:	4.5mph (7.24km/h) max.

Inside the hull it was now extremely crowded. The Ricardo engine drove into a pair of Variable Speed Gear pumps directly coupled to two hydraulic motors that, in their turn, drove pinions in the track frames that linked to the sprockets, by chain loops, in the usual way. Great efforts were made to ventilate the tank, with armoured louvres in the roof, extraction fans inside the tank itself and two radiators in the track frames, one to process the engine coolant, the other for the hydraulic fluid. Petrol was carried in two 50gal (227l) tanks, within the rear frames that were located either side of a rear escape door. The Mark VII was one of the first tanks to be equipped with an electric starter for the engine.

The first Mark VII was completed around July 1918 and orders were placed for the odd quantity of seventy-four tanks, all male, with Brown Brothers and Kitsons of Leeds. In the event only three were completed, all by the Edinburgh firm, and it is instructive to note that a list of all tanks tested by 20 Squadron, RNAS, up to the time of the Armistice, does not include a Mark VII. This would seem to suggest that the mechanical problems, including overheating, were never resolved.

The battle known as Third Ypres, in the long, wet summer of 1917, had nearly brought about the demise of the tank and, as we have already seen, the success of Cambrai notwithstanding, the German counter-attack in March and April 1918 did nothing to restore their stock. One victim of this period, who did not appear on the casualty lists, was Albert Stern. His forthright style and firm advocacy of the tank did not always make him friends and in their period of decline his reputation suffered too. In fact it all came to a head in October 1917 when a clutch of senior officers at the War Office insisted that Winston Churchill,

At first glance the Mark VII was no different from earlier models but a closer look reveals the longer rear horns, revised layout of bearing caps on the hull side and additional ventilation louvres on the roof.

now Minister of Munitions and therefore Stern's superior, should remove him from his post at the Mechanical Warfare Supply Department. The charge was that Stern had encumbered the British Army with hundreds of useless tanks.

Stern still had his supporters, both with the Army in France and in the government itself but Churchill, whatever his feelings may have been, could not ignore the War Office and he persuaded Stern to resign. Vice-Adm Gordon Moore took his place. As compensation Churchill offered Stern the position of Commissioner for Mechanical Warfare (Overseas and Allies) Department, which in effect meant working with the Americans. This was by no means a sinecure. What Churchill had in mind was to harness American industrial power to increase tank production and obtain French help to create a large factory, in France, which could manufacture tanks for all the Allied armies.

Stern was furnished with introductions to Monsieur Loucheur, Churchill's French counter-part, and to Gen John J. Pershing, commander of the American Expeditionary Force. In fact both Stern and Tennyson D'Eyncourt had done their best to get the Americans interested in tanks as soon as they had entered the war, but all they had achieved up to this point was to initiate rivalry between the US Army and Marine Corps over who should have tanks; an argument which is not over yet. Pershing offered Stern the services of two of his officers, Majs H.W. Alden and J.A. Drain, and between them they drafted an agreement that the Americans and French were happy with, to produce 1,500 tanks for allied use. Churchill approved but shortly afterwards the French dropped out since they did not feel that they had the resources to contribute.

THE MARK VIII

The Mark VIII tank that was developed from this agreement, was a joint Anglo-American design, albeit based on British practice that resulted in its nickname of the International. Some planning for what was to become the Mark VIII had already begun, before Stern took up his new appointment. This was done by Tennyson D'Eyncourt and a young man, Lt John G. Rackham, who would subsequently make quite a name for himself in the bus industry – as indeed did W.G. Wilson. The two American officers drafted to the project had different responsibilities. Maj Drain was there to supervise on behalf of Gen Pershing while Alden

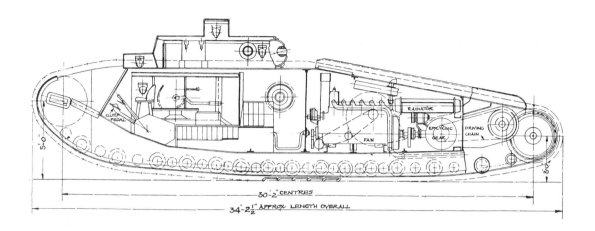

SECTIONAL ELEVATION

GENERAL ARRANGEMENT OF MACHINE Mk VIII

Mark VIII Tank	
Crew:	12
Weight:	37 tons
Length:	34ft 2in (10.42m)
Width:	12ft 4in (3.76m)
Height:	10ft 3in (3.13m)
Armour:	16mm (⅔in) max.
Speed:	5.25mph (8.45km/h) max.

was the technical expert. His main role was to ensure that the design developed in a way that was compatible with American industrial practice but he also produced, and patented, a new type of male gun sponson that was applied to the new tank.

Before looking at the design in detail there are a number of broad points to consider that resulted from previous British experience. The need for wider tracks had already been appreciated but up to this time they had been applied on the original, relatively narrow, track frames with a considerable overlap at each side. In the Mark VIII the gap between the frames was widened, which gave

the tracks better support. At the same time the pitch of the track, the distance from pin to pin, was increased by about 5in (12.5cm). Of course, if one were to widen the track frames without making the hull of the new tank correspondingly narrower, it would not fit the railway loading gauge so this had to be done. However in order to create more room inside, the inner frames were cut down until they were little more than a rim. Central Workshops, in their general summing up of wartime tank design, had criticized the immense strength of the track frames on earlier British tanks as a serious waste of effort, resulting in an unnecessary increase in weight, but this was the first attempt to remedy that fault.

All heavy tanks, built up to this time, were considered underpowered so it was agreed to produce a much larger engine, a V12, for the new tank. The favoured power unit was the American Liberty that had originally been designed for aircraft use, based on Rolls-Royce and Mercedes features. Like the British Ricardo, the Liberty was a state-sponsored design, produced by many different companies. The aero version featured steel cylinders but, in order to keep costs down, the tank engine employed cast iron cylinders. It developed 300hp at 1,250rpm; twice the power of a Ricardo straight six.

In the event, such was the priority on aircraft production, introduction of the Liberty was seriously delayed but this did not greatly affect British plans. Britain had decided to build Mark VIII tanks to its own specification, independent of the International programme, and to this end Harry Ricardo was asked to design a V12 version of his tank engine that had the same power output as the American unit. Whichever engine was used it would be located further back in the tank, quite separate from the crew area from which it was divided by a bulkhead with sliding doors. Beyond the engine was a two-way, forward and reverse, transfer box driving into two-speed epicyclics which not only took care of steering but also gave two speeds in either direction. There were those, even at the design stage, who believed that four speeds would be more sensible than two for a tank of this size but they were disregarded; many later came to believe that they were probably correct.

The Mark VIII was some 2ft (60cm) longer than a Mark V** and something over 1ft (30cm)

taller but a good 12in (30cm) narrower than an earlier male tank of any type. In fact the distinction between male and female did not apply to the Mark VIII since it had the firepower of both, due to an entirely new hull design and layout. In addition to those differences already described, the Mark VIII hull was completely redesigned in outline, being fuller and more rounded at the front with a longer, tapering rear end. The driver sat alone, centrally at the front with his own armoured hood. Above and behind him a long superstructure dominated the top of the tank, pierced in various places for machine-guns, while above that again a small, square look-out tower was provided for the commander. Maximum armour thickness was increased to 16mm but over a smaller surface area than on earlier types. Beneath this superstructure the interior of the front half of the tank was virtually clear and well laid out. There was a large ammunition locker in the centre, roughly where the engine might have been in an earlier tank, and this also served as a platform for the commander and machine-gunners. There was more than enough space left to accommodate up to twenty infantrymen as passengers. A mechanic could pass

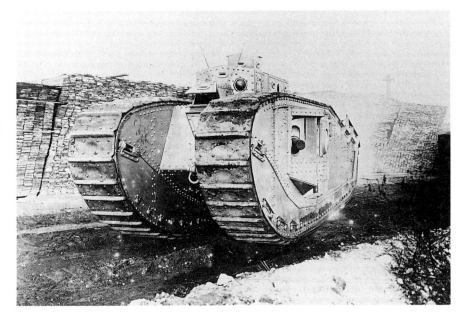

A Mark VIII tank on test in the United States. The sponson is partly folded in which makes the track frames appear even wider. Notice the dimple in each track link which gave added strength to the plate.

through a sliding door in the rear bulkhead and move down either side of the engine, even while it was running. He would find the radiator located horizontally above the transmission and the cooling fan, below it and to the left.

Alden's sponson design dispensed with the rear door and did not even include a machine-gun mounting. Rather a door was provided, abaft the sponson in each side, with a large ball mounting for a machine-gun built into it. The sponsons did not slide inboard, as they did on earlier designs, but were pivoted at the front and swung in from the rear. Alden's patent makes no particular mention of this in connection with railway travel, rather he explains that it is a way of reducing the width of the tank should it need to pass down a narrow passage or similar restricted space.

On the subject of machine-guns America and Britain differed. Tanks intended for US Army service would carry water-cooled Brownings while the British were still committed to the air-cooled Hotchkiss. A typical British Mark VIII would have a machine-gun in each side door and five in the superstructure; two firing forwards, one on each side and another at the rear. The Americans reckoned they could manage without the side firing guns but introduced another refinement in the form of a triangular shaped plate, at the very back of the tank. By firing at the underside of this the rear machine-gunner, in the superstructure, would be deflecting bullets downward at any unfortunate souls who might be cowering in a trench that the tank was passing over.

The international programme called for Britain to produce the structural components of the tank; that is the frames and armour plate. Also the tracks, track rollers, main weapons and weapon mountings. America would provide the engines, transmissions and other mechanical components, all of which would be assembled at a new factory at Neuvy Pailloux in France. In the event, the factory was built but never equipped and the Armistice put paid to further developments.

Even so the British had placed orders for some 1,500 Mark VIII with the North British

Locomotive Company and Beardmores in Glasgow along with Metropolitan in Birmingham, but the only production line to commence work was at North British. They produced a prototype machine that was fitted with a Rolls-Royce V12 engine because the new Ricardo was not then available, followed by twenty-four production machines. The prototype had been tested by 11 November 1918 but only five other tanks appear to have been taken into service, the remainder apparently being scrapped. Armour plate for 100 more machines was shipped across to the United States where they were completed and placed in service, some still being operational up to 1932.

Detailed drawings were prepared for an even longer tank, to be known as the Mark VIII* which would have been capable of crossing trenches up to 18ft (5.5m) wide. It is described as having the same profile and design details as the Mark VIII with an extension at the nose of 4ft (1.2m) and 6ft (1.8m) at the rear. Weight was calculated at 42t (42,672kg). Mention might also be made of a Mark X, described as an improved Mark V in which particular attention had been paid to manoeuvrability, crew comfort and reliability. This also apparently reached the design stage at the time of the Armistice.

The Mark IX, which was the last British heavy tank to be built before the end of the war was, in reality, hardly a tank at all, at least not in the combat sense. Like the Mark VIII it was drawn up by Tennyson D'Eyncourt and J.G. Rackham and, according to W.G. Wilson, the original scheme was for a multi-purpose tank capable of fighting, transporting troops and carrying supplies. This was in the summer of 1917, presumably in sequence with the Mark VIII but, again according to Wilson, the complexities of the design were such that it was reworked into an armoured personnel or supply carrier armed only with a pair of machine-guns for its own defence.

The key to the Mark IX design was to create as much open space inside as possible so the internal track frames were almost removed entirely. Since this could have weakened the struc-

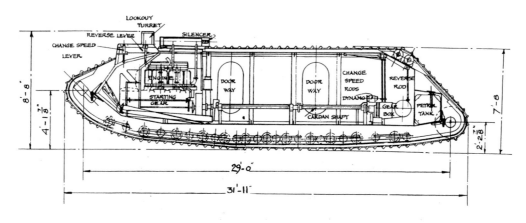

SECTIONAL ELEVATION.

SCALE $\frac{1}{4}$" = 1 FOOT

MARK IX

GENERAL ARRANGEMENT OF MACHINE MK IX

Mark IX Tank	
Crew:	4
Weight:	27 tons unladen
Length:	31ft 11in (9.73m)
Width:	8ft 1in (2.47m)
Height:	8ft 8in (2.64m)
Armour:	10mm (½in) max.
Speed:	4.3mph (6.92km/h) max.

ture to a dangerous extent, heavy girders were installed transversely across the floor in order to stiffen the frames. Space was also created by bringing the engine, the 150hp Ricardo straight six, as far forward as possible and moving the gearbox to the back. Gearbox and epicyclic control rods were run along the roof, on the inside, so the only obstruction on the floor was the long drive shaft that ran right down the middle that everyone had to keep clear of. The profile of the Mark IX was entirely different. It was, in effect, a long, rectangular box with steeply sloped

frames at the rear and a sort of upturned snout at the front, that probably accounted for its nickname, the Pig. In place of sponsons it had two large, oval doors in each side and a smaller hatch at the back that incorporated a Hotchkiss machine-gun mount. There was another at the front, alongside the driver. The Mark IX carried a crew of four and, for the first time in a British tank, the driver sat on the left with the commander to his right. The commander was also provided with a small armoured lookout on top of the cab.

The Mark IX was capable of carrying up to thirty infantry who would probably have to stand if they were all to get inside, but in any case there was nowhere to sit. A series of loopholes, along both sides, enabled some of the infantry to fire their rifles from the tank although the chances of doing this to any effect must have been slim. Conditions inside, with a full passenger load, can hardly be imagined. Fumes from the engine would have permeated the entire vehicle while the men would be packed together in one great, swaying mass, trying desperately to keep from rubbing

A row of Mark IX supply tanks in storage after the war. The letters IC are assumed to stand for Infantry Carrier, which was its primary role. Notice the line of rifle loopholes along the side, the two large doors, roof stowage rack and commander's lookout at the front.

against the spinning drive shaft. When it was not acting as a personnel carrier the Mark IX could carry up to 10t (10,160kg) of stores, mostly inside and in a large tray on the roof. A towing attachment permitted the tank to haul at least three loaded sledges. As noted in the last chapter, the Tank Corps medical officer suggested the Mark IX as a potential sick bay tank and there is evidence from Central Workshop's files that one of the three tanks delivered there before the Armistice was equipped as an armoured ambulance.

Two prototypes were built by Armstrong-Whitworths in Newcastle-upon-Tyne but the main production order for 200 was placed with the traction engine manufacturers Marshalls of Gainsborough in Lincolnshire. Of these thirty-four were built and handed over to the Tank Corps and, although no records survive of their peacetime service some were photographed with the letters IC painted boldly on their hulls, presumably indicating that they were Infantry Carriers.

THE MEDIUM MARK B

During Philip Johnson's visit to Britain in the autumn of 1917 he had inspected, and commented upon the design of, a new Medium tank. This would have been the work of W.G. Wilson that he began in July 1917 and that emerged, as a prototype, from the Metropolitan works in September 1918. Johnson had expressed himself most impressed with the new design although, as it turned out, he was probably misguided. The Medium Mark B, as it was called, was an 18t (18,288kg) tank, intended as a replacement for the Medium A and supposedly designed with the accumulated knowledge of those faults that had become evident in the Whippet.

Wilson had adopted a rhomboid-style hull profile in miniature, topped off by a large fighting compartment, but he had reversed the layout of the Medium A, placing the engine at the back. The engine in question was a four-cylinder version of Ricardo's design, rated at 100hp, that drove through the traditional four-speed gearbox via steering epicyclics to the final drive. The engine and transmission were enclosed in a separate compartment from the crew area that contained four men. The driver sat centrally, at the front, but the commander had no particular lookout for himself. The machine-gunners had five positions to choose from in the superstructure and two more, set in the hull side doors that, themselves, stuck out like miniature sponsons.

169

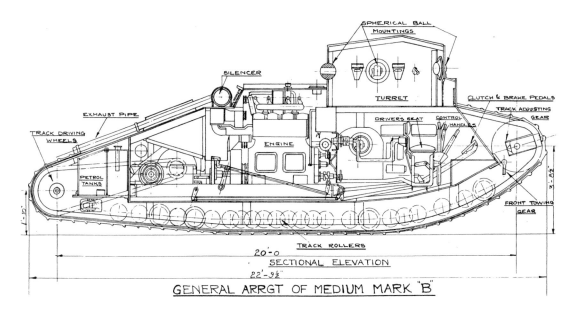

GENERAL ARRGT OF MEDIUM MARK "B"

Medium Mark B Tank

Crew: 4
Weight: 18 tons
Length: 22ft 9in (6.94m)
Width: 8ft 10in (2.69m)
Height: 8ft 6in (2.59m)
Armour: 14mm (½in) max.
Speed: 6.1mph (9.8km/h) max.

Production began at the North British Locomotive plant in Glasgow although orders had also been placed with Metropolitan, the Coventry Ordnance Works and the Patent Shaft and Axletree Company of Wednesbury, near Birmingham. One hundred and two machines had been completed before production ceased, from total orders for around 700. It was when some of these entered Tank Corps service that faults started to manifest themselves. This is hardly unusual, it would be expected with any new tank, but the problem with the Medium B was that any faults concerning the engine and transmission, or even routine breakdowns come to that, were difficult to deal with because the engine compartment was so cramped.

It was bad enough when the engine was cold but, after it had been running for some time it was impossible for a human being to work on it due to excessive heat in such a confined space. It was hardly a situation that could be contemplated in action when a tank might have to be repaired under fire or lost.

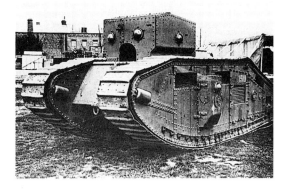

The first Medium B machine to be completed by Coventry Ordnance Works in Glasgow. In fact it still lacks the driver's head cover but one can see the various machine-gun mountings in the superstructure and one of the little sponsons that also served as side doors.

THE MEDIUM MARK C

It is an interesting reflection on Wilson's capabilities. As a mechanical engineer he was little short of a genius but one has the impression that, when he tried to create a complete machine that was functional in ergonomic, as well as mechanical terms, he failed. The confined engine compartment is a good example, but so is the lack of a lookout position for the commander. It is also interesting to observe that the Medium B was Wilson's tank, it was not a Wilson and Tritton design. Indeed while the former was working on his Medium B the managing director of Fosters, now Sir William Tritton (he had been knighted in February 1917), was engaged upon a rival design of his own.

Tritton's tank that naturally became known as the Medium C, also dates from July 1917 as a design but in this case the first prototype, nicknamed the Hornet, was running in August 1918. It was a much bigger tank than the Medium B, indeed it was nearly as long as a Mark V, which

meant that it could cross similar trenches, and weighed 20t (20,320kg). The layout was much the same as the Wilson design but everything was on a bigger scale and there was more than enough room in the engine compartment to accept a six-cylinder Ricardo engine and the standard Mark V type transmission, although in this case the gearbox and epicyclics were ahead of the engine, driving back to the sprockets via a two-stage chain system. The arrangement of driver's cab and superstructure was similar to the Medium B except that Tritton did install a cupola on top for

Medium Mark C Tank	
Crew:	4
Weight:	20 tons
Length:	25ft 10in *7.88m)
Width:	8ft 4in (2.54m)
Height:	9ft 6in (2.9m)
Armour:	14mm (½m) max.
Speed:	7.9mph (12.7m) max.

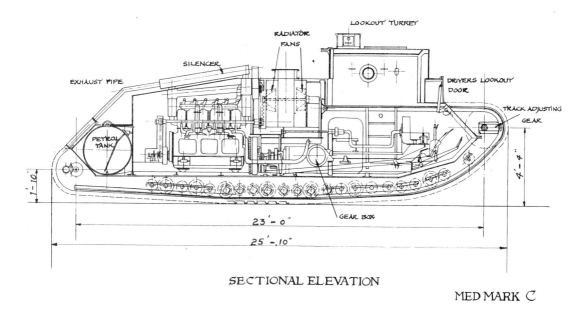

SECTIONAL ELEVATION

MED MARK C

GENERAL ARRANGEMENT OF MACHINE MED. MK. C

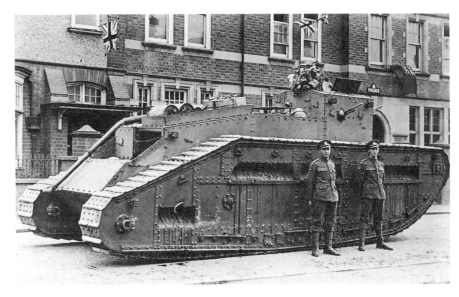

A Medium C tank on tour shortly after the war. The size is quite evident when viewed from this angle, especially when one notes the modest space available to the crew, at the front.

the commander. Despite its greater weight the Medium C could manage nearly 8mph (13km/h) whereas the Medium B would not do much more than 6mph (10km/h), which was slower even than the Medium A. There are those who contend that the Medium C was, taken all round, the best tank design of the First World War. This is quite a claim, especially bearing in mind that it never saw active service, but there is no doubt that it was a good tank.

There is adequate evidence, in the form of official plate drawings, that a male version of the Medium C was planned. This is interesting because with one exception, up to this time, the role of the Medium tank was seen as that of a glorified cross-country armoured car; a fast, anti-personnel vehicle. The exception was an attempt, in 1917, to install a French 37mm cannon into the front mounting of a Medium A but this was never developed. There seems to be little doubt that the male version of the Medium C was intended as a tank destroyer. The gun was fitted into the front of the superstructure, above the driver's head, and in order to reduce the effect of muzzle blast on the driver the weapon selected was the old 40 calibre model of the six-pounder, the long-barrelled version first installed in the Mark I tank.

In the event, the male type was never built and production of the female model was limited to 50 out of 600 ordered, all from Fosters.

THE MARK II GUN CARRIER

The only other new design worth noting at this time was an improved version of the Gun Carrier which was developed to the full-size wooden mock-up stage. Shaped much more like a heavy tank than its predecessor, the Mark II Gun Carrier transported the weapon at the back. Drawings also exist of a salvage tank based upon this hull form. For many years figures quoted for tank production up to the end of the war only dealt with those completed up to the date of the Armistice. Once this had taken effect, as the Treasury was swift to remind the Mechanical Warfare Supply Department, peacetime rules applied and one could not simply carry on ordering tanks as if money were no object. Government and the War Office agreed that just 175 more new tanks would be completed after 11 November 1918. In fact, as the manufacturers pointed out, this did not make economic sense and they would need at least up to the second week in February 1919 in order to wind

A Mark V tank being transhipped from a merchant vessel to a barge for landing at the Black Sea port of Novorossiisk. This was part of the South Russian Tank Detachment.

down production effectively. Thus the total number of tanks completed up to the middle of February was 263, many of which appear to have been scrapped almost immediately.

The Tank Corps, like most elements of the Allied armies, could look back with pride upon its achievements during the war and, if the occupation of Germany was not to everyone's taste it was politically significant. The attempt to stem the tide of Red Revolution in Russia, on the other hand, was pointless and doomed from the outset. Hardly the reward for war-weary troops although they went, all the same. In fact the Allies had been moving troops into Russia since before the armistice, ostensibly to bolster the chances of the so-called White Russians in their anti-Communist struggle, but specifically to try and keep as many German troops as possible on the Eastern Front, lest they be transferred to the west.

With the end of the war, priorities changed and the defeat of Bolshevism became the primary aim, albeit one which was way off target, and the British Government decided to include tanks. The plan, in theory, was for British personnel to act as instructors and then to hand the tanks over to their Russian Allies when they were ready.

The first Tank Corps party to leave went straight from France – ten officers and fifty-five men under the command of Maj Neil McMickling. Leaving Erin in March 1919 they arrived at the port of Batum, at the extreme eastern end of the Black Sea in April. Here they were joined by more men and an initial shipment of tanks; six Medium A Whippets and six Mark V hermaphrodites, or composites. From here they moved north-west to the town of Ekaterinodar, where a training base and workshops were established. It would be interesting to know how this move was achieved. The distance cannot have been much short of 300 miles, as the crow flies, yet there is no evidence on contemporary maps of a railway joining the two towns.

The odds are that the tanks were shipped again, to the northern Black Sea port of Novorossiisk that was on the direct railway line to Ekaterinodar and onwards to Tsaritsyn, on the Volga. At Ekaterinodar they were joined by a further fifty-seven Mark V and seventeen Medium A which, in theory at least, should have provided quite a substantial force to deal with an apparently disorganized enemy. This, however, was the fatal mistake. It was not just a question of underestimating the enemy as a ramshackle bunch of revolutionaries who did nothing without a popular

A Medium B, once part of the North Russian Tank Detachment, later transferred to north-west Russia but here in Soviet hands and apparently in excellent condition. The right side hull door-cum-sponson is open.

vote. It was equally foolish to overestimate one's Allies. Many of the White Russian officers were committed and courageous but they had everything to lose. Their soldiers could rarely be relied upon, even to a modest extent. They were traditionally treated with a minimum of concern by their own officers and lived in perpetual fear of their enemy, which was not encouraging for the British troops.

The Russian commander, Gen Denikin, proposed an immediate advance on Tsaritsyn (a city later to be known as Stalingrad) but, since the training programme was nowhere near complete, the assault was led by a Mark V with a British crew which ensured that it was successful. But it was also a flash in the pan. Training continued at Ekaterinodar but men, under pressure from the Bolsheviks, were deserting almost as fast. By February 1920 it was only the British and their tanks that prevented disaster by covering the evacuation of Russian refugees back to Novorossiisk and then to Sevastopol in the Crimea that was finally evacuated by the South Russian Tank Detachment in June 1920 although all the tanks had to be left behind.

The British also had a Military Mission in the Baltic States and six Mark V tanks were shipped there in July 1919. Known as the North-West Russian Tank Detachment, its task was to support the White Russian Gen Yudenich against the same enemy although in this area there were many undercurrents. The Baltic states all wanted autonomy while the Germans inserted a *Freikorps* unit into the area to protect the predominantly Germanic population. Both France and Sweden also supplied troops but again the weak link was the Russians. Lt Col Hope-Carson, who commanded the British tank force, found the Russians eager for battle and keen to learn how to handle the tanks, but totally incapable of appreciating the need for maintenance. Once again it seems that those tanks with British crews, or at least British officers in command, generally did best. For example, when a tank showed signs of mechanical failure in action, the British commander would withdraw and sort the problem out, since tanks were a scarce resource; a Russian officer would probably keep his machine in action until it broke down. Not that there is a great deal one can achieve with just six tanks, especially when they start to break down, but Gen Yudenich's most ambitious plan, to capture the city of Petrograd (later Leningrad) was not a complete failure in that they managed to get three of the tanks within 22 miles (35km) of the city over very difficult country. In the end, of course, three tanks could not be expected to support weary and dispirited infantry forever and, by late October 1919 they had withdrawn to Narwa. The tanks were handed over and the British troops came home in November.

Maj J.N.L. Bryan commanded another small tank detachment that sailed for Archangel in August 1919. The North Russian Tank Detachment is more interesting for its equipment than for what it actually did. In addition to four Mark V machines they had two Medium B tanks. The role of the detachment in this case was different. The Allies had created a substantial base in the area, around Archangel and Murmansk, and the tank detachment was there to provide additional defence while the troops were withdrawn. Once again the plan was to train Russians to operate the tanks but the Bolshevik forces in this area were relatively weak and opportunities for action limited. With the evacuation complete by October 1919 the tanks were again handed over to the Whites. At least two of the tanks, including one of the Medium Bs, ended up in the Baltic region but two were sunk in the Dvina river to prevent them falling into Bolshevik hands.

This itself was a pointless gesture because, in the end, the Red Army acquired a lot of the abandoned tanks and somehow managed to keep some of the Mark Vs running, and apparently in excellent condition, into the early 1930s. At least one Medium B survived for a while along with a number of Whippets and it is interesting to note that the Russians fitted one of these with the 37mm gun from a Renault. The weapon was mounted in place of the front facing machine-gun, an idea the British had tested in 1917. Soviet propaganda showed the captured tanks being used as farm tractors to break new ground on collective farms but they were also employed in the

A Mark V of the North Russian Tank Detachment with its male sponson fully retracted. Evidence seems to show that all Mark V tanks despatched to Russia were hermaphrodites, just like those that served in Germany.

continuing Civil War. A number of Mark V tanks were finally placed on display in various Soviet cities, at least four of which are known to survive at the time of writing.

The troubles in Ireland that had required 17th (Armoured Car) Battalion to be hurried there in December 1918 showed no signs of abating. The battalion was first made up to strength with sixteen Austin armoured cars, proving that more of this make must have been coming from somewhere because some of the original batch are known to have been destroyed in France. The battalion quickly expanded, the Austins all being issued to A Squadron that went to Limerick while B Squadron, in Dublin, had sixteen Medium A tanks and C Squadron finished up with an unknown quantity of Mark IV tanks. The Mark IVs were subsequently traded for Mark V* and Medium B tanks.

Some tanks took part in the Victory celebrations in Dublin when the Great War officially ended but in general armoured cars must have been more suitable for the kind of patrol work involved. By March 1920 the old 17th Battalion, much reduced, had become No. 5 Armoured Car Company but it still operated a mixed collection of wheeled and tracked vehicles. Some new armoured cars arrived that are outside the scope of this study, but there were still ten tanks in Ireland in January 1921 when 3rd Battalion arrived to administer all Tank Corps units in the country. In fact the 3rd, at this time, was a tank battalion in name only and men to crew the vehicles had to be seconded from infantry, cavalry and Royal Army Service Corps troops. It is not clear how long the tanks remained in Ireland but there is no doubt that armoured cars were proving far more practical and the last of these left Dublin for Belfast in December 1922 following the establishment of the Free State.

Just to round off the subject of foreign adventures involving tanks it should be recorded that one Whippet was supplied to South Africa after the war. Named HMLS *Union* it was used on one occasion, at a time of industrial unrest, but apparently broke down. A few Mark IV and Medium A tanks were sold to the Japanese Government, which was clearly intent upon raising an armoured force of its own. They also purchased some redundant French Renaults and these, proving far more useful, formed the basis for subsequent Japanese designs, just as they did in Russia, while the British veterans were discarded.

THE ROYAL TOURNAMENT

Bearing in mind the horrors that the British public had to face during the Great War and the enormous sense of relief when it was over, it is surprising to discover that a Royal Tournament was held in London in the summer of 1920. One might suppose that everyone was heartily sick of war and the very sight of soldiers yet, by all

accounts, it was a great success and the Tank Corps took part. The show they put on was quite remarkable and displayed the amazing extent to which tanks had been developed in the four years since they were first used. The arena at Olympia was fitted with an arrangement of canvas panels to give the impression of a waterway, some 20ft (6m) wide, with banks at each side. A Mark V** tank approached this obstacle with a long bridge dangling from its prow. The bridge was lowered into place across the 'river' and released from the tank that then rose up and crossed over. Considering the size of a Mark V** tank, all 32ft 5in (9.9m) of it, extended by the length of the bridge, it must have been an impressive sight in the confined space of Olympia and it certainly created a lot of interest.

BRIDGELAYING

The possibility that tanks might be able to carry, lay and cross bridges had been considered at Tank Corps Headquarters in France when the advance into Germany was being contemplated. Experience at Cambrai had shown that the average canal lock in Europe was some 20ft (6m) wide, with firm edges, so a bridge that could be laid across this gap would be a great advantage. At the same time the problem of dealing with broader obstacles was discussed and a method devised for dealing with that. The standard portable bridge of the Great War was the Inglis Bridge, named after its inventor just as the Bailey Bridge was in the Second World War. The Inglis Bridge was a lightweight construction of tubular steel, like scaffolding poles that could be bolted together, and planks for the decking. However the standard Inglis bridge of this period was not really strong enough to take a tank, nor indeed wide enough to permit a male tank to cross without retracting its sponsons. The designer, Maj C.E. Inglis, RE as he was then, came up with a new version that was capable of taking a tank and then developed it further so that a tank could push the bridge ahead

A Mark V* male tank modified as a bridgelayer demonstrates its capabilities over a replica canal lock at Christchurch. Notice how the weight of the tank causes the near end of the bridge to lift clear of the ground as it starts to cross.

A Mark V** male Royal Engineers tank training for the Royal Tournament. The river that it will cross is formed from sheets of canvas, as are the river banks. Bridgelaying, in this case, was only one of the tank's potential roles.

of itself across a gap. The bridge, of course, would have to run on its own tracked undercarriage.

The promise of this work was such that the authorities agreed to the creation of three Tank Bridging Battalions, Royal Engineers that would be established on the river Stour at Christchurch (then in Hampshire) just east of Bournemouth. The officer appointed to command one of these battalions was Maj Giffard le Q. Martel who had served with the Tank Corps during the war. Martel took up his post in October 1918 but, with the signing of the armistice the plan to create three battalions was dropped in favour of a single, experimental company that Martel would command.

Following experiments with a Mark V* that laid its bridge by means of a winch, Martel's team developed a Mark V** that employed a hydraulic

Looking becalmed but with its Naval crew apparently relaxed the swimming Mark IX 'Duck' drifts in the November mists on Hendon Reservoir.

pump, driven off the tank's engine that activated a jib attached to the nose of the tank. This could not only carry and lay the bridge, and act as a link when pushing the Inglis bridge on tracks, it could also be used to trail mine-clearing rollers or support a demolition charge, on a very long boom that could be pushed against a concrete blockhouse and then detonated safely from inside the tank. What Martel had created was a multi-purpose Royal Engineers tank which could perform a variety of functions on the battlefield yet still fight, if the situation so required.

The staff at Christchurch presided over other experiments including another mine-clearing tank that used rollers from civilian steam-rollers, mounted at the front of each track to detonate mines. They also devised a method of rafting tanks across wider waterways using sections of Inglis bridge resting on pontoons and a system for rapidly creating trenches with a tank hauling an enormous, single coulter plough. Yet Christchurch was not the only centre of experimental work at this time.

The staff at Dollis Hill attempted to create an amphibious tank by adapting an existing machine. A Mark IX was used, an odd choice because it would have been brand new, although in terms of weight for bulk it was probably the best available. The tank was made to float by the addition of buoyant drums fitted across the front and down both sides and it was propelled, in the water, by paddles attached to the tracks. A large super-structure was added around the cab area that provided a sort of navigating bridge and from which dangled pipes, undoubtedly attached to bilge pumps. Even without sponsons the idea of making a tank of this era watertight must have been a nightmare, made worse by the four large doors. One wonders how well they were able to prevent every drop of water from getting in and it could be that the thing leaked so much that bilge pumps were essential. The tank was launched upon Hendon Reservoir on the misty morning of 11 November 1918, Armistice Day. Legend has it that, after a short cruise, the engine failed and the crew (most of whom from their uniforms appear to have been Royal Navy personnel) had to be rescued by boat. The fate of the tank is not recorded.

FAST TANKS

Maj Philip Johnson also came home from France some time before the Armistice to pursue his own scheme for the development of high-speed tanks. Johnson took over the Mechanical Warfare Department's experimental ground at Dollis Hill and, by the time of the armistice, had a number of experiments underway. Johnson's main purpose at this time was to produce a tank that would fulfil an ambitious plan to win the war, which had been hatched by J.F.C. Fuller. Known as Plan 1919 it proposed achieving victory in that year by the tactical employment of fast tanks. Fuller claims that the ghost of this idea came to him shortly after he joined the Tank Corps. Leaning heavily on his deep study of military history Fuller studied the trench lines of the Western Front in order to detect a flank, upon which to launch an attack, but in reality there were only two. One was the Swiss border, violation of which would involve a serious infringement of neutrality; the other was the Channel Coast, which had already been considered to some extent with the abortive *Hush* Operation.

The closest alternative Fuller could come up with was on a much smaller scale. All along the front there were bulges, or salients, in the line, facing one way or the other wherever a successful attack had penetrated the opposite line. Fuller saw the sides of the German salients as points ripe for attack and the bigger they were, the more he liked it, because that meant that such an attack would cut off more of the enemy. Fuller brooded upon this for some time but his beliefs were reinforced by the result of the German March attack in 1918. Here Fuller believed he saw total disintegration taking place among front-line British troops who, when they were bypassed in an attack and separated from their headquarters, lost heart and quickly gave up. On this basis, Fuller reasoned, if entire armies could be pinched out and their headquarters destroyed the result would be catastrophic for the enemy and bring rapid victory. He likened it to killing a man by a blow to the brain instead of beating him to death from the toes upwards.

Philip Johnson's converted Medium A tank in its second guise. Features to note are the springs in the track frames, the enlarged engine compartment and the rear end modifications to take the Wilson transmission.

The way to achieve this encirclement, in Fuller's view, was with tanks. In explaining Plan 1919 he describes a situation wherein heavy tanks make a traditional, frontal assault on the enemy lines to fix their attention while lighter, faster tanks penetrate the flanks and destroy their high command and its infrastructure. Plan 1919 was completed in May 1918 and circulated among senior officers in France but it had one, fundamental flaw. The lighter tanks that carried out the flank attacks would have to travel fast, Fuller calculated at at least 20mph (32km/h), and there was not a tank on the planet at that time that could achieve that. This is why Johnson returned to London. His brief was to design such a tank and have it ready for the following summer. It was a tall order.

Johnson realized that two things would be required in order to create a fast tank. Firstly it would have to have springs of some sort and secondly it would need a more powerful engine. There is some evidence to suggest that Johnson had already been experimenting along these lines in 1917 for there are references to a Mark IV and Medium A fitted with springs. In both cases they were heavy-duty, railway pattern leaf springs with a deflection of about 2in (5cm) but there are no records to show how well they worked. In 1918 Johnson reworked the Whippet by linking the track rollers with levers, operating against transverse springs set across and beneath the hull. To provide the extra power the two Tylor engines were replaced by a 360hp Rolls-Royce Eagle V12 and a Mark V type transmission. In this form the tank is said to have achieved 30mph (48km/h), which was even better than Fuller required, but it was not developed further.

Two factors appear to have contributed to this. One was a realization, on the part of Fuller, that it might be impossible to build enough new tanks in time, especially if they were of such a novel type and he was considering how Plan 1919 could be achieved using Medium C machines instead. The second was the armistice. This rendered Plan 1919 entirely redundant, but by this time Johnson

was well into his stride. Upon his return to Britain, Johnson had contacted his old employer, John Fowler & Co. of Leeds and supplied them with a Mark V machine to be modified to his own design. Johnson appears to have become obsessed by two factors directly related to the design of tracked vehicles; one was suspension, the other steering. Work on the Whippet had already proved to Johnson that if one fixes springs to every roller on a tank, the weight would go up; and Fuller had specified that his Plan 1919 tank that he christened the Medium D, was not to weigh more than 20t (20,320kg). Johnson also knew, from his own experience, that the steering of tracked vehicles caused problems. The swinging action not only slowed the tank down, it also set up considerable stresses that would adversely affect a tank with suspension even more than a typical unsprung machine of that period. Johnson sought to solve both problems by using flexible steel wire rope, in which Fowlers specialized. They used it to drag enormous ploughs across fields, between a pair of massive steam engines.

Flexible steel wire rope was not only flexible, of course, it was immensely strong and Fowlers probably knew more about its practical applications than anyone. Johnson employed it on the Mark V in two ways. Firstly he used it as a suspension medium. By attaching the ropes to springs at each end of the tank and then threading them over and under a series of rollers in the track frames Johnson, in effect, created an extra long spring. As the tank moved over an obstacle each track roller would be forced upward against the cables that, in turn, stretched the springs at the ends of the track frames. Thus you had a springing effect at every roller station with springs only at the ends. It was very clever while it worked.

To enhance steering Johnson also employed flexible steel wire rope as the core of the track system, the long, narrow track shoes being threaded onto the cable like beads onto a necklace. This had two advantages. As the tank turned, the track tended to bend with it and created less stress in the lateral plane; further, since each shoe was

The bizarre appearance of Johnson's Mark V, as modified by Fowlers of Leeds. This photograph was taken when the tank was in store at Bovington.

free to pivot on the cable, it would accommodate itself more readily to rough ground and, in theory, be less demanding on the suspension in the vertical plane. The modified tank that was also fitted with a 225hp Ricardo engine, was completed by May 1919 and achieved 20mph (32km/h) on trials but it was an uninspiring sight, not calculated to dazzle the eyes of the uninitiated.

By then, of course everything had changed. The war was over, money was extremely short and the whole Medium D programme became effectively redundant, unless Fuller could do something about it. Fuller, by this time, was resident tank expert at the War Office and he was doing his best to save the Medium D. According to his memoirs,* once the Armistice was established he saw the Medium D as the tank for future foreign wars. To this end he demanded comfort for the crew, who might have to travel long distances to fight, and the ability for the tank to swim without modification. In defence of this latter concept he explained that foreign wars meant landing on foreign shores, possibly against opposition as at Gallipoli, so a tank that could swim from a ship to the beach and subdue opposition was the ideal. This, inevitably, added another difficulty to Johnson's lot. The sequel to the Medium D saga will be told in the final chapter.

*Fuller, J.F.C., *Memoirs of an Unconventional Soldier* (Ivor Nicholson & Watson Ltd., 1936).

15   After the War

The task of clearing the battlefield of wrecked and abandoned tanks fell to the Tank Field Battalion that was formed on 16 November 1918 from the Tank Field Companies and the Advanced Workshops. The work went on for the best part of a year and it is surprising to find, from their records, that they were still recovering old Mark I and Mark II tanks as late as October 1919. If at all possible, the tank was dragged back to the nearest railhead and then returned to Central Workshops but, if this proved impossible, it was simply broken up or even blown up where it stood. German prisoners of war were engaged in this work. There is some evidence to suggest that tanks were sometimes buried although this is not reported in the Tank Field Battalion's War Diary.

From Central Workshops the tanks were shipped back to Britain where a massive scrapping programme began. At Bovington Camp, the area north of the settlement became one huge scrapyard but whether this was simply for tanks then used at Bovington or others brought back from France is not so clear. Private companies were also involved and excellent photographic evidence survives of a huge operation carried out by the Steelbreaking and Dismantling Company of Chesterfield where acres of tanks can be seen as they were gradually reduced to their component parts. Others had a more fiery end, as hard targets on the tank ranges at Lulworth Camp, but it was a lingering death because their rusting skeletons could be seen, scattered across the ranges, for many years.

Many, however, survived. In 1919, possibly at the suggestion of the National War Savings Committee, tanks were distributed among those towns and cities that had raised worthwhile amounts in War Bond sales drives. Since tanks had been used during the war to promote sales it seemed only fitting that tanks should be the reward and there was even a First Prize. This was to be the famous battle-damaged tank *Egbert* that had visited many towns throughout England. It was presented to West Hartlepool, on the East Coast, which had raised a princely sum, equivalent to £31.0s.1d per head of population, during a 'Speed the Guns' War Bond campaign between October 1918 and January 1919. Not every

The end of a legend: Lt Hastie's tank D17 Dinnaken, *the tank that 'walked up the High Street of Flers' is broken up by German prisoners-of-war under the watchful eye of a British sentry at the very spot where the tank came to rest, after breaking down on its return from that epic battle.*

Egbert *gives one final demonstration of his powers before becoming a permanent landmark in West Hartlepool, at least for the next twenty years.*

borough selected for the honour chose to accept a tank and even amongst those that did the gift was not universally popular.

Normal practice was for the tank to arrive in town by rail from Bovington, with a skeleton crew who then drove it to the chosen site. Breakdowns between station and site were not uncommon and handover ceremonies often had to be delayed. Having arrived at the site, once the crowd had gathered, suitable speeches would be made including one by the officer in command who would give details of some gallant action in which this particular tank had taken part. In most cases this was pure fiction. The majority of tanks were training machines and can easily be identified as such, and invariably female Mark IVs. This model was clearly selected in the first place since it was the most common type but it is also claimed that female tanks, with their machine-guns removed, were less of a temptation at a time when Red Revolution stalked the land. Even so some communities got male tanks but there was usually a reason for this. Coventry, for example, where Daimler had produced the tank engines and the City of Lincoln, home of Fosters, naturally. As an additional security measure the delivery crew would remove the final drive chains from the tank before leaving.

In all some 265 tanks were distributed, on behalf of the National War Savings Committee, to towns and cities in England and Wales. Many later became the subject of commercial postcards. All of this is well recorded but it has not been possible to trace similar presentations in Scotland, although War Bond tanks certainly toured there during the war. Some communities received tanks for other reasons. The village of Farningham in Kent was one example. It received a tank because it was where W.G. Wilson and his family were living at the time; another went to the Royal Navy Gunnery School, HMS *Excellent* on Whale Island in Portsmouth Harbour where tank gunners had been trained during the war.

At one point, while distribution was still taking place, a Tank Corps general suggested that these souvenir tanks should be stripped of their mechanical parts, in particular engines, presumably as an economy measure. The idea was rejected by the War Office on the grounds that the Tank Corps did not have the manpower and, in any case, they would need a salvage tank and a lorry to accompany each delivery, to lift the engine out and carry it away. Besides, as someone pointed out, it would not impress local citizens if, having been given a tank, someone came along later and removed large bits of it. Whether that would really have made any difference is debatable. Many communities did not like having the ugly machines in their public parks, complaining that they were neither war memorials nor war trophies, and quite a few were cut up in the 1930s. The rest went during the Second World War as part of a general scrap drive; all, that is, except for the Mark IV female at Ashford in Kent that had been adapted to house an electricity transformer. It is now the only presentation tank to survive in its original location. A number were also presented to communities in France which had strong links with the Tank Corps – Cambrai naturally, Bermicourt and Le Tréport for example.

Britain was spared the horror of Red Revolution although the threat was real enough at the time and there was a good deal of unrest. It

Mark V* tanks and their crews at Seaforth near Liverpool during a time of political and industrial stress in the summer of 1919.

resulted in a General Strike in March 1921 and, in order to play its part in supporting the authorities, the Tank Corps had to call some six hundred men back to the colours. These were mostly equipped with armoured cars and sent to various locations throughout Britain, mainly important railway centres. Some tanks were also sent. A detachment of Medium C machines went up to Glasgow. Whether they had much effect is doubtful. Armoured cars might have made an

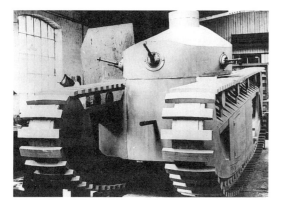

The Medium D first appeared as a full-size wooden mock-up. Real Hotchkiss guns have been fitted into the machine-gun mountings but it is not clear whether the tube, protruding from the front of the hull, represents the gun of a proposed male variant or not.

impression but tanks are unnecessarily clumsy for this kind of work and give entirely the wrong impression. In any case the threat subsided within six weeks and the armoured vehicles all came home.

Writing in 1936, J.F.C. Fuller claimed that, in 1919, he was faced with the choice of building enough Medium C tanks for the Tank Corps or investing the money in Johnson's design for the Medium D. Inevitably Fuller modified the facts to suit his own case. As already noted the Treasury was largely responsible when they reverted to peacetime budgeting conditions after the war, and it was a compromise between the Treasury and industry that decided how many tanks should be completed in 1919. Fuller may have been faced with such a choice in subsequent financial years but by then, one feels, the Medium C tank was getting a bit long in the tooth.

THE MEDIUM D

Whatever the precise truth, there is no doubt that, on the basis of Johnson's very earliest experiments, orders had been placed for ten prototype Medium D tanks before the war ended. According to a Tank Committee report dated August 1919, four Medium D tanks had been ordered from

Fowlers of Leeds in August 1918 and six in September from Vickers, apparently through their Wolseley subsidiary. The design was revolutionary and, from the user point of view incredibly inefficient, but Johnson was clearly obsessed with his ideas on flexible steel wire rope tracks and suspension and gave little real thought to the operational or fighting aspects; it was a trait he seems to have shared with W.G. Wilson.

Tank Corps officers were shown a full size wooden mock-up of the tank at Woolwich but none of their comments appear to have survived. The tank was long and narrow, with a circular compartment at the front, like a turret that did not rotate. Instead it had machine-gun mountings covering the front and sides. There was no male version since a large gun mounting that would have to be placed lower down in the hull, could not be sealed against water and Fuller, as already noted, now wished the new tanks to be amphibious. Having machine-guns at the front was certainly sensible but this arrangement came at a price that now seems ridiculous. This was that the driver, unable to share the front of the tank with a machine-gun, was situated at the back of this turret, looking out at the world from a raised cupola.

In order to provide him with some sort of view the entire tank was arranged as if it were tipping forwards and a consequence of this was that its ability to deal with vertical obstacles was much reduced. Johnson countered this by making the track frames higher at the back so that, when faced with such an obstacle, the tank would turn round and tackle it in reverse. It is impossible to believe that Fuller could have agreed to this, in practical terms it was a complete nonsense, yet neither Johnson nor his designs are criticized in any of Fuller's writings.

The first Medium D was completed in June 1919. An expert, called in from the Admiralty, took one look at it and announced that it would be unstable in the water; however on land it did quite well. Powered by a Siddeley Puma aero engine it managed 23mph (37km/h) on the level and 28mph (45km/h) downhill, which was all Johnson could have asked of it. Even the bizarre wire rope track and suspension systems appears to have held up fairly well. Two tanks from the Vickers order were modified during construction. One appeared towards the end of 1919 as the Medium D* that was simply the Medium D widened from 7ft 3in (2.2m) to 8ft 5in (2.56m) in an effort to make it more stable in the water.

*The Medium D** tank undergoes flotation trials in the river at Christchurch. The crew have wisely attached a line to a Mark V tank on the river bank, just in case anything goes wrong.*

The Admiralty noted this change but were still not happy so another machine designated Medium D** that did not appear until 1920, was wider still at 9ft (2.7m) and slightly longer with additional internal bulkheads. This tank swam quite well in the river at Christchurch, using its tracks as paddles.

Shortly after the first Medium D appeared, the Army Council voted the tidy sum of £1million for seventy-five production tanks but, somewhere along the line, figures had been muddled and in due course it was agreed that this sum would only purchase forty-five tanks that would be fitted with Rolls-Royce engines. This order was later cut back to twenty tanks but, in the event, only three appear to have been built. These were known as the Medium DM (or D Modified) although they were based on the Medium D**. The main visual difference was an extra cupola, on top of the fighting compartment that further limited the driver's view. The tanks were built by the Royal Ordnance Factory at Woolwich and were powered by Rolls-Royce Eagle Mark VIII engines. One of them is reputed to have sunk in the River Thames during trials.

Johnson went on to build another tank to the Medium D design, known as the Light Infantry Tank and then produced three lighter, cheaper machines that were known as Tropical Tanks. These appeared as a result of a visit he made with two of the Medium D machines to India in 1920 where further weaknesses in design were revealed. These new designs were no more successful and, in any case, fall outside the terms of this work. It only remains to say that Johnson continued to develop prototypes until 1923, mainly on the basis of old motor car chassis, before his department was finally closed down.

Some time after the war ended, Britain received another new tank that had been designed with the 1919 campaign in mind. It was known as the Studebaker Tank, after its manufacturer, and it looked like an armoured version of the supply-carrying Newton Tractor that was also being built for Britain at the Studebaker plant. Few records and only two pictures survive but it is believed to have resulted from an offer, to the British War Mission in Washington DC, of a surplus stock of Hall-Scott aero engines; four-cylinder water-cooled units. The tank is said to have been designed by two officers serving with the War Mission although they remain anonymous and their qualifications are not known. It is very difficult to judge the size of the tank from the

The Studebaker Tank apparently photographed in Britain. From this angle it appears to be quite large but in fact it was probably not much bigger than the Newton Tractor from which it was derived.

photographs and so few details survive that guess-work is not much help. However a top speed of 12mph (19km/h) is quoted and the armament is said to have been two machine-guns, which suggested a minimum crew of three. A prototype would appear to have arrived in Britain at some stage but no report has ever been found and it is not even shown in any surviving lists.

WHO ACTUALLY INVENTED THE TANK?

The question of who actually invented the tank was a matter of considerable public interest. Some details had been given in the House of Commons, in response to MPs' questions, but the only way to arrive at the true answer was by a Royal Commission. In fact the Royal Commission on Awards to Inventors was established to deal with a number of subjects and it met to consider tanks, for the first time, on Monday 6 October 1919 at Lincoln's Inn. Thirteen claimants were due to be heard, most of whom retained their own counsel. The Royal Commission was presided over by Mr Justice Sargent with the Attorney-General and the Solicitor-General appearing on behalf of the Crown. While the hearing went on a Mark IV tank was parked outside Lincoln's Inn, presumably as a piece of evidence should a technical query arise.

Winston Churchill appeared as a significant witness but made no claim for himself while Ernest Swinton decided to conduct his own case. It would seem to anyone who has studied the subject objectively, that this was by and large an open and shut case, but that is to ignore the opinions of many individuals who believed, for whatever reason, that their contribution was significant. Among them Cdre Murray Sueter made a case, not just for himself but on behalf of the Royal Naval Air Service in general. Indeed a document survives, dated 16 January 1917, in which Sueter enumerates the details of his 'claim to be the inventor of the Armoured Car fitted with

a caterpillar system of propulsion (commonly called "Tanks")' by saying that he produced the first armoured car in Britain, demonstrated the Pedrail track system to Churchill and discussed, with his officers, certain aspects of submarine design in relation to tanks. It was hardly convincing stuff.

Thomas Hetherington, now Lt Col, also submitted a claim based, apparently, upon his Big Wheel idea. This caused Mr Justice Sargent to comment 'There were two alternative methods, and he was backing 'the wrong horse' which apparently drew forth laughter. Why Hetherington did not make more of the fact that he had also suggested tracks is not clear but there was additional confusion from evidence submitted by F.L.M. Boothby, who clearly remembered things differently from both Sueter and Hetherington.

Boothby, it seems, still championed the cause of MacFie who in turn was still in conflict with his erstwhile partner Nesfield. The latter, who claimed the invention of the upturned nose for climbing obstacles, turned up with the famous model that MacFie had mislaid and even demonstrated it, over a pile of books on a long table in front of the members of the Royal Commission. The meeting lasted for one week, then sat again on 20/21 October to hear the claims of Crompton, Legros, Tritton and Wilson and finally issued its report on 27 November.

While the result – that Tritton and Wilson were entitled to the lion's share of the reward – was beyond dispute the Chairman made some interesting comments. In the case of Hetherington, for example, and in response to his solicitor's comment that work for the Landships Committee was outside Hetherington's normal duties, Mr Justice Sargent said 'It dos not follow that members of the Committee are entitled to reward. They are officers of the Crown, called in as experts. It does not constitute a claim for special remuneration. To say that anyone on the Committee is entitled to special remuneration is a monstrous proposition.' And Hetherington had to admit that Churchill had already recommended

A Medium C participates in a tank-driving competition during Sports Week at Bovington Camp in 1919. Considered by many to be the best tank design of the First World War era they never had a chance to prove what they could do.

One Mark V* male tank must have survived at Lulworth Camp for many years after the war. Here it is seen giving a demonstration during the visit of King Amanullah of Afghanistan in 1927. The king is at the front of the group on the left.

him for a decoration for his work and that he had received the CBE.

Likewise in the case of Crompton and Legros the Chairman took a strong line: 'These claimants were employed for some six months as consulting engineers to the DNC Committee at a substantial agreed remuneration. . . . But they did not in the result, invent or discover the special features subsequently incorporated in the Tanks, and we cannot consider their services as of such an exceptional or extraordinary character as could alone justify an award in addition to their agreed salaries'.

If those who were already servants of the Crown, just doing their duty, and those who were hired to do the work, were to be excluded from

Another Mark V* at Lulworth suffering a more common fate. Parked on the range as a hard target it appears to have caught fire. A Medium Mark II tank keeps its gun trained on the wreck while men rush to put the fire out.

One Mark IV was tested on the Royal Naval Air Station at Pulham in Norfolk as a tug for handling airships on the ground, for which purpose it was fitted with a tower structure on top of the hull. Even so it appears that a substantial ground party was still required to hold the craft. This is Rigid Airship 23r, built by Vickers at Barrow in 1917 and scrapped in 1919.

any reward then, in theory, none should have been awarded. Yet, of the thirteen claimants, Swinton and D'Eyncourt got £1,000 each, Nesfield and MacFie shared £1,000 while Tritton and Wilson shared £15,000. Presumably it was all welcome although one suspects that credit and honour for the invention would have meant more to most of them. Lancelot De Mole, then a Corporal with the Australian Army was in London at this time. He was called as a witness on 20 October and subsequently presented his own claim that clearly made an impression upon the Chairman who, in his final summing up, regretted that he could not see his way clear to rewarding the Australian since his work had no direct influence on the design of the tank as built.

Other claimants were not even considered. A certain Capt Bentley claimed to have designed a tank for Lord Kitchener in 1914 and went to great lengths to prove it. Bearing in mind Kitchener's reaction to the demonstration of *Mother* in 1916, and in view of the fact that he was no longer available as a witness, it is perhaps not surprising that Bentley's case did not get very far. A Mr John Corry of Leeds also went to great lengths but in another sense. He walked all the way to London with a bag slung around his neck with '*John A. Corry, The Tank Inventor, Walking from Leeds to London to Claim His Rights'* chalked upon it. According to the *Daily News,* that rather supported his claim, Corry had submitted a design to the War Office in November 1911. A so-called Land Ironclad that had four 1.7in guns, eight Maxim guns, a crew of thirty and two engines that drove it at up to 20mph (32km) It was described as having two endless chains fitted with massive treads, which shows that it was a tracked vehicle. The War Office turned it down at the time on the grounds that there was no novelty in his design while the Munitions Inventions Department told him, in 1919, that none of his ideas had been used in the tanks as built. And it didn't end there. As late as 1933 a fascinating lady, Mrs Cloete Capron, the wife of an Army

Colonel according to the *Daily Sketch,* claimed to be 'the original inventor of the landships, later called Tanks'. Her claims caused a brief flurry in the national papers and resulted in questions in Parliament but soon faded away.

For four years from the end of the war the Tank Corps led a precarious existence. The War Office was unable to decide whether it wanted an independent tank arm or not so, for that period, only the other ranks were regarded as full-time Tank Corps personnel. Officers were seen as on secondment from their regiments. While Fuller and Johnson between them used up a lot of the available budget, the Tank Corps started to raise armoured car companies for service overseas, particularly in India and the Middle East. The surviving tank battalions at home and in Germany operated Mark V tanks, except for 2nd Battalion that was then based at Farnborough where it operated Medium C machines. A small stock of Mark V and Medium C tanks remained in reserve until the early 1930s and there was a scheme, at one time, to convert some of the latter into armoured recovery vehicles. At least one Medium C was later used for trials of a new patent transmission while a long surviving Mark V** acted as test bed for a new Diesel tank engine, produced by Beardmores.

A selection of key tanks were earmarked for the new Imperial War Museum that was housed at the Crystal Palace in Sydenham for some time. The tanks were not affected when the Palace burned down in 1936 but, with no other home available, all but one of them were cut up for scrap. Fortunately someone with sufficient concern and a good deal of foresight had selected a number of significant tanks from the stock at Bovington and fenced them off on a patch of heath just outside the camp. This became an unofficial museum and, although some interesting exhibits were broken up before and during the Second World War, a representative selection survived to form the nucleus of what is now, in all but name, the national collection.

Glossary

Index